Oh Capitano!

Oh Capitano!

Celso Cesare Moreno—Adventurer, Cheater, and Scoundrel on Four Continents

Rudolph J. Vecoli
and Francesco Durante

Edited by Donna R. Gabaccia
Translated by Elizabeth O. Venditto

FORDHAM UNIVERSITY PRESS
New York 2018

Oh Capitano! The Fabulous Life of Celso Cesare Moreno on Four Continents, 1831–1901 was originally published as *Oh Capitano! La vita favolosa di Celso Cesare Moreno in quattro continenti, 1831–1901*, © 2014 Marsilio Editori® s.p.a. in Venezia.

Visit us online at www.fordhampress.com.

Library of Congress Cataloging-in-Publication Data

Names: Vecoli, Rudolph J. | Durante, Francesco, 1952– author. | Gabaccia, Donna R., 1949– editor.
Title: Oh capitano! : Celso Cesare Moreno—adventurer, cheater, and scoundrel on four continents/ Rudolph J. Vecoli and Francesco Durante ; edited by Donna R. Gabaccia ; translated by Elizabeth O. Venditto.
Other titles: Oh capitano! English
Description: New York : Fordham University Press, 2018. | Includes bibliographical references and index.
Identifiers: LCCN 2018004953 | ISBN 9780823279869 (cloth : alk. paper) | ISBN 9780823279876 (pbk. : alk. paper)
Subjects: LCSH: Moreno, Celso Cesare, 1831–1901. | Explorers—Italy—Biography.
Classification: LCC G276.M67 V4313 2018 | DDC 910.92 [B] —dc23
LC record available at https://lccn.loc.gov/2018004953

Printed in the United States of America

20 19 18 5 4 3 2 1

First edition

CONTENTS

PREFACE

Rudolph J. Vecoli

"Fabulous" can have several meanings. One is that which is totally imaginary, as in a fable; another is "almost unbelievable." In my estimation, Moreno's life embodied both meanings. As his biographer, I have experienced both frustration and fascination seeking to determine where the imagined Moreno ends and where the "almost unbelievable" begins.

Celso Caesar Moreno has been on my mind for quite a long time. I first encountered Moreno while researching my dissertation in the 1950s. A notice in *Unione Italiana*, an Italian-language paper published in Chicago, caught my eye. It reported that a "Prince from Malacca, Cesare Moreno," had arrived in Washington to sell an island to the United States. Moreno's letter, in response to that news, appeared in the issue of August 19, 1868:

> Dear sirs! I read in your paper on August 5th that you wished to honor me with the title Malaysian Prince, which I am not and do not wish to be. Only permit me to tell how it is that I am in America and what I intend to do. In the many voyages which I have made between the British Indies and China, I heard much talk of a very fertile island not yet known or possessed by Europeans. In 1862 I undertook an expedition on my own account and risk. I was successful, landed, and took possession in my name, becoming *Capo e Padrone* (Head and Master), but not *Prince.* I then went to Italy, *mia Patria*, and offered it to the Government to make it a colony, which would have meant a great future for commerce and the Italian Navy, but instead for two years the Ministries of Italy gave me nothing but vague promises, without ever reaching a decision. I am here to sell it to the American government . . .[1]

The letter was signed "Signore Cesare Moreno, Capitano Marittimo."

What manner of man was this, I asked myself, who had the *fegato*, the gall, to claim to be *capo e padrone* of a South Sea island and to present himself to the president and Congress with an offer to sell them an island off the coast of Sumatra?

Preoccupied for the next half century with teaching and administration, as well as research on other subjects, I put Celso on the back burner. Following my retirement, I realized that, free at last, what I really wanted to do was to write Moreno's biography.

Over the years, I had caught glimpses of Moreno in various historical contexts: His campaign against "Italian slavery" in the United States, his exotic adventures in India, the East Indies, and China; his proposal for laying a transpacific telegraph cable; his brief tenure as Prime Minister of the Kingdom of Hawaii; his candidacy for the Italian Chamber of Deputies, and so on. An intriguing figure indeed—but one, however, who has been almost totally ignored by historians in both Italy and the United States. In various studies of Italian colonization and of the Italian diplomatic service, he has been given only brief mention. Even in the field of Italian American history, although he was reputed in 1900 to be the most famous Italian in the United States, he has received only passing reference. Almost all these mentions portray Moreno as a pure scoundrel. Such characterizations did not lessen my interest in Celso Cesare Moreno. Instead, they whetted my appetite to know more about him.

That Moreno kept an archive of his papers, of this there is no doubt. That it did not survive him meant that the research for this book was more difficult and more challenging. Happily, in his numerous polemics, he quoted extensively from correspondence, government records, and newspaper clippings, including his innumerable letters to newspapers. I am indebted to many archives and various databases of manuscript collections that allowed me to gather a goodly number of his letters.

William Nevins Armstrong, who figures in the narrative that follows, knew Moreno in connection with his Hawaiian adventure. In a scrapbook in the Armstrong papers at the Yale University Library, I found a clipping of an obituary of Moreno. Beside it, Armstrong had written: "Someone should write a book about this fellow, but he was an absolute fake."[2] A harsh judgment, indeed. But Celso emerges from my research as a multifaceted, chameleon-like personality not reducible to a single epithet.

PROLOGUE

Francesco Durante

Rudi Vecoli first told me about his project to write a biography of Celso Cesare Moreno in a September 2004 email. Like him, I had stumbled onto Moreno while I was working on something else, and, like Rudi, I considered writing a book about him. So when Rudi told me that he had started his project, I was enthusiastic. The following summer, Rudi retired and found the time to devote himself to it. He kept me updated about his research: his trip to Hawaii, his brief trips to the Library of Congress, and naturally, a trip to Italy, which ended in Moreno's hometown, Dogliani. Emilio Franzina, another great historian of emigration, accompanied him and told me the trip was also a thorough and memorable tour of Piedmont's food and wine.

I enjoyed following Rudi's research from afar and seeing how enthusiastically Rudi undertook it. It was a point of pride for me to see how Rudi valued my opinion on a series of small questions connected to this work.

Then, on December 18, 2007, I received a terrible email. Rudi wrote that he had been diagnosed with incurable acute leukemia two weeks earlier. "It is a matter of weeks," he added. All that, in three lines. The longer part of the message was instead dedicated to his book on Moreno, which risked remaining incomplete. "It would be a great satisfaction for me," Rudi wrote, "if you would agree to be the joint author. There is no other person to whom I would entrust this work."

I responded immediately, with an unbearable pain in my heart. I told him that yes, I would find the time to complete his work. I could not have done anything else because I was indebted to Rudi for his openness, enthusiasm, kindness, and his help with my work on Italian Americans. I had met him more than twenty years earlier in Minneapolis, in his "kingdom," the former site of the Immigration History Research Center. I had decided to research the forgotten literature of the first generation of Italians who emigrated to the United States, and this was the place to do it. On a cold, pale spring morning, I began to consult the catalogs and made request after request. Someone must have told Professor Vecoli, who was the director and heart of that place. He came to see what I was doing, and when I explained, his response was wonderful: He brought me to a door, opened it, and said, "Do it yourself. It's useless to fill out these cards." And so, for a week I was the freest and happiest mouse in the archive. That night, I told Rudi about my progress and asked his advice. At his home, I also had the opportunity to listen to Ruby–De Russo duets on an old LP.

Later, we saw each other in New York, Rome, and Naples, but I regret having spent far too little time with such an extraordinary scholar and a kind and fascinating man. It comforted me to know that perhaps he felt similarly. "Unfortunately, we have seen each other little in the last few years," he wrote in the message in which he thanked me for agreeing to finish the book.

Rudi passed away on June 17, 2008.

More time passed. In Minneapolis, many of the materials on Moreno that he had gathered were carefully collected, a task that was certainly not easy. Rudi had ensured that they would not be available to the public until I had seen them. So I returned to the IHRC's new location in Minneapolis for several days of furious research, many photocopies, and consultations with the magnificent staff who worked there. Soon after I returned to Italy, I received a package of the copies I had requested, and I set myself to the difficult task ahead.

It was not easy. The book on Moreno was a project full of difficulties and surprises. Rudi did a magnificent job in archives on three continents, but I needed to go back to the archives, especially the Italian ones, to check and cite the original documents. Then there was Rudi's legendary handwriting, a kind of hieroglyphics. On top of all that, I also needed to attend to my daily responsibilities beyond Moreno, and this explains why the work was not finished quickly.

And now here we are.

Rudolph Vecoli is the author of this book, and I am, as he wanted, the coauthor. Rudi left me a first draft of the initial five chapters and a sketch of the sixth. I wrote the rest, respecting his plan for ten chapters. Like him, I had the good fortune to find new materials that, in many cases, necessitated my integrating them into what Rudi had already written. And, obviously, I needed to edit the entire manuscript.

The result is this book, whose subtitle retains the working title that Rudi chose. It is my hope that those who read it will be able to experience, in meeting Celso Cesare Moreno, the same fascination that took hold of Rudi and me.

Naples, June 3, 2013

Introduction to the English-Language Edition: "Was Moreno a Sociopath?"

Donna R. Gabaccia

Sociopaths are a hot topic in American popular culture, as any observer of the 2016 American presidential election will have noted. Almost 1 percent of all Internet references to Donald Trump included discussions of sociopathic or psychopathic behaviors or worried more directly the candidate might himself qualify as sociopath or psychopath. Nor did candidate Hillary Clinton receive a pass from armchair psychologists, at least on the Internet. Half of a percent of all references to Clinton also include discussions of sociopathic or psychopathic tendencies and labels. Even professional psychologists disagreed among themselves over the appropriateness of such discussions, and most preferred to reject armchair analyses of persons they had not interacted with in a professional relationship.

As a historian, I knew the 2016 fascination with sociopaths and sociopathic behavior was nothing new. On the contrary, it has been around for quite some time. In 2013 alone, both the *Huffington Post* ("11 Signs You May be Dating a Sociopath," August 23) and *Psychology Today* ("How to Spot a Sociopath," May 7) fed a popular fascination with "difficult" or "toxic" people. Readers who turn to Amazon.com can pursue their curiosity further by ordering *Confessions of a Sociopath: A Life Spent Hiding in Plain*

Sight, *The Psychopath Test*, or the somewhat older book *The Sociopath Next Door*. They can also order books promising a path to recovery from "Emotionally Abusive Relationships with Narcissists, Sociopaths, & Other Toxic People."

Many people have at some point in their lives personally known a person who seemed toxic and that common experience may explain the popularity of books and journalism offering readers help in understanding, explaining, or resisting the amoral, self-centered, or deceitful behavior of individuals who are labeled—often interchangeably—as sociopaths or psychopaths. If sociopaths and psychopaths were merely toxic, however, no one would be fascinated by them, and I would probably not be writing this introduction in the aftermath of Donald Trump's ascendancy to the American presidency. Sociopaths are not just toxic; they are also often deeply attractive and charismatic.

In *Oh Capitano!* Rudi Vecoli and Francesco Durante introduce readers to just one of Italy's 26 million migrants. The migrant, Celso Cesare Moreno, was a man who was simultaneously toxic, deceitful, and charming in equal measure. As a pioneering social historian, Rudi Vecoli focused most of his research and almost all his work as longtime director of the Immigration History Research Center at the University of Minnesota on documenting and understanding the lives of people quite unlike Moreno. He focused not on unique individuals but on the inarticulate mass of ordinary laborers who left Italy in search of work. It was the everyday lives, the political passions of Italy's workers, subversives, anarchists, and close-knit communities that long held Vecoli's attentions.

In his late life, as he moved into retirement, by contrast, Rudi acknowledged and became fascinated with a very different type of migrant—a colorful individual whom he clearly found to be an inexplicable yet deeply attractive research subject. Celso Cesare Moreno was a wild and highly idiosyncratic man. He wandered, adventured, cheated, exaggerated, promoted (mainly himself), and—perhaps this is the most important point—never ceased moving or stopped composing newly invented lies about his past lives as he traveled the world.

Migrants can, and often do, invent and modify their own pasts. But in the book manuscript (which he had not succeeded in finishing prior to his death in 2008), Rudi wanted to tell a different story. In *Oh Capitano!* he sought to create a gripping yarn that could capture both the uniqueness of Moreno and the highly distinctive personality that simultaneously repelled, attracted, and fascinated the people he met as he traveled. Rudi's coauthor, Francesco Durante, respected and to some degree shared the attraction

Rudi felt toward Moreno and his story. This book is a result of their collaboration, much of it unfolding after Rudi's death.

By considering Moreno's appeal to the authors and, I suspect, to readers, too, I want to suggest that personality itself can—and should—be historicized. Was there, for example, anything at all that was distinctively Italian about Moreno's peculiarities, his deceitfulness, or his charm? Or did the era of globalization in which Moreno lived—a time of rapidly expanding empires, trade, and mobility—simply create disproportionately large opportunities for men like him to star successfully, if sometimes only briefly, on the world stage? Moreno certainly sought a role at the center of the globalizing world of the nineteenth century. He claimed at times to have been the ruler of a Southeast Asian island that he then offered for sale to several Western nations. He briefly became prime minister of Hawaii. He testified before the U.S. Congress as an expert witness. He sought to promote a transpacific cable project. He fought with the ministers and leaders of many countries and with fellow Italians and Catholic churchmen almost everywhere. He was more often ignored than feted, and he was accused, probably with cause, of abusing his obligations after claiming guardianship of the sons of King David of Hawaii. Moreno died alone, unloved by anyone and with no significant relations to others (or at least no relations that remain discernible in the historical record that Vecoli and Durante examined).

Vecoli and Durante describe Moreno as a fascinating, baffling, possibly deranged, diabolical man, but also as a deeply attractive, charismatic, and enigmatic human being. In their account, Moreno emerges as larger than life and also as deserving of greater attention—attention that has been lavished on him by the two esteemed authors. (As Vecoli notes in his own preface, traditional social or cultural histories of Italy's migrants scarcely mention Moreno; neither does he figure in most world histories of colonialism.) Whether understood as a fake, a scoundrel, a chameleon, an adventurer, a speculator, a renegade, or simply a nut job (and Moreno was, in his lifetime, slapped with all these labels) or instead accepted as a "dreamer" (Moreno's preferred description of himself, especially when comparing himself grandiosely to Marco Polo or Christopher Columbus), Moreno the man jumps from the pages of this book. Even the paucity of surviving archival material adds to Moreno's appeal, rendering him mysterious. Moreno remains hard to know, hard to pin down, both attractive and repugnant and somewhat elusive, even in the pages of this book.

The power of biography to illustrate and to illuminate the past and the individual life in its social context should never be underestimated. It is certainly on full display in Vecoli and Durante's tale of Moreno's life. In this preface, I do not intend to impose on Moreno the straitjacket of a modern psychobiography. That would be inappropriate, and besides, I am no psychologist. Many readers too will turn to this book simply to enjoy a puzzling and engaging biography and microhistory of a fascinating yet also somehow disturbing and deceitful individual.

Still, I do want to succumb temporarily to the temptation of psychology and to acknowledge the patterns Moreno exhibited as a personality type. I believe the contemporary language of pop psychology and of modern psychiatry can help us to understand some dimensions of Moreno's life and to understand also the powerful attraction people still feel toward him, more than a century after his death. Of course, I turn to the language of psychology as an historian, and I fully acknowledge the dangers of anachronistic thinking. Moreno lived in a decidedly pre-psychological era: in fact, the terms "psychopath" and "psychopathology" scarcely existed at the time of his death in 1901. When nineteenth-century writers discussed the psychopath or the psychopathology of the criminal, they referred broadly to any and all types of mental disturbance and not to any particular cluster of traits. (That identification of clustered traits is instead the marker of modern psychiatry.) Language and terminologies for mental derangement also changed over time. Whereas the use of "psychopath" after 1900 seems to have pointed toward individual, internal, organic, or biological origins for all mental aberrations, the term "sociopath"—which entered popular usage only in the 1950s and still lags somewhat behind "psychopath" in popular discourse—points more clearly toward disturbances in an individual's relationship to others and toward society itself. Modern psychiatry has tried to incorporate both dimensions of these older yet still popular and widely used terms while rendering them more neutral, scientific, and therapeutic through precise catalogues and clusters of behavior.

It is striking, too, that neither "sociopath" nor "psychopath" has found a particularly firm place in the diagnostic terminologies devised by modern, postwar psychiatry. According to the American Psychiatric Association's *Diagnostic and Statistical Manual of Mental Disorders* (DSM-5), persons stigmatized in popular culture as sociopaths and psychopaths suffer instead from "Anti-Social Personality Disorder" (APD). Still, the 2012 revision of the DSM's definition of APD will, I believe, resonate for readers as they meet Celso Cesare Moreno in the chapters that follow.

That definition points toward impairments of both a person's identity (with prominent traits that include egocentrism; self-esteem rooted in personal gain; a tendency toward "goal-setting based on personal gratification" and to "failure to conform to lawful or culturally normative ethical behavior"). APD affects interpersonal relations, which are characterized by lack of empathy and remorse about mistreating others, an incapacity for mutual intimacy, and frequent recourse to deceit in order to exercise power or dominance over others. The person suffering from APD may use subterfuge, or "seduction, charm, glibness" in pursuit of his own interests, and is prone to embellishing and fabricating stories to charm others or to enhance his own position. (I use "he" and "him" consciously here, not because Moreno was a man but because APD is more commonly diagnosed among men than women today.) Dishonesty, callousness, or lack of guilt or remorse (e.g., about the consequences for others of one's deceitful behavior) are also listed among common personality traits, as is anger, hostility and irritability (often through negative responses to "minor slights and insults"). Vengeful behavior is common, as is irresponsibility (for example in making financial or other commitments and agreements with others) and impulsivity. Impulsivity encourages risk-taking. Those with APD are willing to engage in dangerous and even "potentially self-damaging activities"; they pursue risk to escape boredom and because they do not take seriously the possible dangers, even to themselves, of actions impulsively taken. They think big; they act big, and they are cavalier toward others in their pursuit of self-interest. This is what makes them seem "toxic" and "difficult" despite their considerable charm and charisma.

In translating the DSM-5 for a lay audience of Internet users, including those eager to know more about the causes, expressions, and treatment of toxic individuals, the Mayo Clinic in Minnesota notes on its website some of the consequences for self and others of APD.[1] Those with APD are unconcerned with right and wrong; they often have troubles with the law. They can seem exhibitionist and may present themselves as superior to others. The Mayo discussion of APD suggests that children who bully others, who torment animals, and who perform poorly in school because of impulsivity and risk-taking may be diagnosed with APD once they are over eighteen. And as grownups, they may abuse or neglect children and have poor, abusive relationships to their peers. In work settings, those suffering APD are generally irresponsible; they are difficult and uncooperative as coworkers.

Many of the traits associated with APD and the consequences of those traits as described by the Mayo Clinic, will be obvious to readers in the biography of Celso Cesare Moreno. For those scholars who study Italian Americans and the Italian diaspora, however, this summary of APD may also raise large and even more troubling questions. Critics from within and from outside Italian diaspora communities have historically characterized the culture and nation of Italy, or at least the men of that nation, in broadly similar terms—as if masculine personality itself shaped what was once understood to be "national character." Consider, for example, the portraits of men as different as the anarcho-syndicalist Carlo Tresca and the Italian consuls and *prominenti* who functioned as the Italian radicals' archnemeses in the years around 1900. Charm, glibness, personalism (in politics and leadership), and the almost universally and intensely harsh, factional, and intensely individual polemics of the Italian language press (both radical and bourgeois) are not only common themes in scholarship but also viewed as differentiating Italians from leaders and activists of other ethnic or national origins. Popular associations of Italian male migrants with criminality or with the masculine passions (especially passionate recourse to violence) have been associated in Italy and Italy's diasporas with honor, shame, and the defense of female virtue or virginity; they can scarcely be separated from a kind of impulsive and tenacious vengefulness (and attention to one's reputation and desire for "respect") that outsiders, at least—Americans and English-speakers among them—found to be characteristic of Italy's migrants and of Italian culture. The seductiveness, charm, and amorality of Hollywood's and Rome's "Latin lovers" pushes the individual personality traits defined as APD in still other directions that are worth pondering.

Of course, I do not call attention to the overlapping themes of psychiatric and scholarly literatures on Italy's migrants and Italian culture because I wish to revive the concept of national character. Careful readers of this book will see Moreno repeatedly encountering, competing with, and endlessly arguing with other men who seem, as personalities, to have been not so very different from him. And many of these men—even most of them—were not Italians or migrants from Italy. I instead want to urge readers more modestly to think critically about the relation of personality and culture as they explore the intricacies and complexities of Moreno's individual biography and personality. In Moreno's world, it was not uncommon to conflate individual behavior and culture with theories of race. Perhaps that is why modern scholars (or at least the majority who study migration and ethnicity) have been reluctant to reengage with the relationship of personality and culture, for example in the form of psychohistories. Even Vecoli and Durante resisted writing *Oh Capitano!* as a psychohistory of Moreno. They wanted to tell a good story, and they have succeeded in doing so.

Still, their biography of Moreno and the insights of psychiatrists expressed through the DSM'S definition of APD do point toward new, worthwhile, and, I am sure, equally controversial perspectives on the history of colonialism and the spread of a rapacious type of expansive capitalism in early modern and modern eras. Certainly, the life of Moreno was both a global story and one in which both capitalist and colonialist impulses entwined and expressed themselves in particularly dramatic, and self-dramatizing (if ultimately unsuccessful) forms. Writing for Britain's *The Guardian*, William Dalrymple, in a recent article titled "The Original Corporate Raiders," characterizes Robert Clive (1725–74), the manager in India of the East India Company, as an "unstable sociopath" and argues further that "it was not the British government that seized India, but a private company."[2] It is easy to imagine the entrepreneurial ship captain, Moreno, aspiring to the same level of global and transnational influence. Italy, the nation of his birth, early proved to be far too small a stage for his ambitions and his aspirations. The possibility that impulsive, deceitful, and charming men such as Moreno could grasp expanding opportunities during an era of globalization, thus finding a place in the historical record, pushes even more effectively against any easy equation of personality and Italian culture.

While I doubt that world historians will find room in their sweeping narratives for revived studies of personality and culture, they might want to ponder how colonialism and capitalism created the kinds of openings and paths that impulsive, unprincipled men such as Clive and Moreno seized. In doing so they can highlight how the search for personal gain creates openings for humans willing to disregard the moral, ethical, and material consequences of their actions even for people they claimed to represent, guard, or speak for. Rarely does charisma or deceit figure as prominently in global and world histories of capitalism or colonialism as they do in Vecoli and Durante's biography of Cesare Celso Marino. Perhaps it is time for more world historians to take up this complex theme. In doing so they would certainly honor Rudolph Vecoli's lifelong commitments to the ordinary labor migrants and to his analysis of their confrontation with global capitalism and colonialism.

Translator's Note

Elizabeth O. Venditto

O Capitano! proved a uniquely challenging translation. Vecoli left Durante—and by extension, me—drafts of the first five chapters and a few pages of the sixth. However, I could not simply translate Durante's work and add it to Vecoli's original text. Vecoli left early, rough drafts. They included typographical errors, notes about material to add in the future, and multiple possibilities for translating Italian-language citations into English. Durante made nuanced and painstaking contributions to the first five chapters. He clearly tried to preserve as much of Vecoli's writing as possible and translated it directly into Italian. But he also made corrections and additions to many quotations and to the manuscript. In some cases, he added a sentence or two at the end of a paragraph. In others, he inserted several paragraphs of new material into the existing chapter. I decided to translate Durante's final manuscript in order to reflect its polish, flow, and accuracy. The lone exception is Vecoli's preface, which I have included here with a few minor edits for spelling and punctuation.

Yet Vecoli's drafts were central to my English translation. I frequently referred to them for a sense of his voice and, more important, the type of book he intended to write. I carried this sensibility throughout my entire translation. I took my cues from Vecoli in smaller ways too, such as leaving certain non-English phrases untranslated and occasionally including one of Vecoli's particularly vivid turns of phrase.

Therefore, this entire text is a translation, but one in which I carefully tried to convey Vecoli's voice as well as both authors' fascination with, and perhaps admiration for, an audacious and irrepressible man and his larger-than-life biography.

Oh Capitano!

CHAPTER 1

The Traveler's Spirit

Before there was a Capitano Marittimo Moreno, there was the boy, Celso. We could ask what in his childhood instilled in him such wanderlust and lofty ambitions, and what then could have sparked his penchant for exoticism and risk. We could find an answer in his education, both in his family and in school. It would be useful to know what that boy learned from parents and siblings, what his interests were, who were his friends and teachers, which books he read, who were his heroes and who his villains. But if Celso kept a diary or wrote a memoir, it has not surfaced. There is only a brief description of the first half-century of his life as told to the writer Giovanni Faldella. For the rest, for a personality who would turn up in half the world's newspapers, we must not invent but surmise from the environment in which he grew up how youthful experiences molded his character, mind, and spirit.

Celso was born on March 5, 1831, in Dogliani, in the province of Cuneo, about seventy kilometers southeast of Turin, then part of the Kingdom of Sardinia.[1] Although one can see snowclad Monviso from its hilltops, the region in which Dogliani is situated, the Langhe, comprises rolling hills, giving it a pleasing but not dramatic appearance. In a natural basin defined by the Rea, which flows from the Tanaro River, a pre-Roman settlement developed along its banks. The stream ran dry in summer, but in the spring its waters, fed by the spring snowmelt, became a torrent flooding the lowlands. While the mountain air was celebrated as salubrious, the constricted valley received moisture-laden winds from the east, producing violent storms and causing illnesses, it was said, "for the most part of inflammatory nature."[2]

The narrow but fertile plain of the Rea produced grain and vegetables. In the highest subalpine lands, by contrast, the soil produced more meager harvests at the price of hard labor, and herds of sheep and goats survived on scarce pasture. This harsh environment imposed a regime of subsistence farming upon the *contadini*, the peasants, who in any case lacked access to markets. Giuseppe Cesare Abba, the *garibaldino* (Garibaldian) writer from Cairo Montenotte, some thirty kilometers south of Dogliani, seven years younger than Celso, wrote that in these areas, unlike other regions of Italy, "no one died of true *miseria*."[3] Corn was abundant, and the *contadini* used it to produce the polenta that, with a bit of cheese, was the basis of their winter diet. In the other seasons, vegetable soup, chestnuts, mushrooms, and game completed the diet, along with abundant libations. Ill suited for the *latifondo*, or large-scale agriculture, the territory was subdivided into small- and medium-sized properties. The sandy soil on the hillsides was perfect for vineyards. As Casalis's *Dizionario geografico*, published in 1840, explained, although "not very productive in terms of cereals," it "produces wines of the best quality in abundance."[4] The cities of Alba, Alessandria, and Cuneo were markets for the famous Dolcetto di Dogliani, although until the nineteenth century the lack of good means of communication greatly limited commerce there.

Modern Dogliani took shape during the fourteenth century with the construction of a castle on a high point overlooking the Rea Valley. As the population grew, its physical configuration reflected its economic and social hierarchies. In a society that was slowly emerging from its feudal past, there were three classes: the *signorie*, leading families because of their wealth or nobility; the bourgeoisie, middle-class landowners, merchants, and artisans; and the *contadini*. With the aristocracy's decline, more expansive lands were divided into more modest holdings that were often cultivated by their owners. During the nineteenth century, the number of landowners doubled. The most celebrated citizen of Dogliani, the future second president of the Italian Republic, Luigi Einaudi, observed that "the share of the land belonging to the non-farmers is much smaller now than less than a century ago; and it will decrease even further, because the only ones who can profit from the land are the farmers."[5] A class of *giornalieri* (day laborers) did not exist. The tenants who acquired land through annual contracts were called *schiavandai*, a term obviously derived from *schiavo* (slave) and bearing an echo of feudalism. The largest parcels of lands still possessed by the *signori* or acquired by affluent bourgeoisie, were most often cultivated through tenant farming, in which half of the yield went to the owner and the other half to the tenant.

When Celso came into the world, Dogliani consisted of three areas. In the Borgo Castello, enclosed by the city walls, were the palaces of the *signorie*, the residences of those employed in commerce, professions, and skilled trades, and tenements for laborers. As the site of the first church, San Lorenzo, the seigniorial towers, and the marketplace, this district acquired an urban ambiance early on. By the mid–nineteenth century, the population of Dogliani had grown to almost five thousand, most of whom lived outside the walls in two new settlements: Borgo Maggiore, in the valley, and Borgo Airali, on the right bank of the Rea, inhabited by merchants, artisans, and manual laborers. The Moreni family lived in the Borgo Airali.

After centuries of stagnation, feeling the influence of the French Revolution and the Napoleonic Wars, Dogliani experienced rapid changes beginning in the last decade of the eighteenth century. The "new Dogliani," which Celso knew, was no longer a closed community isolated from the outside world. For the old Doglianese, the village had been the *patria* (fatherland), but more current identities gained favor among the upper and middle classes: first "Piedmontese," and then "Italian." The French Revolution was the catalyst for this change, and the Langhe responded more rapidly than other cisalpine regions to the rallying cry "*Liberté, egalité, fraternité*." A contemporary resident of Dogliani lamented that the French had scattered "the poison of democracy of which we had not even known the name, inspiring fanatics with ideas of liberty and equality which were promised but never fulfilled."[6]

The French occupation, which lasted fifteen years, brought even more significant institutional changes. The king of Sardinia was deposed, a republic was born, and the Napoleonic Code was introduced. Feudal rights and primogeniture were abolished. However, all this did not result in a significant redistribution of wealth. The properties of the *signori* were not confiscated, unlike those of the Church. A convent became the site of Dogliani's town government and of a *collegio*, a secondary school founded in 1804.

Abba noted the positive changes brought about by the French presence, but also the problems that sprang from it. Major battles of the Napoleonic

Wars were fought in the Piedmont, and during one campaign Napoleon himself came to the Langhe. The French and Austrian armies left destruction in their wake. Religious conflicts precipitated a civil war between Jacobins and "Catholic fanatics," whom the previously cited Doglianese patrician described as a ragamuffin mass of Christians dedicated to rape and plunder, while the Jacobin creed gave the "plebes" license to attack the "wealthy." In the course of this conflict, however, Dogliani was spared the sieges and sackings suffered by other towns by virtue of an astute policy of "blessed neutrality." Responding to the shifting fortunes of war, the *signori* sang hosannas either to the Napoleonic Republic or to the king, emperor, and Church, depending on which way the wind was blowing.

The peace that followed the French army's defeat in the wastes of Russia and then Napoleon's fall was a cause for celebration. Unforeseen was that the restoration of the Kingdom of Savoy and the crowning of Carlo Alberto would bring decades of harsh reaction. "The time of Napoleon having passed," Abba commented ironically, "life slowly returned almost to what it had been a half century before":

> With a little art, the State and the Church restored everything to the old ways, with much civil discipline, many religious practices, a renewed feeling that each lived to enjoy the little he had and to atone for his share of original sin. . . . True glory had always been and was to be again living humbly content in the place that Providence had assigned to each person, improving yourself only through your own strength without harming your neighbor: interest in and fear of God, loving the Prince, venerating the Pope and the hierarchy, obeying your parents, teaching your children to obey, thinking about your soul, and respecting the authorities under which you had been placed.

The old and familiar forms of respect also returned. The formal second-person *voi* was used between husband and wife, brothers and sisters, while the use of the informal *tu* was reduced to a sign of peasant ignorance. Social conformism and political repression were possibly made more tolerable by the prosperity, until then unknown, which Dogliani experienced in the decades after Napoleon. Among the legacy of that era was public works, including a network of good streets and bridges. In Dogliani, progress took the form of dams to control the flooding of the Rea and bridges to cross it, as well as water pumps and public fountains in the central piazza. Even more importantly, improved infrastructure supported a broader distribution of wine and other products. With three markets a week and five fairs a year, Dogliani became a commercial hub. Outsiders were drawn to the town to trade all sorts of goods: livestock, hemp, mushrooms and the prized white truffles, and mulberry leaves. Harvesting the leaves and raising silkworms for two silk mills provided the *contadini* with welcome extra income. The grape, however, remained the mainstay of Dogliani's agriculture. More than half of Dogliani's cultivable land was dedicated to vineyards, and the growing demand for Dolcetto led to an expansion of vineyards on the hillsides.

In the new Dogliani, increasing prosperity was not enjoyed equally. While the well-being of the *contadini* improved, as indicated by the growing number who owned land, increased rents afforded the gentry more affluent lives. In that time, as Abba commented wryly, "the rich enjoyed themselves." Class distinctions were exacerbated: reduced differences in material wealth had the effect of heightening differences in honorific wealth. By the 1840s, the social and cultural calendar of the *signori* already included performances by a symphony orchestra, musical band, and theater. Opera became the favored entertainment. An endless round of parties, balls, hunting outings, and soccer games kept the "noble heirs of castles" occupied. The festivities reached a high point during Carnevale, when they held challenges to see "who could last the most nights awake, at dinner, in revelry." Nevertheless, the world of the *signori* was not so pleasant. Abba observed that they were "divided by profound jealousy and hatreds," constantly involved in struggles to "triumph and rule." Conflicts erupted around questions like the ownership of church pews and how close they were to the altar. Pleasure was derived from thwarting the ambitions of one's adversaries to become members of the town council or even, heaven forbid, mayor. Derisive nicknames were given to enemies, and malicious schemes involving anonymous letters, satires, and entrapments, were concocted to disgrace them. In this playground of spiteful pleasures, a renewed restlessness among the middle class roiled the waters on which the *signori* were gaily sailing.

The French Revolution, which Abba described as a "meteor" that suddenly exploded in the heavens, was in reality, a thaw that released frozen ideas about liberty and equality. During the reign of King Carlo Alberto, those guilty and also only suspected of subversive tendencies were executed or exiled to the salt mines of Sardinia. In each city, it was said that the mayor, parish priest, and head of the *carabinieri* had absolute power. In this hostile climate, the voice of a young Genoese man sent a shiver of fear through the ranks of the ruling classes. Giuseppe Mazzini became the oracle of a united and republican Italy. From exile, he continued his crusade, recruiting converts everywhere. Bourgeoisie and soldiers, mostly coming from the middle class, joined his secret society, Young Italy. The Mazzinians plotted revolutions against the king, dukes, and popes. If discovered, they were ready to face the firing squad.

Across Europe, 1848 was the culmination of revolutionary movements dedicated to destroying absolutism. The uprising of 1821 and the failed ones of 1833–1834 in Savoy and Genoa were followed by harsh repression with thousands of arrests and hundreds of executions. The spirit of defiance, however, was not defeated. Facing with this indomitable movement, in 1848 Carlo Alberto granted the Statuto, which instituted a constitutional monarchy. Although the right to vote was very limited, liberals greeted the election of parliamentary deputies from Dogliani as the dawn of a new day. Abba celebrated it with an exclamation point: "The ideas won!" Liberty had triumphed over despotism, but the Statuto did not satisfy the republicans, while the *signori* lamented nostalgically for the ancien régime. After an initial victory at Goito in the war against Austria, the first for national independence, Piedmontese forces met disastrous defeat at Novara, causing King Carlo Alberto to abdicate.

Seized with patriotic fervor, Celso Moreno, now seventeen, enlisted in the Savoyard army and was gravely wounded at Goito in June 1848.[7] It was the beginning of his military career. The words of a wounded veteran in Abba's *Uomini e soldati* could have applied to him: "War is a *festa* . . . ! Once one is a soldier, what do you want to do but go to war? It scares those who are at home. I was never so happy as when I was at war!"[8]

After 1848, military defeat and political disillusion were followed by a series of natural disasters in the Langhe. A mysterious disease infected the vineyards, almost destroying the grape harvest. At the same time, the silkworms became sick and died, too. These were black years of depression. The most affluent had to resort to strict frugality. Only a decade later would these ills have passed and a certain level of prosperity returned. Meanwhile, Italian patriotism swelled the Piedmontese forces. In 1859, the second war for independence, they defeated the Austrians with the help of the French and took Lombardy. In 1860, Garibaldi's *Mille* did the impossible, liberating Sicily and the entire south from Bourbon control. Abba was among them, Moreno not. The Kingdom of Italy became a reality.

These then were the turbulent and exhilarating times, but also years of repression and conformity, into which Celso was born and in which his identity and character were formed. What did he think and do during this time? Likely the youth gathered to listen to stories from some old Jacobin war veteran or from a survivor of a revolt. Of fiery temperament, Celso absorbed Mazzini's ideas and made Garibaldi his hero. The Langhe was the world in which he grew up, but obviously the most influential part of that world was his family. Lacking letters or other personal documentation, we encounter a wall of silence. Only through some small gaps is it possible for us to glimpse more intimate scenes. From the archives we learn that Father Vincenzo Garrone of the Church of Saints Quirico and Paolo baptized him on March 5, 1831. The newborn was accompanied by his parents, Carlo Giuseppe Moreni and Antonia Vivalda, and by his godparents, Battista Berrius and Caterina Depero.[9] The fourth of ten children, he was one of five who survived to adulthood.

Although they were not *signori*, the Moreno family was well off. For generations, the family was the owners of sizeable plots of land. Carlo Giuseppe had inherited large properties from his grandfather, Lorenzo Giovanni Battista Moreni. Various documents say that Carlo Giuseppe worked as a shoemaker, but he was also described as a landowner, merchant, or, in one case, with the annotation "*Caproni*," that is, a goat seller. It is, however, rather clear that this was a resourceful and industrious man. Carlo Giuseppe's bourgeois status is demonstrated by the fact that he owned his own home, which reportedly had eight rooms, a shop, two barn stalls, and two workshops, along with a horse and other animals. In 1827, Carlo Giuseppe was at the head of an extended family; along with his wife, three children, and a servant, his lodgers included a veterinarian, a shoemaker, and two weavers, each with a wife and children—in all, fifteen people. Various trades were exercised under his roof, surely also including the cultivation of silkworms.[10] The real estate registries recorded numerous transactions by Carlo Giuseppe, operations that produced considerable revenue in rents and leases.[11] Situated on the alluvial plane of the Rea, the Moreni's fertile soil produced good harvests, more than enough to sustain the family, so the excess was sold at the market. Tenant farmers cultivated vines, grains, and vegetables and tended livestock. Although some sources described him as the son of peasants, Celso instead came from a family of considerable means, and this was sufficient to spare him the hard work of the fields. That does not rule out the possibility, however, that he also cut grapes during the grape harvest or mulberry leaves to feed the silkworms. Judging by his physique as an adult, he must have been a sturdy young man, one who enjoyed climbing the mountains, collecting mushrooms, and hunting hares and partridges. Lacking noble or bourgeois neighbors, his playmates must have been the tenants' children. His position as the boss's son and heir (*rampollo*), along with his dominant personality, must have made him a natural leader in their games. Always combative, he must have been a formidable opponent in any fight. His demonstrated ability as an adult to have a rapport with any person from a culture or class different than his own may be attributable to this type of childhood. Describing his travels in Asia, he emphasized that he never avoided mingling with the natives. "From the highest level of the social ladder to the most miserable *coolies*, I maintained intimate bonds and I conversed with people of any social class."[12] His relationships with the highest-status *Doglianesi*, noted for their arrogance, can explain his intolerance for aristocratic pretentions throughout his entire life. Quick to take umbrage and unforgiving, he was unrelenting in seeking revenge.

We can only hypothesize about his family relationships. The death of his mother, Antonia, in 1843 doubtlessly left a lasting mark on Celso. Among his brothers, the oldest, Lorenzo, became a priest and spent most of his adult life in Rome. Another older brother, Giuseppe Maria, was heir to the family lands. The youngest, Filippo, became a merchant, while his sister Maddalena Carolina (the third child and only surviving daughter) owned land in her own name.

Abba left a vivid description of his education, and it was the same type that Celso received. Most children of *contadini* origin never saw the inside of a classroom. The children of rich or middle-class families went to primary school and studied reading, writing, and arithmetic. Priests ruled the classrooms with slaps and insults; their very look "made students tremble." But Abba idealized one of his teachers, Father Atanasio Canata, who he said managed to open his students' hearts to a love for grammar, literature, and the *patria*. While the children of the *signori* proceeded to *collegi*, where humanities, rhetoric, and philosophy comprised the curriculum, those of middling families rarely went beyond primary school. The few to do so mostly became priests or, as Abba sarcastically commented, "went to learn law and medicine from lawyers and doctors of reputation, then by these marquis were appointed doctors, surgeons, or at least phlebotomists and lawyers and notaries, with the right to work among the people of the area but made to go to war by the real graduates."[13] Moreno and Abba, however, did not conform to stereotypes. Both, in different ways, lived nonconformist lives and resisted supine submission.

Given his tenacity, aggression, and intelligence, Celso must have been a precocious, not to mention difficult, student. As an adult it was said that he knew at least twelve languages. Other sources say twenty-five (including more than eight dialects), still others as many as forty-two.[14] This suggests that he could have excelled in his Latin studies, which he frequently cited in his writings. His formidable polemical talents could have been honed in youthful verbal combat. If the child is the father of the man, Celso's rebellion against the arbitrary and cruel discipline inflicted by the *preti maestri* could explain his animosity as an adult in confrontations with men of the cloth, who "became the Hammer" and "the black beast."[15] But we lack a curriculum vitae, so the question of where and when Celso attended a *collegio* remains unresolved. It may have been the secondary school in Dogliani, which was said to have "good teachers." But in an 1893 letter, Celso expressed his sorrow for the death of Gaspare Buffa, whom he claimed was a relative, childhood friend, and classmate. Buffa, who achieved recognition as a poet and journalist, was born in 1832 in Cairo Montenotte and, along with Abba, had attended the Scolopi Fathers' *collegio* in nearby Carcare. Celso, without a mother and being the difficult son that he was, may also have been sent to school away from home.[16]

In the few places in which he referred to his days as a student, Moreno maintained, with a certain continuity, that his education was paid for by an uncle, the bishop of Ivrea, Luigi Moreno.[17] Occupying the episcopal throne of the diocese of Ivrea for over forty years, Luigi Moreno was an important figure within the Catholic hierarchy. Among the most prestigious supporters of the necessity of reconciliation between Church and State and the main force behind the periodical *L'Armonia della Religione con la Civiltà*, he took part in the First Vatican Council (1869–70).

A family connection between Celso Moreni and Luigi Moreno, however, remains undetermined.[18] In any case, Celso's identity became firmly rooted in this alleged relationship. In a military conscription roll of 1851, he was listed as Celso Moreni. But four years later, in documents certifying his diploma from the University of Genoa, he signed as Celso Moreno, with an elaborate handwriting full of flourishes that seems evidence of a relaxed elegance and a supreme self-confidence.[19] The significance of the name change can only be a source of speculation. Did it signify a rupture between Celso and his birth family? Or was it an expression of his ambition to transcend bourgeois status and claim a more noble ancestry?

What of Dogliani did that young man carry with him when he began adventuring in distant lands? Moreno would only return to Italy twice, in 1864–68 and then between 1880 and 1884. During his last sojourn, having earned fame and notoriety, a local delegation met him at the nearest railroad station. And though he was not present, he offered a dinner to his Doglianesi friends.[20] The weekly *Gazzetta di Dogliani* published descriptions of his exploits and articles that Moreno wrote. Lamenting the fact that he no longer received the newspaper, Moreno wrote to the *Gazzetta* saying that he liked to read the paper that "brings me cherished news from my hometown." The editor reassured him that, even though Moreno had not received the paper for unknown reasons, it was regularly sent to "our illustrious fellow citizen C. C. Moreno."[21] Celso clearly enjoyed the adulation of his compatriots. But there is no trace of a correspondence with friends or relatives.

Describing Sumatra, Moreno permitted himself a rare moment of nostalgia: "Those hillocks, although different in nature, climate, and vegetation, brought to mind those of my native country, the hills of Piedmont, which for some time I had lost the hope of seeing again."[22] But more revealing is that, after decades of absence, he continued to sign his letters "Celso Cesare Moreno of Dogliani."

Youth is the mold in which one's character and sense of one's place in the world is forged. Among Moreno's convictions was, to quote him, "my unalterable belief in destiny." But he also believed that "an individual, as well as a nation, or a government, is as powerful as the force of his will," with a footnote: "*Audaces fortuna juvat*" (fortune favors the bold), which was then the motto of anyone who longed to act daringly.[23] If someone had pointed out the contradiction, perhaps Moreno would have responded that it was his destiny to be bold and to do great deeds.

We do not know exactly when he left home. In his conversations with Faldella, he talked about being a cabin boy, assigned the humblest tasks on a ship.[24] In the 1851 military conscription, Moreno, then twenty, was listed as "employed by the public works office in Sardinia."[25]

All his life, Moreno proudly bore the title Capitano Marittimo, or sea captain. By attending the Scuola di Nautica di Genova, one could earn the license required for that rank. Under the auspices of the city's chamber of commerce, the school trained young men as officers for Genoa's growing fleet of merchant ships. Graduates received a captain's or first officer's license, according to their course of study. The curriculum included geometry, trigonometry, navigation, astronomy, and naval mechanics. The admissions requirements were that the applicant be between fourteen and thirty years old, a citizen of the Sardinian state, have the desire to sail, be able to read and write in correct Italian, have a knowledge of math, including fractions, and hold a certificate of good conduct. The last could have been a problem, but Celso had the rest of the prerequisites. As for expenses, which students had to pay, he claimed that his uncle, the bishop of Ivrea, saw to his education. Although the chronology is unclear, Moreno attended the Royal Naval Academy in Genoa, graduating with the rank of lieutenant.[26] He soon had the opportunity to serve the Kingdom of Savoy in time of war.

According to an article that would summarize these exploits thirty years later, in June 1853 Moreno was a sailor on a Sardinian frigate in the Turkish port of Smyrna (Izmir) during an episode that marks his first "encounter" with America. Martin Koszta, a Hungarian patriot who moved to the United States and became a citizen, was "kidnapped" by the city's Austrian consul, who wanted to take him on board the brigantine *Huszar* and bring him back to Trieste. The captain of the American corvette *Saint Louis*, Duncan N. Ingraham, protested to both the consul and his Austrian colleague, while also anchoring his vessel threateningly alongside the Austrian ship with his weapons loaded and aimed. These were tense days, but Koszta was ultimately returned to the Americans, to the jubilation of all those who had witnessed the charged situation. Among them was Moreno, who was reportedly full of joy at the insult inflicted upon the hated "Germans."[27]

In 1855, Great Britain and France allied with Turkey to stop Russian expansion in the eastern Mediterranean. At that time it was difficult to recruit their own soldiers, so the English hired mercenaries from other countries, including Italy. The English and French were delighted when Camillo Benso, Count of Cavour and prime minister of the Kingdom of Sardinia, sent a force of eighteen thousand soldiers to fight in Crimea. Most Italians had no idea where Crimea was, and they did not understand why Christians should fight for the Turks. But when the Piedmontese troops left Genoa in May 1855, a crowd gathered on the docks to see them off. General Alfonso La Marmora, commander of the contingent, chose his best officers (among whom might have been Moreno) and troops. The expedition disembarked in Balaklava on the Black Sea. Cholera spread through the camps, and many died, including Alessandro La Marmora, the general's brother and commander of a brigade of riflemen. The Piedmontese soldiers proved their courage on August 16, 1855, at the battle of Chernaya, in which Moreno, according to numerous journalistic accounts, was again wounded. In the end, without achieving a clear military victory on the battlefield, the allied forces inflicted a heavy defeat on the Russians. Thanks to the valiant participation of the Savoyard troops, Cavour was able to represent the Kingdom of Sardinia at the Treaty of Paris, where the participants decided the terms of peace. Above all, it earned the benevolent neutrality of the English and French toward the unification of the Kingdom of Italy. Moreno, too, had earned his "red badge of courage." At the age of twenty-four, his experience in battle cemented his notion of being a true warrior.[28]

In the midst of all these activities, Moreno was somehow able to earn a diploma as a *misuratore*, a person trained in geometry to execute construction plans, from the University of Genoa on July 3, 1855. Since January of that year he had been employed in that position under the Genoese engineer Filippo Lanza.[29] He may have exercised this profession for a while, but about this time, he bought a ship. How he was able to do this remains a mystery. Oral tradition in the Moreni family talks about an ancestor who, having stolen a large amount of timber, sold it and bought a vessel with the proceeds. He left for Asia, where he married a very rich woman.[30]

We wish we had a diary that could shed light on what Moreno thought during those formative years. Lacking that, the biography of a contemporary, whose life had striking parallels to Moreno's, might provide some insights. Nino Bixio was born into a wealthy family in 1821. His father was the director of the gold exchange in Genoa. His mother died when he was just nine years old. When his father remarried, Nino did not want to accept his stepmother. Nor would he tolerate school discipline. Strong-willed and rebellious, he incurred the wrath of his teachers, who forced him to sit with his arms folded or kneeling on stones or standing behind the blackboard. Finding him incorrigible, his father set him up as a ship's boy on a brigantine heading for America. Nino ran away and, forced to return home, became even more recalcitrant. At sixteen he was again sent to sea, this time on a warship of the king of Sardinia. Nino learned to obey but also to command. Seven years later, he became a merchant seaman, his eyes fixed on Asia. He embarked on a ship for Sumatra and returned to Italy after numerous misadventures.

In 1848, Bixio plunged into the struggle for the unification of Italy. He became an ardent follower of Garibaldi and one of his most famous commanders during the Expedition of the Thousand. Elected to Parliament, he took part in the unsuccessful Battle of Mentana in 1867 and was appointed senator in 1870. On September 20 he participated in the capture of Rome. Then, to his colleagues' dismay and astonishment, he decided to return to Asia. He left with his ship, the *Maddaloni*, and devoted himself to coastal commerce in Southeast Asia. Contracted with the Dutch, he was at war with the Sultan of Aceh and transported mercenaries from Surabaya to Sumatra. But cholera infected his ship, killing soldiers, crewmembers, and then Bixio himself on December 12, 1873. He was buried on Sumatra.[31]

While the differences in the life trajectories of Moreno and Bixio are obvious, the convergences are instructive. Both lost their mothers when they were still very young. Although Moreno's father did not remarry, the relationship between authoritarian father and uncontrollable son had to be similar. Self-proclaimed anticlericals, both had brothers who were priests. Celso was also a cabin boy in his youth. Both were fixated on Asia, and their travels to Sumatra were important events in their lives, with very different results. Their stars were to meet not in Sumatra but in Florence, then the capital of the kingdom, where Bixio played an important role in Moreno's career. But more astonishing is the similarity in their temperaments. Both were prideful, single-minded, self-confident, to an extreme degree, and had terrible tempers when crossed.

Why the sea? Why Asia? Nothing in Moreno's family history provides a clue to understand these choices. Unlike Bixio, Celso did not grow up breathing salt air. Dogliani is thirty miles from the port of Savona, and while it is more than likely that he visited the coast as a boy, it was not his regular environment. It could have been landlocked life that stoked the boy's imagination with visions of ships with tall masts, stormy seas, and exotic lands. For centuries, ships left Genoa headed for continents across the line of the horizon. Generations of mariners had created a nautical oral tradition of chilling terrors and exotic pleasures. During winter evenings, people gathered in stables to warm themselves with the animals' heat and the stories of local narrators. Surely Celso was among those who listened to these old sea dogs spin yarns that stirred strange yearnings in the young and old.

A reading of Celso's boyhood aspirations by Giovanni Faldella provides a provocative, if tendentious, interpretation. The year was 1881, the place Rome, and Moreno was fifty years old. From lengthy conversations Faldella conjured the youthful dreams and desires that might have formed the vocation of the "Piedmontese Traveler":

> From youth his traveler's soul is irritated by the incessant pounding of the chickens in the barnyard, is irritated by the capers that grow in the liming of the paternal walls and the moldy ground, that cut through the roof tiles of the old church, where he was baptized . . . is even irritated by having always in his way this old Europe with its diplomats in white ties, and he desires and longs to see something else; he knows that there is much more to study, to admire, and to laugh about.

And:

> A country boy, tending sheep, hears the song of a migrant bird, bringing thoughts of distant lands. He sees a dark-skinned boy, brought back by missionaries to adorn a seigniorial coach, and feels the pull of faraway places. He dreams of being a cabin boy clinging to the mast of

> a ship rolling in the swells of the ocean, and then the captain and owner of a vessel bedecked with lofty sails.[32]

Faldella also points out that another brilliant Piedmontese writer who died prematurely, "the gloomy Iginio Ugo Tarchetti . . . feverishly dreamed of being a sultan for twenty-four hours." Moreno likewise "daydreamed of ships loaded with spices, of canals to build, lions to kill, slaves to be freed"—and here his prose takes an erotic turn—"of Indian dancers who receive visitors as long as they leave their swords at the door, indicating that the fortress is occupied, and that others cannot enter." And

> barbarous witches who mingle with apes, of the embraces of so many dark-skinned women, from which he must then fade, silk galleries of odalisques who slip out of hanging gardens. . . . Pushed for the first time in front of some nude savage queen lying on the mats, who sits with her hands resting on a pillow on her knees, she looks with scorn upon that king and pulls the ears of the piglet with which the king of Burma was playing as if it were a puppy.[33]

Moreno's or Faldella's fantasies? Or perhaps the fantasy of an entire generation of adventurous young European men who went in search of not only fame and fortune but also a sexuality free of bourgeois morality?

CHAPTER 2

The Treasures of Asia

By taking to the sea, Moreno was following an ancient and illustrious tradition. Motivated by faith, greed, and glory, Italian missionaries, explorers, and traders had since the thirteenth century been among the first Europeans to undertake the arduous journeys over land and sea to East Asia. The most famous was Marco Polo, whose book *Il milione* (*The Travels of Marco Polo*, 1271) remained the most important source of information about Asia for hundreds of years. Certainly Celso, who cited Marco Polo as his model, had read it.[1]

For centuries, Venice and Genoa were the terminuses of the spice trade with Asia. Each year, tons of pepper, cloves, tea, coffee, and sugar were unloaded on their docks and then sold throughout Europe. As a result of their monopoly of these commodities, the cities enjoyed enormous wealth, visible in the form of lavish churches and palaces. In 1497, though, the vision of Prince Henry of Portugal was realized when Vasco da Gama sailed along the African coast around the Cape of Good Hope and into the Indian Ocean. The new commercial route favored the Atlantic countries: Portugal, Spain, England, and, above all, the Netherlands. Commerce in Venice and Genoa declined, and the cities lost their glamour and riches. By the mid–nineteenth century, however, an increasing number of ships flying the Sardinian flag sailed in the Indian Ocean, the seas of China, and the East Indies.[2]

Moreno followed in the wake of new Genoese mariners when he hauled anchor. In the beginning, the Mediterranean was his zone of activity, but soon after he made his way to the Cape of Good Hope, the Horn of Africa, the Red Sea, and finally, India. Though only in his mid-twenties, he was captain of his own ship. We do not know the precise dates of his voyage, the name of his ship, or the cargo it was carrying, and the news, provided by Faldella, that Moreno traded in India with Garibaldi before 1859, seems rather suspect.[3] It is certain, however, that it was a long voyage. It could take as long as six months to cover a distance of about 12,400 miles. What was he doing and thinking during those many days? Did he fantasize, like many of his contemporaries, of becoming the white lord of a kingdom, worshiped by his dark-skinned subjects, bedecked with jewels, surrounded by maidens ready to fulfill his every desire?

By the 1850s, many Italian sea captains were trading with India, the Malaysian archipelago, Cochinchina, Japan, Korea, the Philippines, and even Australia. As the mercantile center of the thriving commerce between India and Italy, Calcutta already had a modest Italian community. Moreno settled in this cosmopolitan, tumultuous port city, where he soon found himself at the center of a controversy that reached back to Turin. The Kingdom of Savoy established its first Asian consulate in Calcutta in 1841, which in turn spurred a network of consular posts in India, China, and the South Seas. Giovanni Casella, a successful merchant, skillfully served as consul from the beginning.[4] Another well-known and respected representative of the Italian community in Calcutta was a missionary, Father Vincenzo Bruno. A Piedmontese from the province of Ivrea, he had joined the Oblates of the Virgin Mary, a congregation that had sent missionaries to Asia for a long time. In 1839, while still a young man, Bruno was assigned to evangelize a vast territory in India and Burma, a task to which he dedicated the rest of his life.[5]

Arriving in Calcutta in June 1859, Moreno was soon involved in a bitter dispute with both Casella and Bruno. At that time, Italian patriots' passionate opposition to the pope's secular power generated great tensions between the Vatican and the kingdom. In this heated situation, an article appeared in Turin's *Gazzetta del Popolo* on January 17, 1860, that accused Consul General Casella of being the first to subscribe to a fund for the Pope's relief, an act contrary to the government's policy. The article also criticized the morality of the missionaries in Calcutta, describing them as "womanizers." Alessandro Borella, a member of the Chamber of Deputies and the letter's alleged author, announced a parliamentary interpellation into the Sardinian state of affairs in Calcutta.[6]

What had been a clash of personalities in a distant land became a matter of national interest in Italy. Although Casella declared it to be a thing of "little importance," he gave the Minister of Foreign Affairs a detailed report, a ten-page letter in minuscule handwriting. He observed that if the article "had been based on more solid and truthful information, Deputy Borella . . . would certainly have been praised by his country's liberal institutions for his ardor. Instead the honorable deputy slanders me." Casella was convinced that someone else had inspired the investigation: "To prove my hostility to the politics of the King's government," wrote the consul, "the learned writer believes the word of a certain Piedmontese engineer whom I called to the chancellor's office to reprimand him for having said that the priests of Calcutta are womanizers."[7]

Casella then gave a complex and rambling explanation of the facts. He insisted that he had no part in the subscription and described the man to whom, in his opinion, the present scandal could be traced:

> This Piedmontese engineer is a certain Moreno Celso, a native of Dogliani. . . . When he presented himself at the Consulate bearing a regular passport, I welcomed him and was ready to help him with anything he asked. He said that he was an engineer and looking for employment, but that he would have preferred to go to Burma because, as a virgin territory, he would make his fortune more easily there. He made other comments that immediately showed that this young man's mind was somewhat twisted.

Casella then listed the "dishonorable incidents" in which Moreno was involved in in India:

> He was thrown out of one boarding house for not paying for his lodging; the proprietor of another boarding house called him to Court for not paying; he proved a vagabond who had no desire to work; he frequented taverns and theaters etc. etc. One day Rev. Bruno, to whom he presented himself as the nephew of Bishop Moreno of Ivrea, asked me for information, and I could not help but tell him what was said about him, but despite my warnings, Rev. Bruno, a most honest man and exemplary prelate, continued to permit him in his home, believing that he was truly the nephew of the Bishop of Ivrea, with whom he was acquainted and friendly, and so he tolerated him out of respect for his uncle.

Here then reappears the question of Moreno's supposed relationship with Bishop Moreno, which he used, according to Casella, for the sole purpose of spreading venom in the Italian community:

> One day this holy missionary wrote a furious letter to me in which he reported that Signor Moreno told him that my chancellor had told him that the priests of Calcutta are all womanizers, and that Rev. Bruno is the biggest whoremonger. Bruno demanded redress for such a slanderous insult; he identified Moreno, the house where the conversation had taken place, and the people present. Receiving this letter, I knew my chancellor incapable of making up such lies, and I began to suspect Mr. Moreno of such trickery, and I wanted to discuss this affair with my chancellor to find the truth, and he, without getting upset, laughed at the accusations against him, saying that not only could he not have spoken ill of Rev. Bruno, but he had only seen Mr. Moreno a single time, when he came to the consulate to present his passport. . . . So I believed that I needed to peacefully resolve this dispute through my intervention. Therefore I invited Rev. Bruno to come to the chancery on a particular day, and on the same day I also invited . . . Mr. Moreno to come. Moreno did not appear on the appointed day, and I had to repeat the invitation the following day. When they were both there before me, I, without the bureaucracy of criminal or legacy proceedings but in an informal and amicable way, read the aforementioned letter from Rev. Bruno out loud to Mr. Moreno and asked him if he was ready to verify its contents. Without blushing, he denied that he had ever expressed such slander, asserted that it was Rev. Bruno's invention and misinformation, and that he had never heard the chancellor speak either good or evil about the priest. The poor priest was rendered speechless by such claims because he expected a completely different outcome. I did not know what to say, and after such a statement the only thing the chancellor could do was accuse the Rev. Bruno of libel. He could not do anything else and the matter was finished, but not before, however, convincing us that the Piedmontese engineer was the greatest and most shameless scoundrel, and Rev. Bruno forbid Moreno from ever stepping foot in his home again.

So nothing more than a "great and shameless scoundrel." On that point, Casella felt justified in repaying Moreno with some of his own medicine:

> Today the engineer Moreno is the laughing stock of Calcutta, since he is unable to earn a living, depraved to the extreme, after being thrown out of all the places where he looked for lodging, he is reduced to being supported by a public woman, a woman who was first repudiated

> by her husband, then gave herself to the public, and is now supported by a native who, with the mistress, cares for Mr. Moreno. What I am relating is public knowledge in Calcutta, and what is even more disgusting is that Mr. Moreno brags about this adventure, appearing in public with this *disgraziata* acting like he is the conqueror of a new world.

The consul added that Moreno also deceived his "mistress," who, suspicious, wanted information from the consul's office. Moreno had written to the consulate asking it not to give his personal information to anyone. The consul continued his story: "Now he is no longer an engineer nor Moreno but goes by Count Melina, a Venetian aristocrat, and eats, drinks, and sleeps not with his own funds but on the back of his harlot."

What should we make of this? The protagonist of this episode is a person who was subsequently to persuade kings, presidents, and millionaires to embrace his projects and schemes, who influenced the laws and political strategies of nations on three continents, a person who exasperated his adversaries. If only half of Cassella's accusations were true, the man was either deranged or, likelier, a superb if not diabolical actor. This episode reveals Moreno's penchant for reinventing himself and for slandering his opponents. At the same time, it demonstrates his ability to convince others of his honesty and sincerity. It may also be additional evidence of his anticlericalism.

Of greater interest during Moreno's time in India is the question of his role during the Sepoy Mutiny. Beginning in the seventeenth century, the East India Company gradually extended its territorial dominion over various Indian kingdoms. Until 1858, the Company was the effective ruler of the British raj. Its armies were composed of indigenous soldiers called sepoys, commanded by European officers. The Company's principle source of revenue was land taxes imposed on the peasantry. In the nineteenth century, repeated tax increases generated resentment and resistance. Protestant missionaries, proselytizing among the Hindus and Muslims, contributed to the general unrest. Their aggressive brand of Christianity, which denigrated native beliefs, rituals, and customs, aroused hatred among the Indians. Meanwhile, many Brahmin aristocrats, deposed by the British, lost income and position.

The introduction of the Enfield rifle lit the fuse of these smoldering emotions. The new weapon's cartridges, which had to be torn open with one's teeth, were rumored to be greased with fat from cows and pigs. Moreno, in retrospect, rejected that explanation of the "great revolution."

Rather, he observed, the Indians viewed "the English invaders as a horde of shopkeepers and adventurers intent upon ravaging the country, accumulating money at any cost, without the slightest scruple, and demolishing all that the Indians hold most sacred."

Be that as it may, the sepoys, both Hindus and Muslims, reacted violently to this violation of taboos. They rose up and killed their officers, and the revolt spread like wildfire throughout northern India. The ensuing struggle, which lasted over a year, was marked by atrocities on both sides. Among these, the so-called Massacre of Cawnpore in June 1857 outraged the "civilized world." English men, women, and children were slaughtered and their bodies thrown down a well. The British public demanded blood retribution. Their soldiers were encouraged to exact horrendous vengeance, including shoving forbidden meats down the sepoys' throats and shooting them alive out of the mouths of canons.

Nana Sahib, a Hindu nobleman and *Maratha peshwa* (prince), had emerged as the sepoys' improbable leader. He commanded the attack on Cawnpore, and he was blamed for the massacre that followed. Years later, Moreno reported a conversation in which Nana Sahib told him:

> We Indians have neither love nor respect for the British; for two centuries they conquered our land by intrigue and force. We have learned nothing from them about civilization, with the exception of preferring gold to God and gold to any other thing. The prize for barbarity and cruelty committed in India . . . does not belong to us black and barbarous Indians but instead to the white and civilized English. . . . The English are the cause of all our suffering.

Moreno added: "The conduct of the English in the East is sufficient to disgust the conscience, morality, and common sense. A nation which is not noble enough to be magnanimous in victory is not worthy of being victorious and never will be." Moreno turned Gladstone's famous criticism of the Kingdom of the Two Sicilies against the English: "The English government of India, it is appropriate to say, is the negation of God."[8]

Although he was the most sought-after rebel, Nana Sahib escaped to Nepal after the defeat. On numerous occasions, Moreno claimed to have been his aide-de-camp. An article appeared in *Le Figaro* of Paris with a hyperbolic account of his personal participation in these events: "at the battle of Cawnpore [Moreno] had a duel with an English official who cut his forehead with a saber. This gash left a horrendous scar from his right ear to his left eye. Blood dripped and blinded Moreno, who, however, had the strength to draw his revolver and, quoting *Richard III*, 'Despair, and die,' shot the captain in the head."[9]

Fantasy or exaggeration? For Moreno, all the world was a stage, and he was certainly capable of performing such a scene. Although he was proud of his service with Nana Sahib, Moreno's critics used it to tarnish his image. At his death, the *Hawaiian Gazette* memorialized him as Nana Sahib's accomplice during the Cawnpore massacre.[10] But in 1859, while the English were relentlessly pursuing and executing those involved in the Mutiny, Moreno was in Calcutta, circumstances that appear to contradict theories in several accounts that he quickly fled to Singapore.

Although we do not really know when and how, it is certain that Moreno left India with a lifelong opposition to the British Empire and a hatred of the English. At this time, Moreno likely made Burmese acquaintances, facilitated, it seems, by his friendship with some Piedmontese missionaries. One of them, Paolo Abbona, also an Oblate of the Virgin Mary and a quarter-century older than him, was born in Monchiero and studied in Dogliani as a boy. A man of remarkable talents, he had mapped the route from Burma to China and Tibet. It was Abbona, according to Moreno, who introduced him to the court of the king of Burma in Mandalay, a city founded in 1857 in the north central part of the country after the English took over Rangoon. The king in question could be Mindon Min, the penultimate Burmese sovereign, a man of modern views and yet, according to Moreno, the possessor of a harem of two hundred women. Abbona had left Italy in 1839 with Father Vincenzo Bruno, and one can imagine that these men, before breaking ties with Moreno, had introduced him.[11]

Having resumed his trading activities on the coast, Moreno "discovered" Sumatra, an encounter that was to have fateful consequences. A rhapsodic description of "Moreno's Island," recorded (and surely embellished) by Giovanni Faldella, told of finding "precious pearls as big as fists" and "diamonds as big as an ostrich egg":

> He had arrived in those islands like a giant in a kingdom of pygmies; but he took it without conflict.
>
> On the contrary, he learned the language and customs and became Mustafà Vizier. Seeing the Sultan's daughter, he deigned to say, like the Neapolitan Turk: *chissa ma la pappo io.* And he married her; and to compensate the Acehnese, he defended them from Dutch bullets, and then said to his father-in-law: This time we have come out well. But I cannot guarantee you anything next time, since I alone will not be enough to free you from harassment.[12]

Moreno settled for a long stay between Kutaraja, capital of the Sultanate of Aceh, and the island of Pulau Weh off the northern coast of Sumatra. Such was his relationship with Siri-Sultan-Aladin-Sardar-Manshoor-Scander Shàà, as Faldella called him, or, more briefly, Scander, Sultan of Aceh, that he gave him his daughter Prompuan (Lady) Fatima-Fatigia, "the most beautiful girl in the Malaysian archipelago."[13]

The captain, however, held a position as *orang-kaya*, a rich foreign merchant who, by virtue of his wealth, was able to take on a role in the government.[14] And if in Faldella we find him baptized anew as Mustafà Vizir, in another source his Acehnese name is Pootee Tuan Mustapha, White Chief.[15] In this respect, one can compare him to a multitude of other adventurous "white rajahs" who at that time moved through the Malaysian port of Penang and the coasts of Borneo through Singapore and Java, inspiring astonishing stories which in turn inspired literature, such as Joseph Conrad's *Almayer's Folly* (1895) or the extremely popular novels of Emilio Salgari. Twenty years later, destiny, as we will see, would have it that Moreno's trajectory in the Pacific crossed with that of one of the champions of these undertakings, Walter Murray Gibson.

On many occasions, Moreno advised that respect for indigenous people's customs and traditions was essential when dealing with them. He practiced what he preached. Although he was said to have lived for three years among the Acehnese (1859–62), no accounts exists of what must have been at least an interesting experience. By that time, the sultan of Aceh saw his kingdom threatened by Dutch expansion on the eastern coast of Sumatra. A scholar, Anthony Reid, has speculated that the sultan asked Moreno to go Europe and find protection, which could be paid for by the transfer of the provinces of Deli, Langkat, and Serdang, already occupied by the Dutch.[16]

This hypothesis is confirmed by an article reprinted in various international news organs several years later, in 1873, the initial phase of the long conflict between the Dutch and the Acehnese, a war for the total occupation of Sumatra that only ended in 1903. Moreno, interviewed by a reporter from New York and presented as "having acted as prime minister of Acheen during the reign of the late Sultan of that State," explained that he had arrived in Sumatra in 1859, soon after the end of the Sepoy Mutiny. The Sultan of Aceh appointed him to lead a mission to Italy whose scope was to "take possession of the districts between Aceh and the Dutch possessions, where the principal pepper plantations are, so that Italy should make use of her influence so as to prevent Holland from annexing Aceh gradually."

The Sultan and his principle advisers were perfectly aware that the Netherlands sought to conquer all of Sumatra, and so they sought help from other European powers—in vain. Since 1859, the Sultan had a plan for the expulsion of the Dutch: a sort of holy war that united the great Islamic leaders who had escaped the Indian massacres and come to Aceh, "which is viewed as a kind of political Mecca." While Nana Sahib's fate remained a mystery, in the interview Moreno revealed that Mahomet Ali of Muscat, Sheik Abdullah of Aden, Sheik Ali of Madras, Sharvardar Sultan of Karical, Sheik Abu Bakar of Delhi, and Patan Mitteen of Lucknow had sought refuge in Aceh. All had been subadars—the highest rank given to natives enlisted in the British service—and all, brandishing the Qur'an, were now ready to fight until the bitter end against the Dutch too, "as death itself would be preferable to the possibility of apprehension."[17]

Did Moreno fight alongside this distinguished group of Islamic radicals? He told Faldella that he led the resistance of the people of Aceh against the invaders. However, according to his detractors, he had "passed the torch and dagger to the natives of Sumatra."[18] Defeated after a brief civil war, he would have made a hasty escape from Sumatra, perhaps secretly boarding a French ship and leaving Prompuan behind, who died soon after "of grief at the separation."[19]

He established himself in Shanghai, an extremely active port where "Chinese from every province mingle with foreigners of every nationality." In Shanghai he found his kindred spirits in a series of adventurers, speculators, and renegades "who came to China with the goal of quickly making their fortune free from the hindrance of any moral scruple." He did not limit himself to the Euro-American community but pursued relationships with the locals and learned Chinese. Returning to China a decade later, he would capitalize on these contacts to obtain support from Chinese merchants.[20]

Like a moth drawn to a flame, Moreno gravitated toward scenes of rebellion and violence. In the 1860s, China was in the throes of a civil war which had begun in 1850 and which would only end in 1864, after causing the death of twenty million people.[21] The Taiping Rebellion, a mass uprising of peasantry suffering from heavy taxes and the corrupt officials of the Qing dynasty, originated in the preaching of Hong Xiuquan. A messianic figure who claimed to be the younger brother of Jesus Chris, Hong proclaimed himself Heavenly King of the Heavenly Kingdom of Great Peace. Speaking from divine inspiration, he preached communal ownership of property and the equality of men and women. At first his followers triumphed over the imperial forces and gained control over large regions of

China. In this titanic struggle, the Western powers remained neutral until the Taiping rebels threatened Shanghai. It was the largest and busiest port and the center of British, French, and American commercial interests. While they did not intervene directly, their governments provided modern military weaponry and training for the imperial armies. The formation of hybrid units with Western officers and Chinese troops became a means of maintaining a sham neutrality.[22]

A "Yankee adventurer," Frederick Townsend Ward, organized the renowned "Ever Victorious Army," which in fact suffered numerous defeats as well as a series of spectacular victories. Ward's disciplined, well-armed troops played a significant role in the defense of Shanghai. Ward's and Moreno's lives had striking similarities: Both were born in 1831, both took to the sea at an early age, both fought in the Crimean War. Moreno, like Ward, was motivated by a "thirst for action and a hunger for battle," and he was "ambitious, strong-willed, and egotistical."[23]

On September 21, 1862, Ward was shot in a battle at Cixi, ten miles north of the port of Ningbo, and died the next day. Moreno later claimed, "I was talking to him at that moment."[24] What was Moreno doing with Ward that fateful day? Was he serving as a mercenary with the Ever-Victorious Army? Both the Qing and Taiping armies employed Western mercenaries, noted for their tendencies to change sides based on the size of their compensation. An American-Taiping contingent had been formed, but after failing to receive the anticipated "large pay and booty," most of the Europeans and Americans deserted to the Anglo-Qing side. August Lindley, an idealistic young officer in the British merchant marine, attracted by their religious fervor and their promise of social reforms, had joined the Taiping rebellion. Lindley was charged with creating a new unit, the "Loyal and Faithful Auxilliary," led by Western officers with Chinese soldiers. Lindley went to Shanghai in the fall of 1863 to recruit European and American merchants.[25] In his history of the Taiping Rebellion, he described one of his recruits: "Major Moreno, of the Sardinian Army, has held field rank in several armies and has seen much service in Asia, Italy, and Crimea. . . . I wished to place him in supreme military command of the legion because his education as a soldier was complete, and it would have been difficult, if not impossible, to find so well-qualified a man in China."[26]

Lindley went on to say that Moreno, unlike the deserters, was a "man of honor." In addition, Moreno had obtained from "certain European officials" an abundance of supplies and produced a "sample case of French rifles and bayonets." The arrangement that Lindley made with Moreno was that the latter would remain in Shanghai since he was in contact with French officers who were disposed to join the Taiping rebels. Furthermore, since Moreno was fluent in "Hindostanee," he had developed amicable relations with the Indian officers who would follow him.

Did Moreno join the Taiping cause for mercenary reasons, being that officers' salaries were more than seventy pounds a month? Or did he ally himself with the Taiping rebels for ideological reasons or because of his hatred of the English? Moreno later made this revealing statement: "I do not wish to judge whether or not the Taiping have the right to exist. I will only say that they cause great damage to their country. . . . Everywhere they go they devastate, burn, and kill, and they leave desolation and misery and they keep the country in chaos and the people in turmoil."[27]

Moreno's judgment of the Taiping rebels is surprising since the English were waging war against them. On the other hand, Moreno observed that "whenever it suited them, they gave assistance to the imperials, to the mandarins, and at the same time they sold arms to the rebels." However, Lindley's departure for England in 1863 due to declining health brought their venture to an end. His narrative makes no further reference to either Moreno or to the "Loyal and Faithful Auxilliary Legion." Moreno evidently did not assume command of the Legion nor participate in the Taiping military campaign, although a source hints at his relationship with Henry Andres Burgevine, Ward's successor as the head of the Ever-Victorious Army.[28] However, he needed to deepen his knowledge of China. Once again he was helped by an Italian missionary, identified only as "Padre Angelo." This aide to Monsignor Luigi Celestino Spelta, a Franciscan and archbishop of Hankou, originally from Voghera in northwest Italy, accompanied him during a visit to tea plantations in the Yangtze River valley, a trip taken with Monsignor Bigandet, the bishop of Rangoon.[29]

Moreno's return to Italy in 1864 was not a sentimental journey. After a decade in Asia, he had failed to make his fortune, but he did claim ownership of an island, Pulau Weh, off the northeast coast of Sumatra. He arrived in Florence, then capital of Italy, as the *Capo e Padrone* (head and master) of this island, to propose the foundation of a colony in Sumatra to King Vittorio Emanuele II.

At that time, Italy did not possess overseas colonies. Other European powers had obtained empires in Africa, Asia, and Oceania. Italians merchants, explorers, and missionaries had been taking part in these exploits, but theirs was, as Giovanni Iannettone put it, of an "individualistic character." Neither the Kingdom of the Bourbons or the Kingdom of Sardinia had the resources or political will for colonization. Following unification, the Italian government continued to engage in what was called "peaceful penetration," seeking access to markets and resources through negotiations rather than the acquisition of territory. Commerce, not land, was their objective, and they maintained good relations with indigenous peoples, respecting their customs and religion.[30]

By this time, however, the Kingdom of Italy was one of the so-called Great Powers, and ardent nationalists now argued in the spirit of the Risorgimento that acquiring colonies was necessary to maintain this status. Other political leaders, equally patriotic, vehemently opposed territorial expansion. Among them were merchants and ship owners who favored Italian coaling stations and ports along the route to Asia. For the imperialists, however, colonization was a matter of prestige rather than economic advantage. While a civilizing or religious mission was mentioned, it was generally given much less importance than in Great Britain or France. Moreno hardly ever mentioned Christianity or civilization when arguing for Italian colonies, limiting himself to the economic and patriotic benefit to be gained.[31]

During the 1860s, vigorous debates took place in the Italian Parliament, in business circles, and coffeehouses over whether Italy should launch itself into colonization. More sedate and scholarly discussions were held among the members of the Società Geografica Italiana (SGI), founded in 1865, and in the Società di Letture e Conversazioni Scientifiche, founded the following year. Both hosted colloquia, published learned treatises, and even sponsored expeditions in their quest for "scientific" knowledge of distant, mysterious, and exotic lands.[32] In Moreno's mind, these societies, particularly the SGI and its president, Cristoforo Negri, became major adversaries and thus prime targets of his most vitriolic invective.

The construction of the Suez Canal burst into this maelstrom of theoretical debates and political intrigue. The idea of "parting the desert" was not new. Napoleon had pondered such a canal during his conquest of Egypt. A follower of Saint-Simon, Barthélemy-Prosper Enfantin, also designed one, but it was the former French diplomat Ferdinand de Lesseps who had the vision, determination, and ability to finally accomplish this "impossible" feat. After years of planning, de Lesseps won the critical approval of the vizier of Egypt, who ruled the isthmus, in 1854. Overcoming incredible physical and human obstacles, the Suez Canal opened to traffic on November 17, 1869.[33]

Lesseps's achievement was universally hailed as the dawn of a new age, raising extravagant expectations about the spiritual and material benefits that would flow from the canal. But the enthusiasm was even greater in Italy. The Suez Canal cut the journey from Genoa to Calcutta in half, to

10,000 kilometers, and shortened its duration by eighty days. The countries "bathed by the Mediterranean," especially Italy, were expected to be the canal's greatest beneficiaries. In 1855, Genoa's *Corriere Mercantile* predicted that the canal would greatly favor Genoese trade, creating a revolution in the entire Mediterranean and Far East. Surely Genoa would be restored to its former greatness as the center of trade and other transactions between Europe and Asia.[34]

The Suez Canal provided a boost to Italian expansionists. While it was still under construction, Moreno cited its anticipated positive effects to strengthen his proposal for a colony in Sumatra. With Italy serving as a bridgehead for Europe, the canal would channel "the enormous and lucrative trade with the Orient" into the hands of Italian merchants. Moreno added that "nations without colonies [in Asia] would not benefit from the Suez Canal."[35]

Now in Italy, Moreno, "out of love for his *Patria* and devotion to his Sovereign" offered "his" island as the site of a colony in a part of Sumatra "not occupied by the Dutch." Having, he complained, submitted his proposal in writing in "1859–60–61–62–63–64" without receiving a reply (though we lack documentation for these earlier proposals), he had now come to present his proposal to the government in person. Dated February 2, 1865, and addressed to the Ministry of Agriculture, Industry, and Commerce, "Report about the Far East and the Settlement Project Studied There [written by] the Surveyor C. Moreno of Dogliani" was seventeen pages long.[36]

Moreno explained how he came to possess the island that he now offered to Italy:

> During the various times that I traveled between Penang and Singapore, English colonies in the Strait of Malacca, respectable Malays informed me about the nearby Island of Sumatra, so named in the Malay language because of its size, fertility, and beauty . . . the Garden of the Gods, and they assured me it had the richest mines and most fertile soil of all the other islands of Malaysia, and it would be a great resource if some European nation took possession of it. With the intention of rendering service to my *Patria*, I equipped a junk, a little Malaysian boat, which I commanded, with six Malaysians sailors, sailing through the Strait and along the coast of the great Island to Pulau Weh. . . . I sailed a small river, taking advantage of the tide, and reached the residence of the Rajah of the Island. . . . After I assured him that I was neither English or Dutch, he permitted me to visit the other subordinate Rajahs, places where no European or white man had ever set foot.

The sultan, seeking to fend off the Dutch, had been exploring the possibility of an alliance with France or with the Ottoman Empire, to which it was formally a tributary, but Moreno persuaded him to consider Italian protection. Within a few months, Moreno had become the Rajah's alter ego:

> constantly talking about the greatness of my *Patria* and the power of my Sovereign, not omitting the advantages which this island would gain in the future if my countrymen came and settled here under my Sovereign's protection, and always reminding him of the possibility that the Netherlands would also conquer this part of the Island and that Siri Rajah would become the vassal of infidel white men . . . as had many other deposed Rajahs already . . . and after hundreds of conversations, we agreed . . . that Siri Rajah would cede his Kingdom to me, and that I would, in turn, cede it to my Sovereign, and that we would send soldiers to protect it and people to work and cultivate the resources and that all the forces which arrived would support the new Government, and for the gifts I gave him and great service I was going to do for him with my Sovereign, he [the Rajah] gave me forever the Island of Pulau Weh.

The document continued with a lengthy analysis of the colonies that various European countries had established in Asia and the riches they obtained from them. Only Italy did not have colonies, consulates, or merchants in those areas, "but," Moreno observed, "it supplies a good number of Catholic missionaries: Jesuits, Lazarists, Oblates." It was time for Italy to claim its share of the Orient, the "bazaar of the commercial world." A maritime station, providing a commercial depot, shipyards, and moorings, would allow Italian merchants to "throw themselves into the immense and lucrative trade in the Far East" without "having to pay enormous customs duties to other Nations." A stronghold in the Strait of Malacca, the only crossing between India and China, would put Italy in a strategic position. Enumerating the island's virtues, Moreno described the climate as "healthy" ("having only one season . . . always hot, and rarely raining"). Dysentery was the only sickness that affected Europeans ("easy to cure with special tonics.") The land produced an abundance of fruits and grains "breadfruit of various quality, Mangos, Durians, and Pineapples all year long." Moreno listed the island's products, which could be shipped on boats flying the Italian flag: sugar, coffee, "cokonut," tobacco, nutmeg, cinnamon, and so on. There was an abundance of teak, useful for shipbuilding. Citing California and Australia as examples, Moreno anticipated the discovery of gold deposits as well as tin and lead. Tea, silk, and Chinese medicines would easily find customers in Europe. At that time China, although the "cradle of silk weaving," did not produce enough silk, so Moreno proposed sending skilled Italian workers to teach the Chinese, who were "very intelligent in the art of imitation." As for markets for Italian products, since the Japanese, whom he described as Buddhists, had no restrictions on the consumption of wine and liquor, Moreno predicted a lively demand for the "fruit of the vine." Japan would also be a valuable source of the silkworms desperately needed by the Italian silk industry, including in Dogliani, where diseases had killed the silkworms.

Moreno promised a warm welcome from the natives because the Rajah and his subjects held Moreno in high esteem. Since disrespect for native customs and religion had been the principal cause of revolts in English and Dutch colonies, Moreno's guiding principle was never to conflict with indigenous peoples over such matters. Evidently harboring doubts about the Acehnese inclination to commerce, he also stated that he would give full rights to Jewish, Armenian, Chinese, Indian, and Persian immigrants, who could, in a short time, constitute a merchant class "which would fly the Italian flag over their ships and junks."

In closing, Moreno could not resist a querulous reprimand directed at the Italian government and merchants. Colonies were thriving in lands discovered by Italians but in others' possession, and so he vowed that Italy, "instead of the ingratitude, that is, the indifference that it directed toward a great, ill-fated Genoese sailor several centuries ago and now bitterly regrets, it will want to turn toward strong support and encouragement for those who commit themselves to endeavors that will develop Italy's commercial possessions, influence, and honor in remote regions."

Despite the intense interest surrounding the question of colonization, or perhaps because of it, Moreno had to wait two years before he received a definitive response. One obstacle was a rivalry with those favoring expansion in Africa rather than in Asia. Giuseppe Sapeto, an ex-missionary, scholar of Arabic culture, and resident in Ethiopia for many years, was the most famous advocate of establishing a maritime station on the western coast of the Red Sea.[37] Recognized as the leading expert on Africa, the government gave him the task of leading an exploratory expedition to Egypt in 1863. Authorized by the Italian government to buy a site in 1865, he chose the Bay of Assab to establish a port and coaling station for the Italian Navy. Sapeto also believed that it would serve as a commercial hub for products from the African interior as well as the eventual site of an agricultural colony. After years of intense debates, Assab was purchased from local sultans on March 11, 1870, in the name of the Rubattino Shipping Company, Genoa's largest shipping company, through a secret agreement with the Italian government to avoid diplomatic complications. Two days later, Sapeto, who was the envoy during the negotiations, raised the Italian tricolor on a promontory overlooking the Bay of Assab.

Sapeto's choice inspired a decade of polemics. Assab had its supporters, among them Senator Nino Bixio, who, emphasizing its value as a mercantile station, claimed that if it was not occupied "our commerce will suffer and will be required to place itself under the protection of those nations which have already established and secured other stations on the Red Sea and elsewhere." But Sapeto's project also received scathing criticism. It was said to be arid, with temperatures exceeding 104F (40C), with powerful winds and dangerous waters, without vegetation and potable water. One critic concluded, "One could not find a more deserted, more unsuitable, more troublesome place to establish a European colony." Another critic observed sarcastically, "If the Bay of Assab was a bargain, it was because it was worth nothing and is worth nothing now." To Sapeto's dismay, a commission was appointed in 1871 to evaluate its suitability as a penal colony or a commercial base. Sapeto denounced it as "a ploy to make a project that was not sponsored by the government elites fail."

Moreno could not have agreed more with Sapeto on this point. Not until 1879, and again following pressure from the Rubattino Company, did Italy take military possession of Assab. This first Italian colony transformed a policy of "peaceful penetration" into a new strategy of territorial expansion that would culminate in two wars with Ethiopia. The dream of an Italian empire, however, came to a bitter, if temporary, end with the disastrous defeat at Adwa by Ethiopian forces on March 1, 1896.[38]

While Sapeto's ambitions were playing themselves out, Moreno's were on hold. Arriving in Florence in 1864, his initial attempts to interest the government in Sumatra were rebuffed. As he would do many other times, Moreno used his powers of persuasion and his talent as a publicist to circumvent the opposition. He succeeded in gaining an audience with King Vittorio Emanuele II, and the adventurer and the king developed a certain affinity. They were both disinclined to bother with niceties and tedious rituals. Moreno mesmerized Vittorio Emanuele with vivid descriptions of Sumatra's beauties and riches. As Faldella later wrote, "the great King [listened] to captain Moreno and his projects with great inclination." When, at the climax of a speech, Moreno cried, "Eyes and ears, your Majesty!" and "*Avanti* Savoy!"

"the king balled his fist as if to break down a great door; then he widened his eyes, and cried:

—*Androuma a piei-je.*—(Let's go take them!)"[39]

Italy was a constitutional monarchy and real power was in the hands of the prime minister and his cabinet, but the monarch was not without influence. In a note to the Minister of Agriculture, Industry, and Commerce, Moreno claimed that the project also enjoyed the support of Genoa's Chamber of Commerce and that he had personally presented it to the king, who enthusiastically embraced it. Well into his second year of waiting, the royal secretary to the Minister forwarded a letter from Moreno to the king, dated April 18, 1866. An attached, confidential note stated that the king was interested in the proposal of this "praiseworthy traveler," and therefore it would be expedient to treat it with the appropriate attention.

In the meantime, Moreno's attempts to lobby members of Parliament, journalists, and merchants created a public uproar. Articles critical of the government's failure to respond to his proposal appeared in newspapers, while Genoa's Chamber of Commerce officially endorsed his project, as did several deputies. A fervent advocate of Italian expansion, Deputy Bixio asked a parliamentary question which accused the minister of inactivity and called for the establishment of an interministerial commission to review the issue.[40]

In April 1867, the Minister of Agriculture, Industry, and Commerce announced the formation of a commission composed of representatives from his ministry as well as the Ministries of Foreign Affairs and of the Navy.[41] Among the members were Captains Luigi G. Ghigliazza and Bizio, who had both sailed extensively in the straits of Sumatra and Malacca. Shortly thereafter, the Minister of the Navy, Federico Pescetto, issued a preliminary assessment of Moreno's proposal.[42] Three questions, he said, needed to be addressed:

1. Should Italy establish colonies abroad and, if so, what should the Government's role be?
2. Is Sumatra suitable for a colony?
3. If so, are the means proposed by Mr. Moreno acceptable to the Italian Government?

Responding to the first question, the Minister asserted that the Kingdom of Italy "needed depots, stations, and meeting points where a nucleus of Italians who are interested in maintaining contact with the motherland can gather." Since the colonies had to be defended, they "could not come to life in the ordinary way without the Government's will and support." Therefore, before the government could make a decision, Moreno's project needed to be intensely studied. The Minister agreed with Moreno: Sumatra had much to recommend it. In a burst of imperial rhetoric, he opined that it "awaits only the hand and work of civilization to become a great emporium of production." The Malay population's potential to be civilized was attested to by their love of music. Because their language was among the most sweet and melodious, they were known as the "Italians of the Orient."

Two other questions needed to be addressed: the presence of the Dutch and the natives' resistance. How would the Netherlands, which had occupied parts of Sumatra for centuries, view the establishment of an Italian military colony on the island? The minister believed that this "diplomatic difficulty" could be resolved by a preliminary agreement. Regarding the natives, while it might be possible to obtain the acceptance of the rajah and his subordinates with gifts and promises of friendship, the population's submission could only be guaranteed by maintaining superior civil and military forces. In a more pointed criticism, the minister observed that "Mr. Moreno . . . essentially relies on his personal relationship with the Rajah of Aceh." Could the promises of "a Malaysian sultan" be sufficiently relied upon? Moreno's insistence that the project be carried out without anyone's knowledge, leaving the government an undeclared participant, also raised serious political questions. According to the minister, the press would certainly expose the matter and use it against the government.

Continuing his critique, the minister noted that while Moreno's personal acquaintance with the inhabitants' language and customs and his relationship with them would be useful, this knowledge was empiric rather than scientific. Might Moreno have illusions based upon his impressions? At most, he would serve as a "useful auxiliary for the initial exploration and an intermediary for negotiations with the Rajah." As a first step, a warship commanded by a qualified officer would be sent to explore the territory, to enter into negotiations with the king of Aceh, and to ascertain how much money would be necessary to acquire land for initial settlement. "In this work," the minister added, "Mr. Moreno can offer his services."

Naturally, this was not what Moreno had in mind at all.

Seeking expert advice, the Minister of the Navy spoke with captains who had sailed extensively in the South Seas.[43] One of them, Federico Montechiaro, said that he had made over twenty voyages to Sumatra. Captain Giuseppe Scorsono of Palermo recounted his observations in a seven-page report titled "Recollections of Sumatra."[44] With great candor, he admitted that he was not a geologist, botanist, or zoologist, and he was unable to respond to many of the questions posed to him. He had never been to the island's interior, and for good reason, since tigers and other wild beasts inhabited its impenetrable forests. While the heat was mitigated by frequent rains and constant winds, the swamps emitted an unhealthy miasma. The inhabitants of the island of Pulo Paty were docile, as was their chief. All the tribes were subjects of the king of Aceh. The natives cultivated rice, coffee, and pepper and raised chickens, cows, and sheep. They were Muslims, knew how to read, had some understanding of mathematics, and spoke a Malay dialect. His description of their morals was less benign than Moreno's: They all carried knives, were thieves and liars, and were inclined to treachery.

Established on May 24, 1867, the commission produced its report on June 19. Its findings were based on Moreno's proposal, his oral presentation, ministerial documents, reports by Commissioners Ghighliazza and La Mattina, as well as the "verbal testimony of General Bixio."[45] The commission crushed Moreno and his project in just one page. They found his proposal "too vague, uncertain, and suffering from inconsistencies and contradicted by the Members of the Commission who visited those places." They issued a decision that could not be appealed: Moreno's proposals "do not merit the Commission's recommendation to the Government." Truth or legend, it seems that the king was displeased. Leonardo Carpi reported that, sometime later, in a wistful outburst, he exclaimed in dialect: "*Si foeissa stait un di mè antich duchin, Sumatra a'm scappava nen*" (If it had been one of my old dukes, Sumatra would not have escaped me).[46]

Bixio's opinion must have carried weight with his fellow commissioners. Initially a proponent of the proposal, he later told Moreno that pursuing it would mean war with the Netherlands. Later, he questioned whether Moreno had ever been to Sumatra, since his geographic, anthropological, and scientific data were inexact.[47]

This particular point seems to refer to a brief work about Moreno by one of the most gifted writers of the late nineteenth century. Carlo Dossi (1849–1910), who had a brilliant career at the Ministry of Foreign Affairs, was undersecretary of state by the late 1880s. He chanced upon old papers pertaining to Moreno and witnessed the many problems he stirred up to damage the commission. Dossi's commentary on the affair of Moreno's island shredded any remaining hope in the participants' credibility, ascribed without exception to the category (rather dear to Dossi) of "nut jobs." It so humorously mixes the truth with invention that we cannot resist the temptation to reproduce nearly all of it:

> Captain Celso Cesare Morenno—a nut job. All the greatest discoveries and feats of our time were created or foreseen by him. His life was full of adventure. . . . To Ricasoli's Cabinet he presented a plan to occupy part of Sumatra not yet occupied by the Dutch. He asked for 300 soldiers with black beards so that the natives would not mistake them for English or Dutch. He has married—so he says—I don't know if it is the sister or niece of the king of Accin [*sic*]. The Accinese [*sic*] kingdom being occupied, he would have been crowned king *for the moment*, naming Mr. Guttierez of Milan as viceroy, then he would have ceded the kingdom to Italy. In Maraini's house Moreno and Guttierez had an intense dispute over the shape of the crown that Moreno would have made. Moreno then asked the Government for several bottles of coconut oil to grease his soldiers so they could handle the local climate. Ricasoli bent and accepted the proposal. He nominated a commission to examine the proposal, and the majority of the commission seemed to agree. But Moreno squabbled with Nino Bixio, a member of the commission who questioned the accuracy of Moreno's report on Sumatra and the surrounding areas. Therefore C. Moreno's idea ran aground. There was a pretty scene between Moreno and Cristoforo Negri—a comic dispute—about the length of Irawaddy which Negri said, I believe, was 1000 leagues based on a map, and Moreno said 12,000 based on the memory of his own feet.[48]

How did Moreno react to his plan's failure? Was he crushed, demoralized? Not at all. In all his battles, he never waved the white flag. Rejection, defeat, and derision only added new fuel to his ambitions—and to his desire for revenge. Thirty years after the commission rejected his project, he revisited the affair. In an article for the Italian American daily newspaper *Cristoforo Colombo*, he outlined the origins of the colonial policy that led to the acquisition of Assab, which had cost so much but yielded so little: the only result, he commented, was "these sands." Sumatra, on the other hand, offered all kinds of fruits but these had been refused. Who was to blame? "Italy's timid rulers in Florence in the years 1865–1866–1867 allowed this favorable opportunity, which will never come again, to slip through their fingers for the simple reason that the more skillful and courageous Dutch leaders took immediate possession of it after hearing of the Italian government's indecisiveness."

Indeed, Moreno's project made the Dutch intensify their efforts to conquer Aceh. The fate of Bixio, who died of cholera in Sumatra in December 1873 while he was transporting Dutch mercenary troops across the sea, represented the tragic culmination of the project of the captain from Dogliani.

Moreno, however, blamed the failure on Cristoforo Negri and the Italian Geographic Society that he led. Moreno directed his most scathing prose toward what he called the "Italian Society of Geographic Ignorance." As for Negri, "the great geographer in jest," Moreno claimed that he told him in Florence in 1867 that "to know Geography, one must first unlearn the nonsense that one reads in books or the accounts of travelers, explorers, and geographers of no value. Then one most travel, see, and study things as they are, that is to say, the truth." He continued his diatribe: "It was this Italian society of Geographic ignorance that advised the leaders of Italy to prefer the project of Professor Sapetto [*sic*] for the Bay of Assab to Captain Moreno's project for the Island of Sumatra."

In reality, the commission relied largely upon the advice of sea captains who had traveled, seen, and studied things on site. There is no evidence that Negri or the SFI directly influenced the commission's decision. It was true that Negri was an Africanist and particularly interested in Ethiopia. However, he favored commercial expansion, opposing all projects for territorial expansion. Negri chaired the commission, which had adversely judged Sapeto's plans for the Bay of Assab.[49] Then why such criticism? Moreno undoubtedly resented his exclusion from the inner circle of *savants*, that is, the members of the SFI, whose ideas were heard and who influenced government policy, influence which he failed to acquire. Expressing lingering resentment, Moreno took issue with members of the government who believed "ministers, consuls, admirals, and missionaries who, in their reports, erroneously described what existed in these places . . . having little to no practical experience." And again he criticized "the geographers who, without ever leaving their own countries, have written volumes about remote and unexplored regions of Asia. . . . My native country has many of these works, elegantly written but erroneous." The consequence was that "the Italian ministers and the king put more faith in bureaucrats, braggarts, and doctrinarians than in the practical man who offered them a plan, and he was dismissed as a dreamer like Marco Polo and Christopher Columbus."[50]

Moreno had not entirely given up on Italy, but the fall of 1867 found him in Paris, trying to sell his island to Napoleon III. This French parenthesis is extremely indicative of his *modus operandi*, rooted in his consummate ability to befriend the press, create a legend around himself, and then to take advantage of the acceptance he had gained among people of influence. While he was in Florence "at noon on a beautiful day at the Piazza del Duomo" he met the journalist and writer Edmond Texier, whom he impressed. It was Texier, whom he met again in Paris, who introduced him to his colleague Charles Yriarte. Yriarte was a respected writer fond of Italian things, a regular correspondent for *Le Figaro*, and editor of the principal section, namely news about Paris, of the weekly newsmagazine *Le Monde illustré*. In the pages of *Le Figaro*, Yriarte decided to introduce this new character who had debuted on the great Parisian stage and was driven by an iron will to find someone interested in his sensational exotic tales. The trip's objective is immediately clear in the first lines of Yriarte's lengthy article, and the Captain spoke in first person:

> I know an auspicious latitude . . . an island great like France that needs a master and where Europeans have never set foot. It is fertile, it is fecund, and I left that place with an agreement with the ruler to equip Italy with a powerful colony, but Italy turned me down. I begged, pleaded, and gave it all my time, energy, and efforts, but they did not listen to me. I am going to France, and if France also does not believe in me, America is close, and the land that I discovered will belong to the most bold.[51]

Although he claimed that he accepted what Moreno had to say "with a grain of salt," Yriarte was fascinated by Moreno's story, and he paints a picture of Moreno almost worthy of inclusion among his *Portraits cosmopolites*. He started with an almost photographic description: thirty-two years old, Moreno appears as a "colossus" with a low forehead above a face with firm features, marked with "cruel scars," a face that could resemble the emperor Lucius Verus, or also the famous Italian tenor Enrico Tamberlick, although there was in him "something of Lorenzaccio and Vasco da Gama." He was a quiet man, pleasant and elegant in appearance, with manners that revealed his wealthy status. One who had to use cunning as much as force in life, especially the former, which was certainly not his fault. Moreno spoke in a monotonous tone, "like an Arab," perhaps chasing some capricious chimera in the air, and in the meantime his eyes settled on the speaker's forehead as if to avoid his gaze. He rattled off grandiose plans, sketching incredibly audacious prospects, and did so in a whisper, as if confiding a secret, weighing each word as if he was worried about being misunderstood. He gave a hint of a smile only when the listener showed that he was interested in his words, and so he was very far from the Neapolitan's boisterous expressiveness, the Roman's gregariousness, the Florentine's affectionate manner, or the Palermitano's verbal violence. He was a man of the North, and moreover of the mountains, and a calm character aware of his own power.

Moreno was "an astonishing geographer and a first-rate sailor" and above all "an extraordinary polyglot." He spoke "Italian, English, French, Spanish, German, Arabic, Hindustani, Sanskrit, Burmese, Malay, Siamese, and Chinese." And not only those languages. Yriarte recounted a story of how Moreno questioned King Vittorio Emanuele II's Ethiopian grooms in their own language, in the king's presence, astonishing them. The captain had also demonstrated his linguistic prowess in France. At the World's Fair, the Chinese "had abandoned their steadfast coolness" on hearing him speak, and the Turks took him for one of their own. And here Yriarte explains for the first time Moreno's "philosophy" as a citizen of the world, with words that Moreno would later make his own: "He has always followed the peoples' customs. He does not aspire to make converts, he willingly forgets his religion to show respect for that of his neighbors, he eats with the natives, drinks with them, loves like them, loves what they love, and does not shrink from polygamy."

To avoid the English, Moreno went from India to Indochina to explore scantly known regions, to trade with the natives, "to correct maps," to take note of the currents, to fight western prejudices about the anthropology of the people, and finally, in his capacity as a ship's captain, to collect a large quantity of documents and precious information in foreign ports. In Singapore, he heard about an island near Sumatra of boundless fertility eluding Dutch domination. The Malaysians who gave him the information said that they had tried to land there, but the natives forced them to leave. They did not know the latitude, but that was not a problem: Moreno equipped a schooner and, "after innumerable dangers," he landed, finding himself in the midst of a curious population that was pleasant and gentle, ready to welcome him without fear or hostility. They took him to the king, "a very polygamous and scarcely clothed sovereign" who was simultaneously king, father, supreme judge, and executor of great projects. They offered him rice, fruit, a foam rubber mattress, and "a spouse of royal blood."

And so Moreno began to manipulate the king, telling him incredible stories about progress in Western nations, and in turn the king told him about his land's resources, which were abundant and easily accessible. Moreno took note of everything during a journey to the interior, including the place from which came "the gold nuggets that women wear as necklaces": the waters of the river that flowed near the royal residence were full of sparkling specks. Finally, he revealed that he was Italian, and at that point—*coup de théâtre*—the king took out a sealed envelope with French insignias, brought by Malaysians to that remote place twenty years earlier.

It is obvious that what Yriarte reported was Moreno's story. The author of the article could not verify his stories' veracity, and moreover offered them "with a grain of salt." But certainly, this story was really sensational.

> It was a letter signed by King Louis Philippe. Moreno, astonished, translated the letter that had never been read by he to whom it was addressed, and it spoke about France and its sovereign at that time. So his friend, father, and king showed him another envelope, another letter signed by Louis Napoleon III and dated "1853, Saint-Cloud." Moreno translated, and while talking about the power of France, a sword was brought to him on which he could read these words written in French: *Cette épée ne connaît que la victoire.* (This sword knows only victory.) It was a gift that had arrived with the emperor's letter by unknown means.

The first to be astonished was Yriarte himself. He wrote that somehow France had understood that it should have good relations with this island isolated in the seas of Indochina, and in time a French consul was appointed in Penang, Malaysia. That was now what Moreno dreamed for Italy, a commercial base in the seas of China. He shared his ideas with the native king, who welcomed them based on the threat of Dutch dominion and on the condition that the king would maintain spiritual power. In 1862 Moreno was able to write to Rattazzi; he tirelessly pressed him from China, Tartary, Japan, or Tibet. But Moreno received no reply, and finally he decided to return to Italy.

There, Yriarte said, Moreno's stories were received with smug condescension, first in Turin and then in Florence. He was considered a fool, but he did not give up. He finally met with the king, who received him warmly and told Moreno that he should get elected as a deputy from his province of origin to have more influence. The Italian press came to Moreno's aid, and finally the commission looked at his dossier and nominated him. It is here, as we know, that the project stalled.

Based on Yriarte's account, it seems that the captain ultimately considered Nino Bixio his major adversary. *Le Figaro* wrote that the general raised doubts that Moreno had ever set foot on the island—if it existed at all. So Moreno went to France, and on October 11, 1867, Minister of the Navy Admiral Rigault de Genouilly received him. He shared a history with

Moreno, having fought in Crimea; he took part in the bombardment of Odessa and the siege of Sevastopol. Most important, he was very familiar with the seas of China, which he had sailed since the 1840s. During the Second Opium War in 1857, Genouilly was in command and had taken part in the blockade of Macau and the seizure of Canton. He later had an important role in elaborate French-Spanish operations against the empire of Vietnam. He participated in the siege of Da Nang, and in 1859, he took Saigon. Bitterly criticized for how he conducted the operation, he was finally recalled to France.

Yriarte reported that the admiral thanked the captain for saving the crew of the French ship *Augustine-Garnier* of Bordeaux, shipwrecked near Penang in February 1862. The natives wanted to plunder it, but the intrepid Italian prevented them from bothering the crew and obtained a schooner that, commanded by a captain called Kadi-Schaa, safely brought the sailors to the first port with a French consul. There, the sailors reported this act of heroism to the French consul of Penang, Pierre Edmond Mathieu, who in turn reported it to the government. Genouilly therefore knew the heroic captain personally, and he asked him what he wanted as a reward. Moreno, "who has an obsession," replied that his recompense would be a meeting with the emperor, to whom he intended to give the letter that Louis Philippe had signed in 1843 and which the emperor himself had signed in 1853, and to report the native sovereign's response. He would discuss the need to create colonies in Asia, made even more urgent by the imminent opening of the Suez Canal. Moreover, "since Moreno had explored China, Cochinchina, and the seas of Indochina, the Italian seaman explained that our new establishments in Saigon, Bien-Hoa, etc., could be for us what the Indies are for the English, provided we wanted to follow their example."

At the end of his story, Yriarte attempted a provisional analysis. It was valid to doubt; however, there was the French sailors' testimony, the signed letters whose contents the captain knew, the tale of the swords, and the sword itself. All inventions? The conclusion was simple: "*qu'on interroge donc, qu'on examine*" (Let he who wonders do the examination). As for the rest, it was nice to think that, in modern times, there was still "a rajah who had never posed for a photograph, who had only vague notions of the existence of the Treaties, and who nevertheless sought the melding of the races."

Yriarte, whose first article compared Moreno to Marco Polo, claimed that he was even more of a polyglot than Cardinal Mezzofanti, who was supposedly fluent in thirty languages and spoke an additional ten, and that he followed in the footsteps of Mungo Park, the Scottish explorer who reached the sources of the Niger and who met a mysterious end in Africa, somehow "adopted" Moreno. Several months later he was still singing the praise of this "*voyageur d'haute race* . . . whose bold travels, curious expeditions, serious understanding of everything concerning China, Cochinchina, Java, Borneo, the Americas, and above all, the Far East has profoundly struck the men who were the greatest experts about things in those regions."[52]

His new article repeated some of the information from his first, but it mostly discussed the meeting with the emperor. Moreno spent many days waiting in vain for a summons from Napoleon III. During this time, with a behavior he would repeat on other occasions, Moreno "became his shadow, like a man of great will who wanted to achieve his goal," worrying the imperial security services. After all, another Italian, Felice Orsini, had made an attempt on the emperor's life only ten days earlier. Finally, the Minister of Foreign Affairs, the Marquise de Moustier, asked him for an audience, listened to what Moreno had to say, and asked him for a written report.

According to Yriarte, Moreno planned to lay the foundation for a port or at least a "fishery" in that area "for Italy or for France," with the aim of counterbalancing British and Dutch settlements. That was the key to the era's great and sophisticated geopolitical game. And it was the reason that Napoleon III finally received Moreno twice, listening with great attention to what the Italian had to say about India and Cochinchina, as well as to his projects to create a station on "his" island, with his usual recommendation to have the greatest respect for the natives' customs "which one must respect or else risk alienating the country's people."[53]

Although *Le Monde illustré* promised to update its readers about the project's development, the French already had a penal colony and ultimately declined Moreno's offer. But the emperor awarded Moreno the rank of Knight of the Legion of Honor for saving a number of Frenchmen at sea. His time in France, which gave Moreno a certain celebrity, bore fruit, it seems, in the government's support for a mission in Cochinchina.[54]

A substantial outline of what was said during Moreno's time in Paris may be found in an article that the politician and international relations expert Attilio Brunialti published in the magazine *Nuova Antologia* in 1883. At that time, France struggled to conquer Tonkin in northern Vietnam. Brunialti, who was then in contact with Moreno in Italy but who was not aware of *American Interests in Asia*, a pamphlet Moreno published in 1869, recalled how the captain had proposed that objective to Napoleon III. He reminded the emperor "how, since the last war with China, the English have known how to obtain considerable advantages," including "the right to sail the Yellow River up to Han-keu, possession of vast territories in which all ports were open to Europeans, the task of arranging the imperial customs duties." By contrast, France did not know how to take advantage of its presence in Asia. Like Italy, instead of trusting experts, "it has thrown diplomats and consuls there at random from other countries, replacing them frequently." Moreno told the emperor that France could export Indochinese rice to China and that "if the cultivation of opium, indigo, coffee, and sugarcane was introduced and encouraged in Cochinchina, it could be a great blow to the British colonies." Brunialti reported Moreno's words: "It is essential to French Cochinchina's prosperity to take possession of the entire eastern coast of the Gulf of Tonkin in order to control the Mekong and take advantage of its course and those of the rivers which mark the boundaries of the kingdom of Siam, reducing the king of Annam to the condition to which the English reduced the king of Burma."

Possessing only Cochinchina was not enough to convey an impression of power upon the peoples of Asia, nor could one say that the French conquest had produced the promised benefits. In practice, Brunialti wrote, echoing Moreno, "the mandarins were followed by the French, who were perhaps less dishonest but often insulted the natives' traditions, customs, and loved ones through their arrogance and ignorance," and this was the cause of all the war's violence, horrors, and atrocities, and the fact that the "new masters" were "confused with the former in the same hatred."[55] According to Brunialti, the current French colonial adventures also included grave errors and a clear underestimation of China, one possible market for Indochinese resources.

This interpretation was repeated in America, where the *Catholic World*, in a lengthy digression on the French-Annamese conflict, mentioned the conversations between Napoleon III and Moreno and commented on the latter: "Captain Moreno's only mistake—and it was a decisive one—was to believe that the Mekong, whose course the French then controlled, was navigable as far as the Chinese frontier, and that the Yun-Nan province, with all its prodigious riches and fertility, could be opened, through the Mekong, to the world's commerce."[56]

The previous year Lagrée and Garnier had already explored the river's course, chancing upon its impassible rapids. Napoleon knew that, but not Moreno, "whose project thus went justly unheeded." Who knows how Cristoforo Negri would have viewed the affair? However, a few years later, the French favored the Red River over the Mekong to facilitate their commercial penetration into the Heavenly Kingdom's most restless and rebellious province.[57]

We can speculate, however, that after Paris the emperor sent Moreno to Cochinchina or Tonkin, where he resumed his path to the Far East and ended up, almost inevitably, in China. There, he laid the foundation for his own economic fortunes, capitalizing on a network of connections "which stood him in good stead in later years."[58] Moreover, it was from China that Moreno set off for his third continent: North America.

CHAPTER 3

The Challenge of the Pacific

In May 1868, Moreno disembarked in San Francisco after a long Pacific crossing and presumably finished his trip to New York on the recently completed transcontinental railroad. Why America? As he would write thirty years later, he had come at the request of William H. Seward, then secretary of state, through the intermediaries General John A. Dix, the U.S. ambassador to France, and Wisconsin Senator James R. Doolittle. He intended to "negotiate the United States' acquisition of Pulo Way, known in the Malaysian archipelago as Moreno's island." Dix's letter of recommendation stated that Moreno "has lived for many years in the Far East," adding that Senator Doolittle "was greatly impressed by his intelligence and his familiarity with eastern business and interests."[1]

It did not take long for Moreno's presence in America to become known. As news of his mission spread, thanks to his tireless self-promotion, it provoked different reactions. The *New York Times* took a skeptical tone and wrote on August 23, 1868, that an Italian adventurer

> has for some time been trying to get a hearing from Secretary Seward, in order to ventilate a scheme for selling to this Government an island

> which he claims to have discovered somewhere in the Pacific Ocean. He wont [*sic*] tell anybody where his island is, but he has revealed the fact that it is of enormous value, and all the rest he will make known after he has been paid something like a million dollars for the information. The whole thing is so preposterous that we are surprised any paper should be deluded into speaking seriously about it—even in dull times.

The next day Moreno responded to the article, challenging the aspersions cast on him. The truth was, he claimed, that "I propose when Mr. Seward places a United States war vessel at my disposal to go there, and plant there the glorious American flag, giving undisputed possession to your Government." He denied that his asking price was a million dollars and insisted that a June 11, 1868, memorandum from Congress showed that he had asked for $750,000. Moreno concluded in an injured tone: "Without ever having seen me and without knowing anything about me, you publicly brand me as an adventurer, seeking to swindle your government out of $1,000,000. Such treatment of a stranger seems unworthy of the editor of a great American newspaper."[2] No apology was forthcoming.

Even the young Italian American press was not entirely welcoming. San Francisco's combative *Voce del Popolo* posed a question:

> Mr. Moreno, who claims to be a sea captain, is negotiating . . . with Seward, the great real estate dealer, the sale of an island to the United States which he claims is as big as France. . . . He says that the island is inhabited by a numerous population, with many Rajahs, princes, and kings of all kinds. How is it possible that these *pagnottisti* (promoters) submit to the "rights" of this Italian captain and to being sold to the Yankees like a flock of sheep? The incredible, marvelous, and almost supernatural adventures of Mr. Moreno raise doubts, uncertainty, and skepticism.[3]

However, among those who welcomed the Capitano Marittimo—as Moreno signed himself in the *New York Times*—were some of the most eminent mariners of any time. One of the leading Italian-language newspapers, *L'Eco d'Italia*, which was owned and edited by Giovanni Francesco Secchi de Casali, dedicated an entire column in English to the "Italian contribution to Civilization." Listing Italian achievements starting with Columbus, it observed, "Also in our days audacious, enterprising, and intelligent Italian travelers have contributed greatly to the growth of geographic and archeological knowledge. Beltrami was the first to explore the valley of the Mississippi . . . Belzoni and Botta were in Egypt and Africa, Moreno among the great and countless islands of the Indian Ocean."[4]

In time, Secchi and Moreno would become bitter enemies. A disillusioned Secchi described how the Captain deceived him and other newspaper editors:

> A few days after having deigned to visit the humble offices of *L'Eco d'Italia*, presenting himself as the great maritime captain and former deputy of the Italian parliament, initially lavishing every possible kindness on our countrymen and above all to new arrivals, taken in by his fantasies and the quantity of articles about him in newspapers in Italy . . . we fell into his web and placed the columns of our newspaper at his disposal, which he abused without restraint.[5]

Meanwhile, Moreno pressed on to Washington to sell his island. Although Secretary Seward was an expansionist in favor of opening new markets and acquiring territories in the Pacific, he did not immediately support the idea of bringing Sumatra under the stars and stripes. The timing was not favorable. In March 1876, Seward bought the territory of Alaska from Russia for $7.2 million, an Arctic expansion of almost 600,000 square miles whose potential value was not particularly appreciated by his American compatriots. Noting that "the Italian Moreno has come to Washington with a Malay island in his pocket," the *Times* snidely commented, "Now that the money for Alaska has been paid down, we may expect to find a great many other outlying fragments of the earth offered to our Secretary for purchase."[6] With the quip "Seward's Folly" ringing in his ears, Seward was not receptive to the offer of a Pacific island, even at a "bargain price," and particularly not from an "Italian adventurer."

Moreno, as we have seen, was not the type to be easily discouraged. As in Italy, he launched a media campaign that included the 1869 publication of a pamphlet, *American Interests in Asia*. It began:

> During the fifteen years that I passed consecutively in all the various parts of Asia—the European possessions and the kingdoms and tribes governed by native rajahs, on the continent as well as on the islands—my principal object was ever to practically study their countries, learn their languages, associate myself with their customs, interpret their ideas, and tendencies, respect their faith and religions.[7]

What came after was a description of the voyage, including the topography, flora and fauna, resources, trade, and people of the countries situated between India and Japan, with ethnographic observations that seemed to have been gathered in the field, and descriptions of the religions and cultures of various peoples. Some observations were extended and vivid, others brief and unimaginative.

Of the Malay character, for example, he said:

> The Malay never thinks of to-morrow, and contents himself with the maxim *Allah kerim* (God is great). The Malay contents himself with a *Roomah* (a little wooden house), surrounded by a few betelnut trees, some cocoanut, mangoe, mangosteen and banana trees, sugar cane, a few plants of tobacco, a black goat to furnish the necessary milk and keep off *Shaitan* (the Devil), some rice when he can get it, vegetables, salt fish and curry, fruits, one or more *prounpuans nonas* (wives). Then he is happy . . . The Malay sleeps sixteen out of twenty-four hours, and when awake, chews the betel, which is made from the betelnut, arrak, a strong green leaf called paanh, a little lime, some cinnamon and cloves. This mixed together, put in the mouth, chewed, and spit out red, gives a good flavor to the breath and preserves the teeth, but makes them quite black, which is there considered a beauty.[8]

Moreno held the Chinese in particularly high esteem as "the most expert, laborious and industrious people of all the Asiatics; they are the soul of colonies in Asia, and the prosperity is in proportion to the number of Chinese inhabiting it." They

> exercise every profession, eat everything—even hog's-flesh, so much detested by the other Asiatics, is their favorite dish. The Chinese live at little expense, and earn much; work eighteen hours of the twenty-four; they are not inventors, but possess the art of imitation in the highest degree. . . . In cunningness he excels even the Armenians, and can lie or dissimulate at convenience; and to make reverences or pass compliments he is the Parisian of Asia, and when he desires to bow profoundly, takes his tail of hair in his hand, which he regards as the national flag.[9]

Given this positive opinion, he did not hesitate to endorse Chinese immigrants, "who will be very useful for the Southern States, and will very likely introduce the cultivation of tea, and mulberry plantations for silk worms."

Other ethnic profiles were dedicated to the Parsees, "the descendants of a crowd of fugitive Persians who fled from Teheran on the fall of their monarch." They "are very numerous, and wealthy merchants," and "many occupy elevated positions under the English government in India." The

Sikhs "are the inhabitants of the Punjab, courageous soldiers, and of great physical strength. They were great enemies of the English . . . now they are their best subjects and friends" to such a degree that "if Great Britain is still in possession of the great empire [a reference to their role in suppressing the Sepoy rebels], she owes it, to a great extent, to the bravery and fidelity of the Sicks [*sic*]."[10]

The descriptions of other ethnic groups are less colorful and little more than sound bites: Muslims are "very turbulent . . . excited by a religious and warlike fanaticism," while "the Burmese are good architects" and "good agriculturalists." Although he had visited the cities of "Nagazaki, Jokohania, Kanagawa, and Hokadadi," Moreno resorted to this enigmatic aphorism: "the more they [other strangers] seek to learn from them and about them, the less they will ultimately know." Concerning the Annamites, Moreno confessed that having visited only their capital, Saigon, he could say little. Anticipating objections, Moreno declared: "My assertions may encounter incredulity, but time will render me full justice."[11]

While *American Interests in Asia* shared commonalities with the many writings about the Orient by missionaries, diplomats, and explorers, Moreno's primary purpose was not to educate and entertain his readers. His pamphlet had two underlying objectives. The first was exposing the disastrous impact of European—particularly English—colonization upon the peoples of Asia. The second was engaging Americans, and especially American capitalists, in the economic development of China.

With respect to the encounter between Western and Asian cultures, Moreno offered a perspective which has a modern ring to it.

> The civilization of the West can be offered to them [the people of Asia], but not imposed on them. Nothing is more sacred to the Asiatics than their castes, customs, and religions, particularly to the natives of India . . . Holland and England, which violated this fundamental principle in governing their colonies in India, have made the dire experience.[12]

Force was not the way to make inroads in Asia. "Obedience and respect towards our Government can easier be obtained by prestige, good example, and benevolence . . . than by force, laws, and punishment."[13] Examining the rule of European colonial powers, Moreno found them all, to greater or lesser degrees, guilty of exploiting the bodies and violating the spirits of their subjects. He reserved his harshest judgment for the English, who kept "millions of the unfortunate inhabitants of their Oriental colonies under the most abominable, cold and odious tyranny—treating them more as tools or things placed at their disposal than as human beings."[14] For their part, the Indians "judge the English invaders as a horde of shopkeepers, adventurers bent upon ravaging their country, accumulating money at any price, and, without the slightest scruple, overturning all that is most sacred to an Indian, and appropriating whatever suits them."[15] He noted, "England cannot boast of any other glory than that of having accumulated great wealth at the cost of the poor wretches under her dominion, and of being the principal cause of that implacable hatred and disrespect evinced by the Asiatics toward us people of the West."[16]

Moreno drew upon conversations with Indians to flesh out his indictment of English colonization. Of particular interest is his 1868 interview, during the Sepoy Mutiny, with a Brahmin fakir in Benares, "an octogenarian, who dwelt at the back of a pagoda, situated on the right bank of the sacred river":

> Inside of this pagoda, just within the door, stood a black cow, made of metal, placed on a pedestal of masonry, with two lamps filled with coconut oil . . . Further on the right, on a high pedestal, stands an upright figure of Brama [*sic*] about eleven feet high. Close by, seated on a mat, this old fakir passes the greater part of the day reciting prayers and acknowledging the salutations of his co-religionists, who hold him in great esteem for his dignity, wisdom, and being a distinguished learned man.

The fakir asked Moreno what had been his opinion of India before his visit. Replying that it had been based on reading papers and books by the English, the ancient scholar observed: "Our conquerors, by means of the press and books, give but false and perverse information about us and our country to the rest of the human race; their mission is to ruin and defame us."

Assuring the fakir that he sympathized with the Indians, Moreno asked, "But why do you people of Asia hate us Europeans?" The Brahmin replied:

> If the English, who boasted to be the best among the white race, have thus devastated and ill-treated us, it may be but logic on our side to place the rest of the white race on the same level . . . We know that, according to the Christian religion, pardon draws a man nearer to his Creator . . . But it is evident that the English in this country forgot to practise this maxim, and behaved more like Pagans than Christians.

Moreno, launching into a defense of the "Latin race," commented that the Anglo-Saxons pretended to be the heirs of the Romans, "who were a great people, virtuous, and warriors, and governed by wise principles," while the English "like the Carthaginians, only leave traces of their pride, egotism, and avidity to make money." Moreno also recounted his visit to the Sultan of Delhi, "the last occupant of the throne of the Great Mogul" shortly before his death:

> that caused me an emotion that will ever remain indelible in my memory. Above all, when this venerable old man, with his flowing white beard . . . related to me his misfortunes caused by the English invasion, with an emphasis and confidence as if speaking to a friend, in which manner he treated me because I hastened to inform him that I was an Italian and not an Englishman . . . the last words that he addressed to me I well remember—"I live in the hope that, should my countrymen fail, Allah will avenge me sooner or later. Salam, sahib."[17]

What did all this have to do with the United States? In imagery meant to appeal to Americans' belief in the redemptive role of their nation, Moreno called upon them to overcome the evils of European imperialism while simultaneously making a great deal of money. Moreno also cited the recent emancipation of blacks:

> That magnanimous and humane act of the American Government—the abolition of slavery—drew applause from all the generous hearts in the universe, and will insure a permanent title to the consideration of the Asiatics, who will joyously welcome the unfurling of the Stars and Stripes on any part of their territory, as the herald to a new era of liberty, equality, and justice, till now denied to them by the native sovereigns and the European conquerors.[18]

Being "entirely free, America tolerates every kind of religion and habits in her States and extends equal rights and privileges to all races" and was uniquely suited to fulfill "the glorious mission" of healing the wound between East and West, which would as a consequence secure great benefits "to the great Republic of the United States."

Moreno believed the United States could prevail over Great Britain and France in dealing with the Chinese because it had obtained equal commercial privileges by treaty, rather than by force. "Without firing a gun," it was the first Western power to show "justice, humanity, toleration, and even international decency toward the Government and people of China."[19] Shifting easily from morality to self-interest, Moreno assured his readers that China would be a source of enormous wealth for Americans, who would simultaneously "assist the Chinese in the development of their social-political-economical order."[20] Moreno returned to his theme of pacific penetration and reiterated that China was not to be conquered by arms, but "by the inventions of the age." The telegraph, railroad, and steamship would be more effective than cannons in securing access to Chinese markets and resources. Here, then, was a limitless and fertile field for the investment of American capital.[21]

While Moreno's prescription for America's relationship with Asia appears enlightened, humane, and benevolent on its face, as a "practical man," Moreno was not above crude calculations of profit. For example, he recommended employing Malays on the increasing number of merchant ships in Asian waters, not only because they were excellent sailors, but also because a monthly salary of 9 to 12 rupees would be more than adequate for them, since "they live on rice, salt fish, and vegetables, which does not exceed 5 rupees a month per man."[22] In his market approach to opium, Moreno most explicitly revealed the contradiction between altruism and financial gain. Since, he reasoned, "the Chinese prefer buying opium to smoke than rice to eat," Americans should imitate the English and "push forward the cultivation of that plant [poppy] in the eleven kingdoms."[23]

China had not always been "a nation of opium eaters." In the nineteenth century, British India was the major producer of the narcotic, which became an important and profitable commodity in trade with China. As one critic put it: "The British Indian Government . . . cultivates, prepares, and sells [opium] expressly for the Chinese market, without regard for Peking's efforts to suppress the commerce." When the Chinese tried to prohibit the importation of opium because of its debilitating effect on its subjects and the drain on its gold bullion, the British forcibly broke down such barriers. The opium trade with China increased greatly following the first and second Anglo-Chinese Wars of 1840 and 1857. Recognition of the narcotic's "morally and physically deleterious" effects fueled an anti-opium movement in England. It maintained that "the horrors and evils of the traffic . . . render it unbecoming for Great Britain as a Christian nation to . . . permit its continuance, whatever may be the merchants' *apparent* profit."[24] The English debates were reported internationally, and Moreno must have been aware of them.

Moreno's support for the opium trade, though it was under English control, contradicts his expressions of affection and empathy for the Chinese people. Even while advocating for increased poppy cultivation, he denounced opium dealers as "the worst enemies of China" in a letter dated August 30, 1869.[25] The mask of benevolence had fallen from Moreno's face to reveal the visage of a callous imperialist. It should be noted that he did hold out hope for opium addicts. The craving of the Chinese for "tonics and stimulants," he foresaw, could be satisfied by tobacco which, "in time would take the place of opium."[26]

Moreno's alluring portrayal of Asia as an arena in which "the energy and enterprising spirit of my fellow American fellow-citizens can have full scope and obtain vast wealth" fell on receptive ears. While the Civil War had left the South in a state of desolation, the conflict had stimulated northern industry and the construction of cities and railroads. The resulting accumulation of great fortunes ushered in the era of the robber barons, a time when unrestrained capitalism sought profitable investments both domestically and abroad. "Ambitious capitalists," in Mason's words, "hoped to develop China's natural resources by introducing modern methods of mining, building railroads, and the use of steamboats on China's great rivers."[27]

The response to Moreno's manifesto was overwhelmingly favorable. The Piedmontese adventurer had become the darling of Wall Street overnight. *American Interests in Asia* received favorable reviews in the *Times*, *Sun*, and *Express* in New York, and in newspapers in other cities. The press praised the author for raising questions about Americans' knowledge of and readiness to develop trade with Asia. President Ulysses S. Grant was urged to take advantage of Moreno's expertise. A Washington newspaper, reviewing the pamphlet with enthusiastic adjectives, proposed giving its author a diplomatic role in China.[28]

The pamphlet secured Moreno an invitation from the New York Chamber of Commerce to speak to its members. Among the distinguished attendees was Andrew G. Curtin, president of the China Telegraph Company; Thomas Clark Durant, president of the Pacific Railroad; and Louis McLane, president of a mail steamer company on the Pacific coast. America was fascinated by the prospect of playing a role in the great Asian game in which England and Russia were protagonists, with one's approach being "pillaging" and the other's "usurping." The United States could insert itself into this game through a civil project of trade expansion, as some American capitalists had done by working with the East India Telegraph Company. One day, the construction of Chinese railroads would provide a formidable infrastructure, such that "we will feel that our mission in Asia has begun," as one newspaper commented.[29]

Shortly after his arrival in the United States, Moreno began a correspondence with Charles Sumner, the great senator and abolitionist from Massachusetts. While his initial letters were written in Italian, by March 1869 Moreno was writing in English with an impressive command of grammar, spelling, and vocabulary. Presumably he had learned his English during his sojourns in India and other countries. Still, his letters demonstrate an extraordinary linguistic facility. They also exemplified the flattering and astute style with which Moreno cultivated important people.

Expressing admiration for Sumner's eloquence and wisdom as an orator, writer, and patriot, Moreno voiced his great desire to know him personally. In a letter on September 20, 1868, he asked for a meeting in order to "verbally tell you the details of the 15 years during which I traveled in Asia, the fruit of which I offered to *Mia Patria d'Italia* which did not know how to adequately appreciate it, and now I am here in America, my adopted *Patria*, for the same purpose."[30] During these months, Moreno seemed to be traveling back and forth between New York and Washington. His wish was fulfilled in the latter city in May 1869. In a subsequent letter, Moreno thanked the senator "for the kind manner in which you received me."[31]

In March of that year, Moreno sent him a copy of *American Interests in Asia* and called its publication "of great significance to the interests of this Great Republic, *my adopted country*, which is destined to be the herald of a new era of Civilization in Asia." He then asked Sumner's opinion.[32] Moreno attached a clipping of one of his op-eds that appeared in the *Mercantile Journal* titled "American Supremacy in the Far East." In it, he reiterated ideas presented in the pamphlet. Given its geographical position, "with able Ministers and Consuls, and a steady policy," the United States would "infallibly attain supremacy in that part of the world."

In 1863, Moreno had met Anson Burlingame in Peking. Burlingame was the American ambassador to China. Among the results of his work was a Chinese diplomatic mission to the United States in the spring of 1868 that negotiated a treaty guaranteeing China most favored nation status. China enjoyed this status until the beginning of the 1880s, when the United States implemented various measures to stop Chinese immigration.[33] Moreno's assiduous courtship of Sumner—to whom Burlingame was more than a friend—produced the desired results. (In 1856, Burlingame had humiliated the southern congressman Preston Brooks by provoking him into challenging him to a duel. Brooks had publicly and viciously beaten Sumner unconscious in the Senate chamber.) In the subsequent years, the senator's support was vitally important to the advancement of Moreno's various initiatives.

Moreno was not only a visionary. As a "practical man," he repeatedly sought to transform his ideas into concrete realities. Having preached that limitless opportunities in Asia awaited only the energy and ambition of bold men, he took the sermon to heart. China, with its vastness and huge population, was a treasure chest that only railroads, steamships, and the telegraph could unlock. Moreno understood that communication was the key to the transnationalism of the modern age. Therefore, the construction of a transpacific submarine cable between America and Asia was essential.

Samuel F. B. Morse's invention of the telegraph was one of the wonders of the era. Messages could now be transmitted across hundreds and then thousands of miles in a matter of minutes. Entrepreneurs and statesmen alike seized upon its importance for business and strategic purposes. In the United States, a web of lines extending thousands of miles was laid, culminating in a transcontinental cable. Though the federal government subsidized the latter, unlike in Europe where telegraphic networks were built by the state, in the United States this was left to private enterprise. Great Britain, given the telegraph's value in binding its far-flung empire together, dominated the world's cable industry. While submarine cables were soon laid across short distances, spanning oceans encountered financial and technological obstacles. An American, Cyrus W. Field, undertook the construction of the transatlantic cable with English capital. It took a decade, but the line was completed in 1866.

At the same time, the Russian-American Telegraph Project undertook the connection of the Eurasian continent and North America across the Bering Strait. Created by Perry M. Collins, a United States consular agent in Russia, the Western Union Company began construction in 1864. Surveying crews braved the wildernesses of Siberia and the Northwest while ships took soundings of the straits. After expending $14 million, work came to a halt. The completion of the Atlantic cable, amidst other setbacks, took the wind out of the project's sails.

The laying of a transpacific submarine cable, extending some 7,000 miles, was indeed a daunting task, but Moreno was not fazed. Beginning in 1869, he threw himself into the project with great enthusiasm and energy. Even though he had not mentioned it in *American Interests in Asia*, he had surely conceived of the project by that time. As the driving force behind the enterprise, the burden of securing supporters, potential investors, and the blessing, if not dollars, of the federal government fell upon Moreno's shoulders. On January 30, 1873, he appeared before a joint committee of the Senate and House of Representatives as a representative of the America, Japan, and China Telegraph Company, a name soon changed to the American and Asiatic Telegraph Company. On that occasion, Moreno repeated, with almost identical language, the thesis of his book. The effect of laying the cable would be "shortening the distances; the words would complete the trip to and from Asia, which is now 25,000 miles long, in only six thousand miles, greatly reducing costs and placing everything under American control."[34] He added: "The Pacific Cable will be the pivot upon which will turn our supremacy in Japan and China . . . It would place us in immediate communication with the Far East, give a wonderful impetus to our commerce there, add prestige and influence to our name . . . inspire confidence and security to governments and people connected with a powerful and friendly nation."

"The Chinese and Japanese," Moreno claimed, "feel a warm friendship for America and the Americans." Taking advantage of this friendship and "this magic power of this wonderful Italo-American invention . . . let us avail ourselves of the present opportunity to reap some of the fruits of our early pioneering in the Orient."[35] With a passionate appeal to a patriotism that transcended mere financial gain, Moreno declared that the project "should stir the pride of every American citizen, and animate them with the noble desire to witness the completion of the great pathway toward the East, which had its foundation in the daring and skill that overcame the obstacles of the Rocky Mountains."

"Gentlemen, do not leave this work unfinished and incomplete! Crown its summit with this electric cap-stone," Moreno exhorted. "Establish the last line needed for embracing the entire circumference of the Globe with the telegraphic wire." Though new to the country, Moreno had intuited the frontier ethos of Manifest Destiny and tapped into this vein of American aspiration. But he offered a more universal justification for the Pacific cable, making a rare appeal to religion: since a "marriage" of America, China, and Japan "will be the extension of our civilization, the increase of our commerce, the maintenance of our national comity, the diffusion of christianity [*sic*], and the common good of mankind."

The astute Italian reassured the congressmen that he was asking for the blessing of the U.S. Congress, but "no subsidy or privileges." The bill did stipulate that the secretary of the navy would provide vessels and steamships "for surveys and soundings" and provide "such assistance as may be calculated to promote the success of the enterprise." As for financing, Moreno declared: "We have full confidence that we can furnish the capital necessary." He bragged that the collective wealth of the board members of the American and Asiatic Telegraph Company was "far superior to the amount of money required to complete this enterprise." The states on the Pacific coast would especially benefit from the cable, and, in particular, San Francisco would become "the clearing-house and the intermediary point between Eastern Asia, the United States, and Europe." The presence of some of California's wealthiest businessmen on the AATC board attested to the project's financial support.

It was to be expected that even the Chinese and Japanese would "vie with Americans in buying shares." Moreno decided to impress the congressmen with his description of Asia's wealth:

> There is no lack of money in China and Japan. I have seen, with my own eyes, vast sums of money, both in gold and silver, hoarded for years without use, waiting for investment. . . . Mexican and Spanish silver dollars, as well as the East India rupees, . . . and our trade dollars, have found their way into China and Japan—*le casseforti del tesoro del mondo così a lungo chiuse* (the long-closed treasury house of the world). (Italian in original)

Expressing his own animus, but also appealing to the Anglophobia that resulted from Great Britain's favorable disposition toward the Confederacy, Moreno touted the ATTC project as a means of breaking the English stranglehold on telegraphic communication with the Orient: "A strong effort is being made in the interest of British corporations to wrest from the American Flag the supremacy upon the great Pacific ocean—which by manifest destiny ought to be an Americo-Asiatic lake."

America, he argued, was sandwiched between Europe and Asia, which forced the Americans, willingly or unwillingly, to use the lines of communication "established and controlled" by English corporations, this being the "genuine, old monopolistic policy of the British capitalists." The bill before Congress would "prevent the English from driving us away from the Pacific ocean, as they did from the Atlantic."

Despite his optimistic outlook, Moreno saw storm clouds gathering on the horizon in the form of a "general bill" which had been introduced regarding the Pacific cable. Denouncing it as "a plan of the agents of British corporations," he claimed it would "kill forever this Pacific cable enterprise in the hands of the Americans" and "afford to our greedy rivals, the English . . . the possibility of perpetuating in their own hands the monopoly of telegraphic communications from the Far West to the Far East," following the old policy of "grabbing everything."

Moreno's appeal to pride and prejudice provoked sustained applause from the members of Congress and from the national press. On his side were Senator Sumner, his old pen pal, and Congressman J. Packard of Indiana, who endorsed the bill, declaring that the submarine cable was of the "highest importance," since it would "open to us the treasures of Asia, so closed to the world." Packard described Moreno as "of Italian birth, but devoted to American interests." He said, "No man understands the Chinese better than he does, having conversed with them for years in their native tongue."[36]

Naturally, Moreno's project received the highest praise from Californians. The *San Francisco Examiner* referred to "his able speech before Congress on behalf of the enterprise" and called him "the indefatigable promoter of the sub-Pacific cable enterprise." It included much of his language in its article, as did other newspapers, which suggests that Moreno had widely distributed the text of his speech.[37]

Congressional maneuvers delayed enactment of the bill for many years. Although it passed both houses of Congress in 1873, a motion by Senator Eugene Casserly of California, intended to reconsider the question, killed it. But, as one journalist reported, "Signor C. C. Moreno is not at all disheartened. He does not belong to that class." In fact, during the next session of Congress, he resubmitted the bill and his brief before congressional committees. But after the Senate approved it unanimously, Senator Henry Dawes of Massachusetts recalled it from the House of Representatives. In this case, however, the delaying tactic did not work, and the law finally passed on August 15, 1876.

All due credit was given to Moreno for the persistence and commitment with which he fought for it. The captain had made various trips and inspections for the project's preliminary study. In 1874, for example, he went to the Seal and Aleutian Islands in Alaska "on board the U.S. warship *Tuscarora,* for Sounding, ordered by Congress."[38] These months had to have been really wonderful for him, and finding himself on the advancing frontier of modernity must have been exhilarating. There are some clues in letters to Bettino Ricasoli, the steel baron who was Cavour's successor as the head of the government of the Kingdom of Italy. In the first, Moreno wrote: "Now I am here in California to play the great game that is proceeding perfectly, to connect the Far East with the Far West. What would the so-called great geographer Christopher Columbus have said about my undertaking? He would call it a dream or madness, as others did when I was in Italy." In the second, Moreno claimed to have written while he was "1550 feet below the Earth's surface" in the belly of a Nevada mine "where there is a great volume of gold, silver and mercury that has been undiscovered until now." It was almost a "postcard," perhaps a way of knowing that his career had taken flight. Moreno closed with a joke: "According to my calculations in the vein where I am now writing this letter there is $1,000,000,000=50,000,000,000 francs. With this Minghetti could balance the budget of Italy."[39]

But where did the opposition to the cable come from? On August 20, 1876, the Washington paper *Forney's Chronicle* published an exposé of those behind the machinations. It identified the British Ocean Cable Company, which had a monopoly over telegraph communications with Asia, as the culprit and Cyrus Field as its chief conspirator. The *San Francisco Examiner* called for his head: "The only object of Mr. Cyrus W. Field is to place obstructions in the way of other persons obtaining the franchise from Congress for a sub-oceanic telegraph enterprise. Mr. Field is the agent of English capitalists who, at any cost, want to preserve their monopoly."

For almost a decade, the BOCC had exercised delaying tactics, including the Senate's two reconsiderations, "to gain time and defeat its passage in the House." On the most recent occasion, it was done so that the Senate could not proceed unless it did so unanimously. According to the article, Senator Hewitt, the son-in-law of the president of the British Atlantic Company, had induced Indiana Representative William S. Holman to act has his accomplice: "This pseudo reformer threatened to use his privilege in the interest of this British monopoly unless he was allowed to amend; as to allow any other company to share the same privilege, ostensibly to make his movements a very liberal one, but in reality to defeat the measure itself."

The intent was foiled when the supporters of the Pacific Cable bill accepted the amendment. *Forney's Chronicle* rejoiced at this "great triumph over British capital [and] its paid agents" and savaged Holman, who "while pretending to be a great friend of the people, lent himself as the tool of the most rapacious monopoly in existence" and this "for a few 'barrels' of New York money to influence the Indiana elections."

Passing to the architect of this triumph, the *Chronicle* lavished lengthy praise upon Moreno, who "will be to this new project what Morse was to the telegraph, Fulton to the steam engine, De Lesseps to the Suez Canal. . . . Like these men, Moreno has encountered many obstacles in the last eight years, in trying to open the eyes of American statesmanship to the rich resources of the Orient . . . The struggle was a hard one, not only with Congress, but with the arrogant British monopoly, and at last Mr. Cyrus Field found his match."

Celso Moreno of Dogliani would have basked in that universal adulation, which had been denied him in Italy. Less than ten years after his arrival in the United States, he had become a key player in the country's politics and economy, negotiating with statesmen and tycoons. As on other occasions, he personally added a final flourish to his portrait, solemnly declaring: "The transpacific cable and the transoceanic canal across the

Isthmus of Panama will revolutionize world commerce. They are two of the greatest opportunities of the present and will be two great achievements of the future." It was dizzying. The sky was the limit. However, as in all his adventures, Moreno had an Achilles heel.

The Trans-Pacific Cable Act of 1876 granted Celso Caesar Moreno and his associates the right "to construct, lay, land and maintain a line or lines of Telegraphic or Submarine Cable or Cables on the Pacific Coast of the United States of America, to connect the American and the Asiatic coasts by telegraph lines or submarine cables." Since the act carried no appropriation of funding, the task of securing the necessary capital fell to Moreno. Initially, it appeared that he would easily succeed at this task as he had with Congress. In his words, "the respectability of the gentlemen at the head of the American and Asiatic Telegraph Company . . . is proverbial on the Pacific slope . . . and their collective wealth is far superior to the amount of money required to complete this enterprise."

On November 15, 1877, the new board of directors of the Transpacific Cable Company met at the Merchants' Exchange Building in San Francisco. It was a select company that included personalities of the caliber of Leland Stanford, the ex-governor of California and president of the Central Pacific Railroad, as president; Celso C. Moreno, first vice president; J. F. Miller, president of the Alaska Seal Company, second vice president; A. S. Hallidie, secretary; and Mark L. McDonald, treasurer, along with George S. Dodge, O. H. La Grange, M. L. McDonald, A. J. Bryant (mayor of San Francisco), W. Simon, Frank Pixley, Eugene Sullivan, William Norris, N. K. Masten, Central Pacific Railroad President Mark Hopkins, and J. C. Flood, one of the "Bonanza kings" of the silver mines of Nevada and California. As its first order of business, the board of directors set the corporation's stock at ten million dollars, divided into one hundred thousand shares for one hundred dollars apiece.[40] Certainly this capital was within the capacity of such deep pockets. But in spite of the initial, euphoric response to the project, the necessary funds were never raised. The reason for the resignations of some board members is unknown. The legislation had specified that Moreno and his associates "shall begin to lay said cable within three years from the passage of this Act." The 1879 deadline was not met, but Moreno repeatedly sought and secured congressional measures to revive and extend the Act of 1876, the last in 1899, two years before his death.

In 1897, an article by George Ethelbert Walsh in *New England Magazine* described earlier efforts to lay a cable in the Pacific, without mentioning Moreno or the Trans-Pacific Cable Company. On the contrary, he claimed that "the first and only project of a cable in the Pacific has failed and no company has dared to revive it," with evident reference to Collins's project in the Bering Strait. Ironically, Walsh reiterated Moreno's appeal: "It is manifestly the duty of the United States to cable the Pacific in the interest of its own citizens. . . . A Pacific Ocean Cable is only a matter of time."

It was true. The Act of 1876 provided "that nothing in this act shall be construed to limit the United States in granting to other persons or companies similar privileges." Much to Moreno's chagrin, interest in a Pacific cable revived in the 1890s. In 1891, by an act of Congress, the Hydrographic Office of the U.S. Navy was directed to take soundings between San Francisco and Hawaii "for the purpose of determining the practicability of the laying of a telegraphic cable between those points."[41] A few years later, the Pacific Commercial Cable Company (PCCC), a conglomerate of telegraphy and cable-manufacturing companies, was founded. Following a report to the Department of the Navy, the PCCC was authorized to begin construction in 1899. The first section of cable was brought to Honolulu in 1902 and then extended to the Philippines, Japan, and China. The transpacific cable was inaugurated on July 4, 1903. The first words, spoken by President Theodore Roosevelt, took nine minutes to go around the world.[42]

Moreno, who had died two years earlier and whose name was not mentioned during the opening ceremony, would have been pleased. However, he would also have been furious to know that the English had sneaked into the project again. An eight-thousand-mile cable in the Pacific, connecting Vancouver, with Australia and New Zealand via Fiji (since the United States had not granted permission to go via Hawaii) was completed on November 1, 1902.[43]

Because the project's most important sponsors lived in California, Moreno spent the majority of his time between 1872 and 1876 in that state. His testimony before congressional committees during these years indicates that he made several transcontinental trips by train. The trip from Washington to San Francisco took seven days. What were his thoughts while the train puffed across the prairies and mountains toward the Pacific? We can be sure that his fertile mind was imagining new ventures. In the 1870s there were in San Francisco a couple of thousand Italian restaurant owners, gardeners, fishermen, fruit sellers, and saloonkeepers. Moreno would have found few investors among them. Instead, King Kalākaua of Hawaii captured his attention during a visit to San Francisco in 1874. After they met, Moreno sent a portrait to Ricasoli and wrote that "this sovereign . . . is a bit more civilized than my father-in-law the Sultan of Acheem [*sic*] on the island of Sumatra."[44] It was a meeting ripe with unforeseen consequences for both men.

Among the leaders of the Italian community in California was Carlo A. Dondero, an ardent nationalist and Garibaldian republican. When he arrived in New York at only thirteen years old, Dondero fortuitously found work with Secchi de Casali, the editor of *L'Eco d'Italia*, beginning a long career as a printer and journalist. Still young, he went to California in search of gold. He did not find any, but he set up a press in San Francisco. Along with others, he founded *La Voce del Popolo*, and for many years he was its editor and publisher. A fervent Mazzinian, his attacks against the monarchy brought him into a "knife fight" with the Italian consuls, the king's representatives. Moreno was attracted to this independent-minded man, and the two became friends. Many years later, Dondero would offer a description of Moreno very different from that of his mentor Secchi de Casali. To Dondero, Moreno was a man of great culture, prodigious memory, good character, indomitable courage and energy, great determination, generous and kind with everyone he met, who treated the most humble and the most proud alike. He was a most charming man, and affectation was completely unknown to him.[45]

Despite his absorbing work with the Trans-Pacific Cable Company, Moreno participated in the life of the *colonia italiana* in San Francisco and in the Mutual Benefit Society Dondero founded.[46] He became a defender of Italian interests in Sacramento, though it is not clear if he worked as a paid lobbyist or as a volunteer. According to Dondero, he was "the first to obtain from the State Government a decent harbor location for the Italian fishermen of San Francisco." Moreno claimed authorship of a bill that banned the destruction of small fish in San Francisco Bay and the Sacramento River by the Chinese, who used small-mesh nets. An 1876 California law stated, "Any person who shall set, use, or continue, or who shall assist in setting and using or continuing any pound, weir, set-net, stake-net, trap, or other fixed or permanent contrivance for catching fish in any of the waters of this State, is guilty of a misdemeanor." Although the provision did not specifically refer to the Chinese, another law, passed in 1880, said, "All aliens incapable of becoming electors of this State are hereby prohibited from fishing, or taking any fish, lobster, shrimps, or shell fish of any kind, for the purpose of selling, or giving to another person to sell."

Since at that time only Chinese immigrants were excluded from citizenship, they were obviously the law's targets. Moreno, who was in Italy at the time, had no responsibility for the law's passage. Both laws, clearly intended to exclude the Chinese from the benefits that Italians and other Europeans enjoyed, were expressions of racist nativism in California. The sources however do not say anything about the way that Moreno, the great friend of the Chinese (in China), reacted to this sinophobia.

In 1870, the Risorgimento had culminated in the annexation of Rome to the Kingdom of Italy. During these years, Moreno's involvement in homeland politics had been marginal. As we have said, as soon as Moreno arrived, he described America as "my adopted fatherland" and thereafter used the expression "we Americans," perhaps as expedient rhetoric. In a letter to Sumner dated September 28, 1870, he wrote, "I know that you will rejoice with me that Italy is now mistress of her destiny and I hope that we Italians soon will be able to imitate the example of our forefathers and establish in the Capital of Eternal Rome . . . a Republic." He went on to say that the republican form of government "in my opinion ought to make the whole circuit of the World and you Americans are fortunate to have set the example in this modern age." (What about his "very good friend" King Vittorio Emanuele II?) Always ready to point out economic advantages, Moreno observed, "Now Italy and America ought to be closer united by commercial relations which are the more fit for promoting friendship." As an example, he cited a steamship line to be established between New York and Genova that "will unite the birthplace of Columbus and the land of Washington." Shortly thereafter, writing in Italian on the letterhead of the Comitato Italiano per la Gran Festa Nazionale Roma Libera (The Italian Committee for the Great National Celebration of Liberated Rome), to be held in New York on October 28, Moreno extended an invitation to Sumner to participate, assuring him a welcome "worthy of your Honorable Person."[47]

In the meantime, the Piedmontese gentleman was participating in a campaign to save Corporal Pietro Barsanti from execution. Barsanti was a twenty-year-old soldier in the Italian army who in March 1870, during a failed attempt at a Mazzinian insurrection in in Pavia, had taken some soldiers prisoner and cried "*Viva la Repubblica*!" He was court-martialed and condemned to death. A protest movement in Italy and among Italian expatriates called on the king to commute the sentence. According to Dondero, Moreno "not only helped me to collect signatures among the Italo American mothers of California . . . but being a personal friend of King Victor and his brother, the Duke of Genoa, he sent a heart rending personal appeal to spare the life of the youth."

But the appeal was in vain. "The merciless monarch," Dodero continued, "paid no attention to the petition and prayers of nearly 200,000 souls," including more than 300 Italian mothers and 1,500 "prominent American mothers" from California. "Barsanti was shot . . . but that young and ardent patriot went to his death to be vindicated by a superior Italian civilization! May it come soon, for hypocrisy and barbarism have already plagued it enough." According to Dondero, "Moreno swore never to return to Italy in his just hatred for the perfidious monarchy that he had devotedly served in his gallant and energetic youth." But he did not keep the promise.

Now forty, he had spent more than ten years in the United States. Despite his heroic efforts, he was unable to realize either of his objectives: the sale of "Moreno's Island" or the construction of the transpacific cable. Moreno, however, did not renounce either project. The latter would take him back to China and then to his fateful rendezvous with King Kalakaua. In the meantime, he discovered another cause to which he could dedicate his restless spirit and boundless energy: a passionate campaign in defense of those he called "the Italian slave children." In the end, this "distraction" became the defining issue of the remainder of his life.

CHAPTER 4

The Little Italian Slaves

> It was a bitter cold night of February, 1871, when at the corner of Owen House and Pennsylvania Avenue, at about 11 o'clock, where I found a squad of little Italian wandering musicians, two boys and girl from 7 to 8 years of age, crying, suffering from the cold, hunger, and fear of their cruel *padroni* . . . if they should go home without the sum of money fixed, one dollar, that they ought to bring each of them every night to their *padrone* after wandering all day through the streets, squares, alleys, bars, beer saloons, and other worse places playing their instruments, singing, and begging. . . . The two boys playing the violin, whose arms being too short, placed it against their stomachs, and the girl playing the triangle . . . the pitiful story of . . . the three little creatures . . . was heartrending and made me cry with them.[1]

Moreno, the bold sea captain, the lusty lover, the battle-scarred warrior, the forceful entrepreneur, reduced to tears at the plight of exploited "little creatures"? Here, another persona in Moreno's repertoire stepped onto the stage, the compassionate protector of the weak and helpless. Eschewing the pious rhetoric of the time, he used vivid prose based on personal observations. Accompanying the children to a shanty, there Moreno found two "ferocious looking *padroni* playing cards and drinking beer . . . waiting for their little slaves . . . to bring them the money they had earned and begged." Questioning the *padroni*, he learned that they were from Marsico Vetere in Basilicata and had twelve children in their care. Insisting on seeing their sleeping quarters, he entered a stable in which boys and girls were lying, pell-mell, on dirty straw full of vermin and covered with rags. "At such a sight," Moreno wrote, "my forehead became red with shame and my heart full of indignation, and from that very moment I made up my mind to do all in my single person against a compact multitude."

In this heartfelt language, Moreno described his "discovery" of Italian child slavery in America. With the energy and zeal that characterized all of his endeavors, he undertook his crusade against the "great wrong," which would last for the rest of his life.

Italian street musicians, both those who played musical instruments and others with hand organs, had been familiar figures for centuries in Rome, Naples, and Genoa as well as Paris and London.[2] It was one of many ambulatory trades that enabled hill folk from the Apennines to eke out a miserable existence. While children often accompanied relatives or *paesani*, an increasing number of very young street performers were indentured to *padroni* by the 1860s. Formal contracts specified the terms of service. The parents received modest annual payments, and the master was obligated to provide food, shelter, and clothing and to teach the children to play an instrument. In towns where *miseria* reigned, families with too many mouths to feed found this tempting. For money and, perhaps, the belief that the child would learn a trade and live a better life, young ones were entrusted to the *padrone*. Contrary to the provisions of an apprenticeship, the system lent itself to abuse, cruelty, and neglect.

By the 1860s, the growing presence of Italian child musicians in European cities caused outrage, inspired philanthropic initiatives, and resulted in ameliorative legislation in several countries. The plight of the "Italian slave children" made good copy for newspapers and models for picturesque paintings that appealed to the Victorians' sentimental humanitarianism. In Italy, the nationalists, exalting in the triumph of the Risorgimento, were perplexed by the international outcry surrounding their little compatriots. They, too, raised their voices in protest, more often out of concern for the honor of Italy rather than for the children's fate. In 1868, several publications raised the level of public concern. A report by the Società Italiana di Beneficenza in Paris drew attention to the "shameful speculation" in "*petits italiens*" in France.

That year, Ferdinando De Luca, the Consul General of Italy in New York, sent a detailed report to the Ministry of Foreign Affairs describing, in detail, the modus operandi of the *padroni*'s system and the horrendous suffering it entailed for the children. De Luca expressed his personal distress at the plight of these "small musicians," so poorly fed and abandoned "that the most neglected of domestic animals receive better treatment":

> Each night when they return home, they are stripped of their clothes and searched, including their shoes and hair, by the *padroni*. Woe to anyone who has hidden even five cents. The delinquent is furiously beaten to serve as an example to others.
>
> It is a sad spectacle to see them . . . dressed in rags, exhausted, pale from hunger and sufferings, freezing in winter snow, feverish in heat of the summer, stopping to look hungrily at any food display, eyeing open doorways in hope of receiving the remains of dinner. A sad spectacle indeed to hear them bring forth from their instruments gay notes and raise their infantile voices in song. Then to watch them trudging along without any sign of that noisy vivacity which characterizes all children. . . . How many have I surprised swallowing their tears, crouched in a corner. I remember once near New Orleans finding one on the edge of a woods, who could not have been more than five or six years old, and who had lost his way, trembling from fear and crying for mamma.[3]

De Luca found the moral dangers to which the children were exposed even more threatening than their physical ills. Deprived of any religious influence, they resorted, without qualms, to lying, thievery, begging, and even worse. Since saloons and brothels were the most profitable venues for their performances, they acquired the habits of swearing, drinking, and observing obscenities "which muddied the purity of their minds." Anticipating the skepticism of some, the Consul General acknowledged that "the colors of this picture may appear exaggerated, but what I write is regrettably the absolute truth, nor am I doing anything more than frankly reporting what I have seen for many years and see today, and what others have seen before me."

De Luca closed his report with a cry: "In the name of God is there no law which can prevent these horrors? . . . the national dignity is offended every day and in every part of the world by such vile business. . . . Where natural paternal protection is lacking is it not the duty of the Government to intervene?"

These were not the words of a disinterested bureaucrat, and De Luca's appeal did not fall on deaf ears. Initially printed in the *Gazzetta Ufficiale del Regno d'Italia*, the report was published as a pamphlet and widely distributed by the Ministry of Foreign Affairs.[4]

Giuseppe Guerzoni's novel *La tratta dei fanciulli* (*The Trafficking of Children*), also published in 1868, was most influential in stirring the sympathy of the upper classes. Guerzoni, like Abba, was one of Garibaldi's *Mille*, and he became a popular writer and member of the Chamber of Deputies. In the book's preface, he described the circumstances of its publication: "These were the days when the theme [of the wandering children] was on the lips of all: the press discussed it, Parliament discussed it, the country as a whole was affected by it; therefore even a small book written in an affecting and popular style, on one of many episodes in this pitiful childhood odyssey, would not be found unwelcome and superfluous."[5]

The book proved popular, and eager readers snatched up many editions. One of note was published in the San Francisco Italian American newspaper *La Voce del Popolo* (1868). It was a melodramatic account of the sorrowful lives of Carluccio and Stefanella, brother and sister, who were sold to a *padrone*, taken to France to sing and dance, endured untold woes, and came to a tragic end. It particularly tugged at feminine heartstrings. In the preface, Guerzoni anticipated his book's effect: "If a gentle tear should stain the story on these pages, it will be a testimony to the saintliness of the cause," but he reassured his readers that the children's deliverance was close at hand: "The public consciousness is raised, the truth is well-known . . . and even the government, which is always the last to be convinced and to intervene, is taking steps!"

Not satisfied with literary success, Guerzoni became the leading proponent of government action. In 1873 he and his colleagues realized their goal with the passage of a law voiding all employment contracts for children under eighteen years of age in the ambulatory trades (including acrobats, fortune tellers, animal trainers, peddlers, singers, and musicians). A specific provision subjected persons taking children abroad, or employing them in such jobs in other countries, to strict penalties. Even harsher sentences were to be imposed upon those who abused the children. Instructions were sent to diplomatic and consular agents about the law's enforcement, including cooperating with officials in countries of immigration to suppress the "infamous trade in children." Despite good intentions, the law proved unequal to the task. Subsequent instructions addressed the difficulty of ascertaining which children practiced bona fide employment, especially if they had emigrated with their parents.[6]

Mingling with politicians and journalists in Rome in the 1860s, Moreno was certainly aware of the impassioned discussions about the trade in Italian children. During his sojourns abroad, Moreno kept abreast of developments "at home" and publicized his projects back in Italy by subscribing to Italian newspapers and corresponding with public and literary figures. His correspondents included such luminaries as Angelo De Gubernatis, professor at the University of Florence and a leading intellectual; Francisco Protonotari, editor of the *Nuova Antologia*; and Deputy Guerzoni himself.

Moreno wrote to Guerzoni in 1872, claiming that what the writer called "child slavery" he had previously labeled "white slavery." 7 As evidence, he referenced two letters and a report that he sent Cesare Correnti, as well as a message to Princess Dora of Istria,[8] in 1871. Moreno urged the Chamber of Deputies to put an end to that "scandalous traffic which inspires horror among Americans and dishonors Italy."

By the 1860s, as Consul General De Luca reported, the sight of Italian child musicians on the streets of American cities caused scandal. Their presence was noted and commented upon even earlier in newspapers and sermons. Since the 1850s, Charles Loring Brace had conducted a mission among New York City's poor immigrant children. Despite his opposition to "bigoted Italians"—priests foremost—Brace and A. E. Cerqua, an immigrant teacher from Umbria, a "Protestant and patriot," founded an Italian School in 1855 to deliver children "from the wretched street-trades," and instead teach them "useful trades." Despite initial skepticism, Brace gained the support of a number of affluent Italians. When their committee shared with the Italian government the work being done on behalf of its "destitute and ignorant subjects," they received approval and support. After visiting the Italian School on October 23, 1867, Marcello Cerruti, the Italian ambassador to the United States, wrote to Brace and said that he was convinced because "by your efficient and humane exertions, hundreds of poor Italian children have been redeemed from vagrancy and turned into industrious and useful members of the community." Brace was among the first to call attention to the nefarious *padrone* system, first with an 1869 letter to the *New York Times* and then with his book *The Dangerous Classes of New York, and Twenty Years' Work Among Them* (1872).[9] Brace dedicated a chapter to the "The Little Italian Organ-Grinders," and with words analogous to Moreno's wrote:

> Some of the little ones suffered severely from being indentured by their parents in Italy to a "Bureau" in Paris, which sent them out over the world with their "*padrone*," or master, usually a villainous-looking

individual with an enormous harp. The lad would be frequently sent forth by his *padrone*, late at night, to excite the compassion of our citizens, and play the harp. I used to meet these boys sometimes on winter-nights half-frozen and stiff with cold.[10]

Meantime, in the pages of *L'Eco d'Italia*, Giovanni Francesco Secchi de Casali had been exposing and campaigning against the abuses of street children since the 1850s. He may have been the first to call them the "white slaves" of New York. His newspaper printed an account, *Il piccolo genovese* (*The Little Genoese*), about one of these children.[11] In 1872 Horatio Alger Jr. published a novel, *Phil the Fiddler*, part of a series about poor but determined children who, with courage and luck, succeeded—like the trailblazing "little Genoese"—in overcoming every obstacle and achieving respectability and a well-to-do life.[12] Twelve-year-old Phil (Filippo), after having endured the harshness of the streets and the *padrone*'s blows, fled to New Jersey, where Pat and Bridget McGuire sheltered him from his pursuers. Caught in a snowstorm, he was not only saved but also adopted by a doctor and his wife. Among other blessings that follow, the good doctor takes him on a trip to Italy to visit his mother. Alger assures us that Phil has "bright prospects for a prosperous career." Alger achieved a degree of verisimilitude in his descriptions of the lives of the "white slaves" because of the assistance of A. E. Cerqua and G.F. Secchi de Casale. In his preface, Alger introduces the hero of his book: "Among the most interesting and picturesque classes of street children in New York are the young Italian musicians, who wander about our streets with harps, violins, or tambourines." His purpose—other than selling books—was to show the American public their suffering and to "excite an active sympathy on their behalf."

Some artists also found these children "picturesque," and they became popular subjects of many paintings and drawings. John George Brown, the most successful of these artists, created dozens of works about Italian street musicians in the 1870s. Inspired by a series of *New York Times* articles about "Italian slaves," his pictures "captured an especially grim and widely publicized form of child labor that reached its height of public recognition in 1873 and 1874 mostly because of extensive coverage in the press."[13] In Brown's paintings of these street urchins, the children are sometimes covered in rags, sometimes not, but they are always attractive: "sad—but clean and healthy." Brown's paintings sold well. Like Alger, he no doubt hoped to "excite an active sympathy on their behalf."

Others therefore preceded Moreno's "discovery" of "white slavery" by several years, a fact that the Captain never recognized. But his ability as a publicist ensured that the issue was on the front page of both the American and Italian American press, so much so that the Captain claimed to have introduced the word *padrone* into the English languages. It passed from his private correspondence to official acts of Congress and to the courts and was even used by President Cleveland.[14]

Whether out of credulity or cynical exploitation, *the New York Times* became Moreno's megaphone, publishing his letters as well as engaging him as an informant and translator. Moreno accompanied its reporters into the Five Points neighborhood, the main concentration of poor Italians, in search of the dens of the *padroni*. In June 1873, the newspaper carried no fewer than twenty articles and letters under the rubric "Italian Children as Slaves." The prestige of the *Times* allowed Moreno to control the narrative about the "Italian slave children."

The sensational reporting captured the public's attention. (One wonders how much of the purple prose was due to Moreno's "translations.") The descriptions of the moral and physical squalor that the children endured appealed to altruistic sensibilities, and probably also to a certain voyeurism. A reader praised "your bold and open denunciations of the abuses which so long disgraced the first City of America and are read and quoted and commented upon favorably everywhere."[15] One article in particular caused a stir: it stated that "between 7000 and 8000" children were "kidnapped from Italy and held in a state of slavery in American cities." Later, the article described how the children were sold at auction for between $100 and $500, except girls "who are exceptionally pretty," who could be sold for as much as $1600, suggesting that the girls were also subject to sexual exploitation. The article ended with the manifest of a ship that had allegedly disembarked 317 Italian children in the past two months.[16]

Though others had made the analogy between African slavery and "white Italian slaves," Moreno made it a central theme of his publicity and lobbying campaign with references to kidnappings, slave ships, auctions, and runaway slaves. It is unclear how much of this was fact and how much was the invention of his fertile imagination. It is certain, however, that Brown's images also "derived much of their potency from their allusion to conditions of slavery" and "anti-slavery feelings continued to fuel public reaction to the musicians." Advertisements for the discovery of fugitives appeared in newspapers almost as if they had returned to the era of slavery. One read: "$10 REWARD—Runaway, an Italian boy, eleven years of age . . . plays violin; had on striped pants and vest, and cap without peak." There were even rumors that boys were "marked" by a cut on their lip or by having their tongues cut so that, like birds, they might sing more passionately in the street.[17]

Moreno, whatever his genuine concern for the children, had an ulterior motive. In the opening shot of what was to be a thirty-year war, Moreno not only denounced the "scandalous traffic in Italian children" but also announced that following "detailed research," he had concluded that Consul General De Luca was "responsible for this dishonor to the Italian name." Moreno then attacked De Luca without restraint: "The presence of this individual as Consul at New York," he wrote, "is an outrage to the conscience and patriotism of every Italian who has the national dignity at heart." He claimed that the Italian Ministry of Foreign Affairs was undermining the Italian Parliament's recent law prohibiting the "traffic in white children" by refusing "to remove the cause," namely De Luca himself.[18]

The next day, A. E. Cerqua, C. L. Brace's partner, intervened in the consul's defense. He wrote that De Luca had been "indefatigable and unflinching in his exertions to eradicate this evil, and time and time he has called the attention of the Italian Government to the scandalous traffic in children." Cerqua attributed the law's passage "in large part to the consul himself."[19]

In a June 15 letter, H. D. Monachesi, a journalist for the *Times*, called for an investigation by the Italian and American governments without explicitly endorsing Moreno's accusations against the consul. Monachesi argued that De Luca's reports should have been sent to the American government to bring the issue to American authorities' attention. If it had been, "the traffic would have been stopped long ago."[20]

Monachesi became Moreno's collaborator in his campaign against De Luca. When a *Times* editorial claimed that the Consul General could no longer deny the existence of the phenomenon, De Luca was forced to break his silence. He did not find any exaggeration in the descriptions of the children's suffering. However, he defended himself, saying, "no Italian official abroad has more continually than myself exposed them to my Government, without the smallest palliation, and insisted on the adoption of energetic and immediate measures for their suppression."

As previously noted, De Luca had submitted a report to the Ministry of Foreign Affairs in 1868. In it, he described and denounced the trade in Italian children in language even stronger than Moreno's four years later. His claim that the Italian Parliament's law of May 1873, which made child trafficking a felony, was due in no small measure to his reports appears justified. The Consul closed his letter with a touch of irritation, saying, "I will be deeply thankful to God for all those unjust attacks against me, if out of them may arise some efficient measure by which America may be enabled to co-operate with Italy in suppressing this evil."

Moreno, however, was not to be persuaded or placated. Ignoring De Luca's self-defense, he resumed his attack with an ad hominem invective. He criticized De Luca for not having brought "this nefarious traffic" to American authorities' attention. If no Italian representative abroad had done more than him to oppose the enslavement of children, this simply proved "they altogether are harmful nullities." Furthermore, whereas De Luca had served the corrupt Bourbon Kingdom of the Two Sicilies as Vice Consul in New Orleans; whereas he came from the same province from which "most of the stolen children are taken"; and whereas the evil had appeared after he became Consul General in New York, it was a guilty verdict, case closed. Unrelenting, Moreno held De Luca responsible along with the *padroni* "for the tears shed by a thousand mothers who have been deprived of their children."[21]

Moreno followed the same tactics that he used in his many other controversies: ignoring the contradictory evidence and burying his adversaries in an avalanche of allegations and innuendoes. Following Consul General Casella and Father Bruno in Calcutta and Professor Negri in Rome, De Luca now had the misfortune of becoming the target of his venom in New York.

On June 21, five letters appeared in the *Times* under the heading "The Traffic in Italian Children." In one of them, Secchi de Casali jumped into the fray. Regarding Moreno's accusation that the commerce had begun when De Luca became Consul General in New York, Secchi claimed that *L'Eco d'Italia* had been exposing it for the past twenty-four years! The children, moreover, were hired under written contracts with their parents, and not one of them came from the same province as De Luca. He had arrived in the United States as Consul General of Italy in New Orleans in 1864. Charles Loring Brace joined the chorus the same day with a letter commending the *Times* for adding its "powerful voice in the reform of this issue of the Italian children." Since the *padroni*'s claim of parenthood or guardianship made it almost impossible to enforce a prohibitory law at the port of embarkation or disembarkation, Brace proposed a city law requiring "every child to carry a certificate from a responsible teacher showing that he had half-time schooling every day." Lacking this, the child "would be arrested as a vagrant."[22]

Provoked by a continuous barrage of criticism, Consul General De Luca once again felt obliged to refute the accusations of Moreno and others. Regarding his failure to call upon the American authorities to address the problem, he explained that, as consul, he was prohibited from communicating directly with the State Department. It was neither within his power to arrest Italian nationals nor appropriate for him to tell American officials how to do their duties. De Luca supported Brace's proposed municipal law to regulate children's employment in street trades, as well as a revision of the Treaty of Extradition to enable the *padroni*'s deportation to Italy.[23]

The controversy fell heavily on the Italian residents of New York. A letter writer went so far as to accuse them of collective responsibility for the "infamous traffic": "It is high time that the Italian colony in this country should take strict measures in order to cure an evil that has long disgraced their nationality. . . . Now the Italians should at once seek to remove from our streets the painful spectacle which hundreds of unfortunate children offer from morning until night."[24]

In the early 1870s, the Italian community, which had fewer than fifty thousand people, largely comprised merchants, artists, musicians, language teachers, and artisans. The wave of *contadini* from southern Italy would arrive later. The Five Points neighborhood, however, had already acquired a reputation as a slum inhabited by poor and ignorant Italians. Crosby Street was the *padroni*'s favored haunt, and here journalists sought them and their little slaves. The *prominenti* who prided themselves on their elevated social and cultural status and their northern Italian origins feared that the daily exposés of this sordid business stigmatized "respectable" Italians.[25]

As the *Times* reported, "many of the leading Italian citizens complain bitterly of the disgrace that has been put upon them." They were frustrated by the Italian and American governments' paralysis, and directed "a severe criticism" at the Consul General's apathy.[26] De Luca responded, injured, and cited the "extremely flattering address," he had recently received from prominent Italians (whose names he listed), commending him for calling on the Italian Government to act against the "shameful traffic" of children.[27]

Contrary to the observation that Italian residents had decided "more firmly than ever to work together and stop this growing evil," they became embroiled in a bitter conflict amongst themselves. Once again, Moreno was at the center of the controversy. He had made De Luca, rather than the children, the issue. The "little Italian slaves" became pawns in a struggle between Moreno and De Luca for leadership of the Italian community. The Italians polarized into "pro" and "con" factions that mirrored personal grudges and political ambitions among the *prominenti*.[28]

The Associazione Donnarumma, "one of the most prominent and influential bodies of Italians in the City," excluded the Consul General from its deliberations and called upon the U.S. government to suppress the trade in children. On June 30, the group held its annual picnic in Sultzer Park, which was gaily decorated with American and Italian flags. After food and dancing, Mr. Donnarumma introduced Moreno as the person who started the movement against the importation of Italian children. The Capitano Marittimo called upon the "community" to end its silence on the "slave trade . . . between *the southern provinces of Italy* and the United States," a silence which was "a weapon in the hands of our enemies." He would "appeal to the generous American people who have . . . shed torrents of blood for the emancipation of the negro, to assist us in the deliverance of the whites." Moreno concluded by wishing "confusion, remorse, and contempt" upon those who had failed in their duty (that is, De Luca). Those assembled unanimously adopted a resolution "to do all in our power to bring about the abolition of this new system of slavery," and censuring the Consul General for failing in his duty. It also warned against a meeting of De Luca's supporters, the members of the Republican Society of Italian Citizens of New York, as a "trap to catch the unwary."[29]

Secchi de Casali, one of the Consul General's staunchest allies, defended him on the pages of *L'Eco d'Italia*.[30] He sent one of his reporters, Giuseppe Vallosio, to the Associazione Donnarumma's picnic. Vallosio was a member of the Republican Society of Italian Citizens of New York and a self-described "Mazzinian and Volunteer for liberty." Five times he responded to the "odious resolutions" with shouts of "*Non è vero*! (It's not true!)" only to be denigrated and threatened.[31] He also reported that Moreno had approached him, first to complain about money owed him for articles contributed to *L'Eco*, and then to repeat his attacks on De Luca. An unfriendly exchange ensued. In the midst of their humanitarian appeals, New York's Italians lost sight of the children's plight as they engaged in vicious polemics.

As Moreno used one hand to stir a cauldron of emotions in New York City (and not just there: the issue also provoked an uproar in Chicago),[32] he cultivated alliances in Italy with the other. He claimed to have written to the king, four of his ministers, and various members of Parliament and journalists since August 1871.[33] He seemed delighted with the uproar that his lobbying on behalf of the "slave children" and against Italy's representatives abroad caused.

In his pioneering 1874 analysis of Italian emigration, Leone Carpi observed:

> The year 1873 will perhaps have its praiseworthy aspects, but it was a year of infamy with respect to Italian emigration. All our newspapers have carried news of the pitiful condition of more than 3000 emigrants, for the most part from the southern provinces, tricked and seduced by detestable agents, and thrown into the miserable squalor of the slums of New York. To such a scandalous episode, which is reminiscent of the brutal recruitment of Indian and Chinese coolies, a commission of notable Italians of New York calls the attention of our Royal Consul to those who abuse the ignorance of that population and who traffic in a shameful way on the honor of our country and the lives of their countrymen.[34]

An article by Pasquale Villari contributed to the furor. Published in the *Nuova Antologia*, one of Italy's most influential magazines, it described the miserable conditions of New York's Italian children. Carpi referenced an article in *L'Eco d'Italia*, "The Italian Slaves in the United States of America."[35] Although he did not mention Moreno, it is likely that his exposé, disseminated in the Italian press, was at the center of the outcry in Italy. In this context, Moreno wrote a letter to King Victor Emanuel on June 24, 1873:

> It may interest Your Majesty to know the type of person to whom the honor and interests of the Italians of New York are entrusted. The Consul of Italy has been condemned by public opinion with respect to the continuous arrival of children of both sexes kidnapped and bought in Italy and sold as slaves in the major cities of America, and to defend himself this Consul dishonors the Entire Nation by his Statement published yesterday, June 23, on page 8 second and third column of the *Times*, and reprinted in the American press. He claimed that since no Italian law prohibited child slavery, Italy had been declared by its official representative in New York as a nation that considers white slavery legal, just like Zanzibar.[36]

The letter was forwarded to the minister of foreign affairs, who replied:

> Mr. Cesare Moreno . . . is well known to this ministry as a dangerous person devoted to intrigue. Since he did not receive support for his project to establish a colony abroad, he has incessantly opposed the Italian government, personally attacking some functionaries of the State. The ministry is aware of the unsupportable accusations that he has directed at the consul of New York about the traffic in migrant children. . . . I believe that silence is the only possible response to his attacks which present facts which cannot be proven.

But silence, as the minister would learn to his dismay, was not enough to stop Moreno. His letter to the king was a clear indication that he was more concerned with a vendetta against his "enemies" than in saving the "little white slaves." Still, Moreno was not satisfied with merely using the issue to cudgel De Luca. In the midst of his intense lobbying on behalf of the transpacific cable, he launched a campaign for a federal law against the "enslavement" of Italian children. With his canny political instinct, he enlisted the two people best identified with the abolitionist cause: Senator Charles Sumner and Frederick Douglas.

Summer, as we have noted, had already succumbed to Moreno's charms and sponsored his bill for the transpacific cable. How could he refuse the appeal of the "indefatigable worker on behalf of these poor children?" Moreno began his letter:

> You, the Moses of the late Slave why do you not rise [*sic*] your voice in behalf of oppressed infantile humanity? Seven thousand, 7,000 Italian children of both sexes are kept in the most abject slavery after having been kidnapped in Italy and brought here and sold to heartless *padroni* . . . I have done all in my power to bring this curse before the public opinion. Now it is to you that have done and suffered so much for the freedom of the colored people, I ask to help me to free thousands of my helpless little countrymen.[37]

The august senator replied after just one day. "I like your idea. Such a wrong is infamous, and it ought to be corrected. . . . I should be glad to do something."[38]

True to his word, Sumner introduced a bill in the Senate in January 1874. Speaking to his colleagues, he submitted a petition from naturalized Italians representing organizations in New York City "to emancipate these unfortunate children from unjust and tyrannical rule . . . which no lover of freedom can contemplate unmoved." Meanwhile, Moreno persuaded James Scott Negley, a major general in the Civil War and then a Representative from Pennsylvania, to sponsor the bill in the House.[39]

But Moreno's masterstroke was securing the support of the renowned orator, writer, journalist, and abolitionist, Frederick Douglass. On January 2, 1873, when the campaign was just beginning, Douglass's newspaper, the *New National Era*, ran a front-page article with the headline "Children Brought in Italy for the New York Market."[40] Subsequent articles were effusive in their praise for the Italian agitator:

> Celso Caesar Moreno is the name of the liberator of Italian children . . . from an oppression and captivity not unlike that abolished by the

> thirteenth amendment . . . [he] has labored with an energy and zeal not surpassed by abolitionists of other days, and he has been denounced by other Italians as a fanatic . . . He has done the work that the Italian Ambassador and Consul are paid for and should have done.

And:

> Moreno . . . is deserving of the highest encomiums for his indefatigable zeal in the cause of his oppressed countrymen. He has expended his money and given his time without stint for the liberation of the little Italian children from the rapacity and cruel oppression of the *padroni*.[41]

With such prominent sponsors, the "Moreno bill" enjoyed smooth sailing. In the closing minutes of the first session of the Forty-Third Congress, the measure was approved by the Senate and rushed to the House, where it was considered and passed unanimously on June 23, 1874. Senator Sumner, who died on March 11, would have been pleased. Captain Moreno, who was said to have "devoted three years to this work, and expended on it thousands of dollars," was admitted to the floor of both chambers and "congratulated heartily by many Senators and Representatives."[42]

The law was intended to "to protect persons of foreign birth against forcible constraint or involuntary servitude" and prescribed severe penalties for those who brought to the United States "any person inveigled or forcibly kidnapped in any other country, with intent to hold such person so inveigled or kidnapped in confinement or to any involuntary service."[43] Although it did not specifically identify Italian children, it was clear that they were the law's intended beneficiaries.

Although Moreno celebrated its passage, the law proved no more effective in eliminating the presence of the wandering child musicians than the 1873 Italian law. The first and only conviction of a *padrone*, Giovanni Ancarola, was achieved in 1879.[44] By then, Moreno was again in China. Nevertheless, the "*padrone* statute" became enshrined in American jurisprudence and would be cited in cases involving involuntary servitude and peonage.

Interestingly, the *New York Times*, which had served as a vehicle for Moreno's campaign, did not celebrate the law's passage. The *Times* seems to have become disenchanted at his moment of triumph. It advised Senator Sumner to be on guard against "half-considered legislation . . . which would only do mischief." It cited a Children's Aid Society report by Cerqua, who had recently received a knighthood from the king "for his lengthy humanitarian commitment to the Italian children of New York" (a fact which must have bothered Moreno, since he never earned similar recognition). The report claimed that the number of children was seven thousand across the entire world, not seven thousand in the United States, as Moreno claimed. Moreover, the use of the term "kidnapping" was inaccurate, since the children were entered into apprenticeships by their parents. The article praised the Italian Consul for having made "the strongest statements against this cruel and infamous trade in children." It was, in sum, a studied rebuke of Moreno. But when the Italian government considered honoring Ambassador Luigi Corti and the Consul of New York for their efforts to get Congress to pass the law, another New York paper, *The Sun*, pointed out that the credit was not theirs at all, but Moreno's.[45]

However, the newspapers' interest in the issue decreased dramatically from 1874 onwards, though the issue briefly resurfaced in February 1874, when Moreno warned the editor of the *Brooklyn Daily Eagle* that the *padroni* who left New York had moved to Brooklyn. The newspaper sent a reporter who found hundreds of Italian children begging. They came from Mulberry and other streets in Little Italy, crossed the East River each morning on the Catherine Ferry, and returned in the evenings.[46]

John Zucchi, a historian of Italian child musicians, has concluded that their number began to diminish in the 1870's, and that the musicians almost entirely disappeared from American cities during the following decade.[47] He attributes this decline primarily to economic changes that demanded adult labor, not to government action. Yet as the immigration of *contadini* increased dramatically, so too did the number of Italian children who worked on the streets of American cities in great numbers, if not as minstrels, then as newsboys, flower girls, bootblacks, fruit vendors, etc. The difference was that they were no longer exploited by a *padrone* but by their own parents.

How can we assess Moreno's role in this convoluted episode of high-minded reform and low-minded politics? Zucchi finds him "usually dishonest in his claims and accusations," and though eccentric, also "an excellent publicist."[48] We would agree with this assessment and add that Moreno once again demonstrated his political acumen, strength of personality, enormous energy, and ruthless will. While beguiling Wall Street with his vision for American interests in Asia and obtaining a congressional charter and California money for his transpacific telegraph cable project, he captured the public's attention and secured an act of Congress on behalf of the "little Italian slaves." Certainly, his motivations were not innocent. If he stirred up outrage that improved the children's lives to some degree, he also maligned Consul General De Luca. If he mobilized Italian immigrants, he also sowed dissension among them. His exaggerations and lies encouraged negative stereotypes that influenced Americans' attitudes towards the tens of thousands Italian immigrants now arriving in the United States. But Moreno declared victory, and shifted his attention back to his affairs in California. However, he was not done with the "Great Wrong," and he later returned to it with even greater zeal.

CHAPTER 5

The Enchanter of Hawaii

On November 14, 1879, Moreno disembarked in the balmy port of Honolulu to a warm welcome. Nine and a half months later he departed hastily under threat of lynching. In less than a year, he became a central figure in the political crisis that culminated in the overthrow of the Kingdom of Hawaii.

Unlike many episodes of his career that left no enduring mark on the historical record, Moreno has been immortalized as a "fascinating but baffling figure in Hawaiian history."[1] Ralph Kuykendall, the leading historian of Hawaii, devoted a chapter in his monumental history to the "Moreno Episode," which he described as "one of the most curious and at the same time one of the most important incidents in Hawaiian history."[2]

Moreno arrived on the steamship *Ho-chung* from China, where he had been "disgusted," according to a source, because he realized that he would not be able to sell his island or carry out the transpacific telegraph. In Shanghai, he was well connected with new Chinese capitalists who, moving away from traditional markets in tea and silk, were turning to modern ventures. Some of them had cut their teeth in California and had traveled in Europe. They were buying Yangtze River steamships built by Americans and German and English ships for coastal trade, and they wanted their ships, flying the banner of the dragon, to eventually reach the Golden Gate. Moreno "was selected as the agent of the Chinese capitalists," who, though they were not yet ready to finance their cable project, told him that this enterprise would be possible with the Hawaiian government's support.[3]

Most important, Moreno won the confidence of Li Hung-Chang, the most influential man in late nineteenth-century China. A celebrated general in the war against the Taiping rebels, Li rose within the Empire's governing elite to the position of Governor General of the region of Chihli. He was also an accomplished diplomat who conducted China's negotiations with Western powers. His most significant initiative was the policy of "Self-Strengthening," a response to the threat of imperialism from those powers. China, he argued, had to modernize and acquire technology and scientific knowledge. To this end, Li sent young scholars to the United States and to other countries. He also constructed the first Chinese railway, telegraph line, and cotton mill. In 1872, he established the China Merchants Steam Navigation Company (CMSNC) to conduct coastal trade, which had been in foreign hands. Now, he was contemplating expanding the merchant fleet to carry Chinese laborers to Hawaii and South America.[4]

When Moreno set foot on Hawaiian soil, he presented himself as a special agent of the CMSNC. In his role as lobbyist, he came seeking, among other things, a subsidy from the Kingdom for his steamship line.[5] With his customary grandiloquence, he declared that directly connecting Hawaii to China and the United States would make the Sandwich Islands "by manifest destiny . . . the Singapore, Java, and Sumatra of the western Pacific," that is "a commercial depot of crucial importance between Asia, Australia, and America."[6] The primary cargo would be Chinese laborers. Moreno's shipmates on the *Ho-Chung* were 451 coolies destined for the island's sugar plantations.

The Hawaii Moreno found was no paradise. Following its "discovery" in 1778 by the ill-fated Captain James Cook, the rapid incursion of Western influences, which Lawrence Fuchs has described as "the introduction of venereal disease, firearms, and the idea of trade for profit,"[7] decimated the physical and cultural constitution of the Kanakas. Hawaii was not conquered by bloody battles. However, the scourge of smallpox, measles, leprosy, cholera, and syphilis (Hawaiians lacked immunity to all of them) killed thousands upon thousands. Between 1778 and 1878, their numbers decreased from 300,000 to 50,000.

Following initial colonization by the Polynesians and isolated from the rest of the world, a complex Hawaiian culture had evolved, adapted to the benign environment of volcanic soil and ocean. Though certainly not a Garden of Eden—cruelty and exploitation were also part of the Hawaiian way of life—it was a life lived according to established beliefs, traditions, and values. *Kapus* (taboos) as enforced by *kahunas* (shamans) dictated all aspects of life. This fragile cultural system crumbled under the onslaught of a motley assortment of *haole* (foreign) adventurers, speculators, and plunderers, attracted by the islands' riches and motivated by greed and lust. As Fuchs explained, *haoles* were Caucasian foreigners of northern European origins. Even *haoles* born in Hawaii remained foreigners. The Portuguese, who were not considered *haoles*, were given an "intermediate role in the Hawaiian social order between the Orientals and the *haole*." The Hawaiians and the *Kanaka* ("human beings" in Hawaiian) were the original Polynesian inhabitants. In a letter to an English friend, King Kalākaua explained the meaning of race:

> While the whites openly demonstrated their contempt for people of color, the people of color hid this and nourished it in other ways . . . Kanaka showed his contempt for the whites by calling them *haole*. This word came to be interpreted as *white pig* when Captain Cook first landed in these parts, since white was immediately ascribed to the species that oinks. When the Kanakas' passions were excited . . . they frequently said "*Ka! Kahi haole pupuka ino! Ugh!*, that is, what a wicked (or ugly) white pig!"

The king closed, "Although we are very dark as a race, we feel the same repugnance towards blacks that the whites do."[8]

Other *haoles* came to save souls. The first missionaries came from New England in 1820, bringing a Calvinist creed that salvation could only be obtained by embracing their brand of Christianity and its repressive discipline. In their view, the natives were heathens and their behavior was shocking. They denounced and prohibited traditional beliefs and practices like polytheism, *kapu*, *kahuna*, the *hula*, and circumcision. It was said that the natives' high mortality rate could partially be attributed to their loss of will to live.[9]

The Kingdom of Hawaii came into being in the early nineteenth century when Kamehameha I, with the aid of Western advisors and arms, conquered the other islands. As a monarch, he and his successors enjoyed absolute power, mediated through reciprocal obligations with their chieftains. A constitution was created in 1840 under the missionaries' influence. It affirmed the king's authority and provided for an elected assembly and hereditary council of nobles. Faithful to their republican principles, the New England missionaries made sure there was a broad electorate. Since native Hawaiians constituted the overwhelming majority of the population, they were in a position to control the representative body. Since the *haoles* dominated the king's government, the stage was set for conflict.[10]

All the land belonged to the king, who allocated it to chieftains, who in turn oversaw its use by the members of various tribes. Until introduced by the *haoles*, the ideas of real estate, land transactions, and their profits were foreign to the Hawaiians. The "Great Mahele" of 1848, which introduced the division of land by grant or sale, marked the institutionalization of these capitalist principles. In less than a century, the ownership of Hawaii ended up in the hands of a small *haole* minority, among them many missionaries and their sons. In Hawaii's system of agricultural capitalism, land produced wealth through a marketable staple, sugarcane. The key to prosperity was access to the American market, which, however, levied a duty on imported sugar. A reciprocity treaty with the United States that would permit Hawaiian sugar to enter the United States duty-free was one of the island's central political questions for decades. While planters lobbied vigorously for it, the opposition, especially the Hawaiians, resisted it as a step toward annexation by the United States.[11]

When President Ulysses S. Grant finally signed the reciprocity treaty on August 15, 1876, he set a sugar boom in motion. Plantations spread across Hawaii and the plantation owners, who included no native Hawaiian, soon dominated the island's economic and social life. As a result of "reciprocity," Hawaiian society was transformed into a caste system with a *haole* oligarchy and a mass of wage-earning Asian workers. The natives no longer had a place in this new economic order.[12]

Growing and harvesting sugarcane required an army of cheap and compliant field workers. Hawaii's population was declining rapidly, but the natives did not want to work on the plantations. Immigration could meet this need, so recruiting foreign workers became a persistent preoccupation for the planters and the Hawaiian government. The most obvious source was Asia, and from the 1850s onward the Chinese arrived in growing numbers.[13]

William Nevins Armstrong, Kalākaua's childhood friend and later his prime minister, grasped the reciprocity treaty's consequences before the king did. He wrote, "It is a money-making business and a hammer that will drive nails into the Hawaiian race's coffin. . . . Soon we will be overwhelmed by the Chinese." The king replied:

> I am not afraid. They are a peaceful race and easily governed and controlled. . . . We still have enough room to receive them. The Chinese will be very prosperous under our autonomous institutions and a positive element to introduce in a country that is not able to attract other workers. If they are well treated, they will be excellent citizens. Thanks to the ingenuity, industriousness, and low cost of Chinese manpower, we will be able to compete in commerce with other nations.[14]

Within a few decades, the population's racial and cultural character was transformed. While 90 percent of the population was Hawaiian in 1876, in 1900 the percentage had fallen to 26 percent, while Asians were already 56 percent. Although they constituted a small minority, *haoles* controlled all areas of life. Echoing the brutal anti-Chinese movement in the United States, the "white" men of Hawaii, increasingly hostile to the growing presence of "yellow" men, tried to attract immigrants from other places, particularly from Europe.[15] They had some success recruiting Portuguese from the Azores and Madeira, but a steadier influx of Japanese ensured that Hawaii would become increasingly Asian. Unsurprisingly, native Hawaiians developed a growing resentment of "white" domination.

Although some Americans called Hawaiians "niggers," early relations between the two groups seem to have been relatively free from racial prejudice.[16] Mixed marriages between *haoles* and high-status native women were not uncommon. Children of royal or high *ali* (chieftain) birth attended the High Chiefs' Children School along with the missionaries' children. But in the last decades of the nineteenth century, growing racial tensions worsened relations between the natives and the *haoles*. In the 1870s, an organization of Young Hawaiians raised the cry "Hawaii for Hawaiians."[17] Among the leaders were the *hapa haole*, sons of unions between white men and native women. One of these was Robert William Kalani-hiapo Wilcox, who would play an important role in Hawaiian politics and in Moreno's subsequent career.

Hawaii's political situation was further complicated because it became the target of the competing imperialisms of Great Britain, France, Germany, and the United States. The European powers were busy grabbing islands in the Pacific, and the United States soon joined them. Their rivalry for influence over the Kingdom of Hawaii was demonstrated by their legations in Honolulu and their warships anchored in its harbor.

They interfered in Hawaiian politics, and at times American and British marines came ashore to quell "uprisings." In 1874, during the hotly contested struggle over succession to the throne between the pro-British Queen Emma and David Kalākaua, bribery and 150 American marines decided the issue in favor of the latter. Ironically, Kalākaua, an opponent of annexation, owed his crown to American bayonets.[18]

This was the Hawaii that Moreno encountered in 1879: a society undergoing rapid change, marked by divisions of race and wealth, and a government tarnished by corruption and nepotism and entangled in a web of internal political struggles and international intrigues. Though hula dancers did not greet him at the dock, Moreno's reception was auspicious. His reputation preceded him, and the American press printed articles praising him.[19] In the words of one historian, "Moreno overwhelmed Honolulu." Glowing articles described the "the gentleman from Genoa" as flamboyant and handsome. A more severe critic, General James M. Comly, the United States ambassador to Hawaii, noted his more attractive qualities: "Mr. Moreno is a subtle, crafty, and extremely clever Italian, of an imposing and insinuating manner, a big, burly man, six feet high, with an air of some distinction."[20]

Always attentive to his public image, Moreno's principal objective was to win King Kalākaua's confidence and support. Previous meetings in San Francisco in 1874 had paved the way. Kalākaua recalled the occasion as pleasant. He found Moreno "polite and intelligent and he seemed to be deeply interested in ocean telegraphy, as I was."[21] Ten years later, Moreno described their conversation: "We were in agreement on many points in regard to modern innovations that should be introduced in the Kingdom."[22]

Although a full-blooded Hawaiian, David Kalākaua grew up bicultural. From his *Kanaka* grandmother he gained great knowledge and love for Hawaiian culture and tradition.[23] Of noble lineage, he attended the High Chiefs' School, and this Western education served him well, enriching his intellect and polishing his social graces. At the same time, rigorous discipline and beatings from the headmaster instilled in him wariness toward priests and their religion. Endowed with a lively and curious mind, Kalākaua pursued many interests, ranging from music to science, from technology to history.[24] Once king, his healthy appetite for women, alcohol, and gambling won him the sobriquet "the Merry Monarch."

As king in a time of diminishing royal authority, Kalākaua proved adaptable, resilient, and resourceful, but also impulsive, yielding, and extravagant. Population decline, the threat of annexation, and the steady encroachment of capitalism worried him, but he still embraced policies that facilitated these trends. In his first message to the legislature in 1874, Kalākaua declared: "The subject that awakens my greatest solicitude is to increase my people." Under the slogan "preserve and increase the race," he sought to encourage a permanent immigration of families of "cognate" races, that is, Polynesians.[25]

Yet his campaign for the Reciprocity Treaty resulted, as we have seen, in a mass influx of male Chinese sojourners: immigrants without women whom the missionaries disapproved of because they were supposedly addicted to masturbation. As Dye has observed, the missionaries had turned "sexually deprived" men into "sexually depraved" men.[26]

Kalākaua also sought to revive native Hawaiian culture, including the roles of the *kahunas*, the hula, poetry, and music. Reflecting his antipathy toward straitlaced New England sobriety, this policy brought him into conflict with the missionaries' contemptuous attitude toward indigenous culture and their campaign for total assimilation.[27] Despite his commitment to Hawaiian traditional culture, Kalākaua was himself a cosmopolitan and an admirer of Western art and music. He recognized the need to educate young Hawaiians in science, technology, and art and established a program that sent students abroad for advanced studies.

Kalākaua soon became involved with the ambitions of Claus Spreckels. A German immigrant who made his fortune as a sugar refiner in San Francisco, Spreckels arrived in Honolulu on the ship that brought the news of the Reciprocity Treaty. He acquired a vast tract of land and, with the king's help, secured an abundant supply of water. Soon after, Kalākaua received a gift of $10,000 and a low interest loan of $40,000 from Spreckels. Given the king's frequent need to borrow and the sugar king's readiness to lend, Spreckels became the richest and most powerful capitalist in Hawaii by the 1880s. It was said that he had both a monopoly of the sugar industry and the government of the islands in his hands. It was even said that "the government of the United States, in the matter of the Reciprocity Treaty, is only an instrument of Spreckels."[28]

Moreno also had to contend with a rival as he sought to win the king's affection. Walter Murray Gibson was ten years older and had arrived in Hawaii in 1866. Like Moreno, Gibson had a past full of adventure, one woven out of fact and fiction. His biographer summed him up as follows: "Gibson, the romantic visionary with his dreams of Pacific empire, and a resourceful man of many talents, could always be counted on to find a connection with the holders of power."[29] Moreno's doppelgänger!

An English-born American farmer and businessman, Gibson answered the irresistible call of the sea. Initially engaged in piracy in Central and

South America, his true destination was Sumatra. In short order, the Dutch authorities charged him with inciting the natives to rebellion and he was condemned to hang. After a dramatic escape from a prison in Jakarta and his return to the United States, he converted to Mormonism. He became an elder in the Church of Jesus Christ of Latter Day Saints and president Brigham Young sent him to Malaysia as a missionary. When he landed in the Sandwich Islands, Gibson found them to his liking and remained there for the rest of his life. He established a Mormon church and colony in Lanai, which he ruled as the High Priest of Melchizedek, but he was soon excommunicated because of controversies over church lands and unorthodox teachings. Reinventing himself, Gibson began a career in Hawaiian politics and journalism. In this new guise, while lobbying in Washington for the Reciprocity Treaty (which he later vigorously opposed as a step toward annexation), he met Moreno in 1868.[30] His biographer Helena G. Allen writes that Moreno presented himself as a member of the Italian legation and that Gibson's account of the opportunities in Hawaii aroused his interest. Unfortunately, aside from the vitriol that, as we will see, Moreno published twenty years later, no record survives of their conversations, which must have been fascinating.[31]

While Gibson was an influential defender of the "darker races" against Anglo-Saxon pretensions, he was as an ardent proponent of immigration who favored the "red races," including Hindus, but not "Mongolians." But recognizing the sugar industry's need for labor, he lobbied for immigrants from China. He rapidly became a champion of the Hawaiians. He attacked the planter-businessmen oligarchy and the "missionaries of Americanization" in the newspapers and legislature. He was one of the few *haoles* elected to the legislature, and he soon became the indigenous majority's recognized leader. He was accused of fomenting "racial hatred"[32] for his advocacy of *Kanaka* rights.

Although his ideas were closely aligned with those of the king, and despite his staunch support of royal policies, Gibson's aspirations to enter into Kalākaua's inner circle were frustrated. By playing on his ambitions, Moreno was able to enlist Gibson's essential support for his projects. Gibson and Moreno were described as "equally tall, well-spoken, masters of language and the art of persuasion," yet the king kept the former at arm's length while embracing the later.[33]

Years later, Moreno maintained that Gibson had entreated him again and again to convince the king to accept his personal council. Gibson, he claimed, had even suggested overthrowing Kalākaua to crown Queen Emma so they both could be ministers.[34] True or not, one can imagine

Gibson's chagrin as this Italian interloper became the king's confidant within weeks of his arrival.

Moreno was quickly invited to the drinking and card-playing evenings in the king's boathouse. While Moreno assiduously courted Kalākaua, their relationship appears to have been based on a real affinity. They were both bon vivants with a taste for fine wines. Both could be convivial and charming, and both were easily carried away by grand ideas. The king was supposedly "dazzled" by Moreno's ability to breathe life into his fantasies. William Green, an English merchant who twice became the Hawaiian Minister of Foreign Affairs, observed that "those who were acquainted with his magniloquent language, the elaborate style, plausibility, and audacity" of his stories, would not be surprised if "unsophisticated Hawaiians, of royal or plebeian origin, were charmed by him," noting, "I think that in Washington and elsewhere much more seasoned men were duped by his arts."[35]

Among the dreams discussed during these meetings was unifying the Polynesian people in a Pacific Empire over which Kalākaua would reign. It was not a new idea, but it was the Italian enchanter who "ignited this flame of ambition in the king's mind." [36] In an open letter to Kalākaua in 1886, Moreno reminded him of:

> the great, human, and generous idea of uniting under your scepter the whole Polynesian race and making Honolulu a monarchical Washington . . . Remember, these are the precise words I had the honor and courage to tell your majesty on November 16, 1879. . . . The formation of a Polynesian kingdom . . . was the principal theme of our numerous and long conversations of the following year, 1880.[37]

Another idea attributed to Moreno that might have appealed to Kalākaua as a panacea for his dwindling finances was admitting a million Chinese immigrants, each paying a $10 entry tax. Voilà! Ten million dollars![38]

Recovering from their initial infatuation, the planter-business establishment regarded Moreno with increasing apprehension as he, in a contemporary's words, "gained unbounded influence over the King by servile flattery and by encouraging all his pet hobbies."[39] Wild rumors flew. One rumor was that Moreno was a Chinese spy whose true mission was negotiating the sale of Hawaii to China.[40]

The powerful "missionary element" also had good reason to view the anticlerical Italian as a threat. Moreno soon concluded that the old missionaries and their perfidious sons were "the ANTITHESIS of their Christian profession, a disgrace to American civilization, and a calamity for the primitive and good race of Hawaiians. . . . I told [King Kalākaua] that he should get rid of them or they would eventually destroy both his government and his people."[41]

As animosity toward Moreno grew, the American ambassador, James M. Comly, played a decisive role in fomenting the political upheaval that followed. Comly, a Republican newspaper editor, had supported Lincoln in 1860 and subsequently served as the colonel of an Ohio regiment during the Civil War. He was a staunch supporter and friend of Rutherford B. Hayes, who appointed him ambassador to Hawaii following Hayes's election as President. Comly was a seasoned political observer who kept a watchful eye on the relationship between the newcomer and the monarch. Initially remaining neutral, he reported that Moreno was said to be "the inspiration under which His Majesty's statesmanship is developing." Later, he added that Moreno was "a familiar visitor at the Palace, and has gained more influence with the King than his constitutional advisers."[42]

When Comly realized the nature of Moreno's "advice," he and others sought to break the Italian's spell over the monarch. They looked into Moreno's past and learned that the international agreement for laying the transpacific cable had expired. As to Moreno's claim of personal friendship with James Garfield, Comly's inquiry brought a sharp denial from the president-elect. Despite the Ambassador's warnings that Moreno was "a false pretender and a dangerous adventurer . . . and not a fitting associate for him," Kalākaua "continued to smile on the rogue."[43]

Asked why he had such steadfast faith in Moreno, the king replied that he found him

> a very entertaining companion, a man of large and novel views in political and state affairs; that he had been frequently surprised to discover how exactly Mr. Moreno's views coincided with his own; and that he had put him in office because of this harmony and sympathy; and because he thought him the best agent to carry out some of his own views—namely increasing Chinese immigration; establishing a line of Chinese steamers; laying a Cable to connect the Sandwich Islands with China; and so on.[44]

During the 1880 legislative session, the ill-fated ship *Kalākaua-Moreno* crashed upon the craggy shores of the *haole* opposition. Given the solid majority of "king's men" in the assembly and Gibson and Wilcox's support, smooth sailing seemed assured for Kalākaua's proposals, including all of the above and more. A $24,000 subsidy for the CMSNC was allocated (although never paid), as was a bill, passed but vetoed by Kalākaua, granting a two-year license to import, manufacture, and sell opium, previously forbidden, to a Chinese merchant for a $120,000 fee. It was said to be Moreno's plan to give Hawaii control of the Pacific narcotics trade, and it would also have given the royal coffers a little relief.[45]

Ambassador Comly reported to Washington that "Mr. Moreno has secured these results [the passage of the opium bill and the subsidy for the steamship line] with money provided by a lobby . . . of some Chinese merchants of Honolulu."[46] Bribery was not uncommon in Hawaii, so this alone was not remarkable. But Kuykendall portrayed the practice as particularly sinister in this case, observing that "Moreno's lobbying activities cast dark shadows over the legislative hall." The *Pacific Commercial Advertiser*, denouncing the "open and wholesale bribery," and accused a "certain impecunious adventurer" who "boasted power to out the Ministry [which] may satisfy his egotism, but will never enhance the brilliance of his fame, or add one title to his influence. He has been judged by a discriminating community [which] will be heartily glad for the opportunity to bid him a final farewell."[47]

During the 1880 election, a broadside called *A Reply to the Ministerial Utterances*, whose authorship was attributed to Kalākaua or Moreno, was published in English and Hawaiian. It endorsed subsidies for a steamship line and transpacific cables. It also proposed that Hawaii borrow $10 million to build two forts and purchase several warships. The proposal was ridiculed by those fearful of imperialistic designs and the law was defeated.

Moreno had other unfinished projects. A newspaper account of his first meeting with Kalākaua in San Francisco in the fall of 1874 described him as a "most persistent visitor . . . speaking incessantly and bombarding the king, who listed patiently to plans to build a trans-Pacific cable."[48] Five years later, the Italian reaped the fruits of his labor. The lobbyist used every stratagem in his tool kit, even publishing a Hawaiian translation of *The Trans-Pacific Cable: A Project of Celso Caesar Moreno*.[49] A bill was introduced that would have earmarked a $1 million bonus in gold to be paid to "Moreno and his associates" for the completion of a cable between Hawaii and California. He submitted a copy of the Congressional act chartering the project, signed by the U.S. Secretary of State, as evidence of its legitimacy, even though its three-year limit had expired. The bill was dead on arrival.[50]

Stymied on all fronts, the king, allegedly at Moreno's urging, next took action and shook the very foundations of his throne. On August 14, he suspended the legislature, dismissed his cabinet, and appointed a new cabinet. Moreno became a naturalized Hawaiian citizen that same day and was appointed prime minister and minister of foreign affairs.[51]

Several letters written by Louis L. Rice, a retired journalist living in Honolulu, reported the subsequent events from a *haole* perspective. On August 23, 1880, Rice wrote:

> The last two or three weeks has been an exciting time, politically, in Honolulu, and throughout the Kingdom. The current King . . . is a miserable fellow, at best, the weakest in talent and lowest in character, of any ruler since the establishment of this form of government. His Ministry, for the past two years . . . has been the ablest and best and most popular that has ever existed. But a week or two ago he summarily removed them, and replaced them with a group of totally unqualified men whose character is, in all respects, greatly inferior to their predecessors. At the head of this new cabinet as Minister of State he put one Moreno, a Foreign Adventurer, an Italian, or a Spaniard, who by some means, had gotten the King's ear and confidence, and who, it is supposed, was chiefly responsible for inducing the King to change his Cabinet. Moreno is so destitute of character and so despised by everybody that the Foreign Ministers and Consuls unanimously refused to hold any official relations with him. A number of public meetings were called by both natives and foreigners and resolutions were passed denouncing the change of the Cabinet, and calling on the King to remove Moreno . . . For several days a general riot was imminent . . .

Fearing for his life, Kalākaua mounted cannons to protect his palace. Rice continued:

> The foreign ambassadors led the King to understand they would hold no official relations with his Cabinet so long as Moreno was its head. As a result Moreno was removed, at least until things would calm down . . . and now, anonymous printed communications are scattered in the streets daily, intended to stir up the Natives against the Foreigners to expel the latter and place the government entirely in the Natives' hands. Moreno is supposedly behind these appeals.

Several weeks later, Rice reported:

> The object of Moreno, and the King under his manipulations, was evidently to substitute Chinese for American interests in the country's business. Hence the sensitivity of the businessmen, who are chiefly American, at King's actions under Moreno's influence.

And on February 12, 1881:

> The excitement here about political matters has entirely subsided . . . since the King left on a trip around the world . . . but the acts of that disagreeable fellow, Moreno [persist]. It is very evident that the mail from Honolulu which followed Moreno's departure has been tampered with, either here or on the steamer which carried it to San Francisco. . . . Many are fearful that the King has planned to meet Moreno some place on his foreign tour.[52]

Williams Nevins Armstrong, Kalākaua's former schoolmate, who had recently returned to Hawaii after a successful legal career in the United States, recorded the king's account of the 1880 political implosion and of the events that followed. The king thought the opium bill was the work of an agent of a Chinese company "to give the Chinese a hold in these Islands." The king said that he and Moreno "had no scheme whatsoever, except about the cables." He had adjourned the assembly and dismissed the cabinet because of a legislative impasse. The position of minister of foreign affairs was offered to Moreno without his foreknowledge "so that his plan of an ocean telegraph might be carried out." Rather than a devious plot to plunder the country, he and Moreno were trying to enact important legislation. Kalākaua responded angrily to the protest meetings, complaining that he was being treated unfairly. To resolve the crisis, the king told the Italian to reach an agreement with Ambassador Comly, but instead the two men got into an argument, and Comly told Moreno that he must leave. Kalākaua then asked Armstrong, his childhood friend, what he should do. The Attorney General advised him to apologize, acknowledge his mistakes, promise to amend the constitution, and invite the "best of the whites" to a luau. The sovereign agreed to all of this. To his summary, Armstrong added: "I am convinced that the King has more brains than people give him credit for. Of course he is a native, and doesn't understand constitutional government."

Armstrong also reported a conversation with Moreno in which the latter declared, "There will be a new ministry appointed. I shall be Minister of Foreign Affairs, but only for a time." He went on to say that "the reason Comly opposed [his appointment] was that he did not offer the Minister any interest in the underwater cable property."[53]

As Rice testified, the *haoles'* reaction to the king's coup was outrage. A mass meeting adopted a resolution condemning the king's action and denouncing "Celso C. Moreno, a stranger and foreign adventurer . . . who has neither the confidence nor respect of the community nor of the

Representatives of Foreign Powers."[54] Moreno risked a lynching. According to Armstrong, a group of frenzied young merchants gathered in front of his house yelling threatening things. Moreno showed up at the port asking, "Hey, what do you want?" and the youth withdrew in short order.[55] Moreno added details to that scene. Confronting the crowd that reached his house on Fort Street, "I grabbed two revolvers and went out to meet them. I told them to come forward, that I had just the pill that they needed. They stopped, and no one came closer to me that night."[56]

The British, French, and United States ambassadors refused to have any contact with the new Minister of Foreign Affairs. Spreckels threw his considerable influence on the negative side of the scale and told Kalākaua that "he had surrounded himself with a precious set of fools."[57]

Naively, Kalākaua sought to facilitate a "reconciliation" between Moreno and Comly. Rejecting the olive branch, the U.S. ambassador lectured the king and told him that the Italian was not a fit associate for him, saying that Moreno was "universally loathed and considered a scheming adventurer, living by his wits, without property or visible means of support, a mere tramp and vagrant."[58] He then implored the king to win back "the love of his subjects by calling the wisest and best men of the Kingdom to him" and to leave "the vile and corrupt to the position they have competed for."[59]

His fate was now in the American ambassador's hands, and Moreno insistently requested an audience. Warned of possible physical violence if he did not accept, Comly agreed to meet. In vain, Moreno asked the Ambassador to withdraw his opposition ("he implored me in a tiresome way"). In a dispatch to the Secretary of State, the Minister described what happened next:

> After wonderful patience and self-control . . . Mr. Moreno at last burst out passionately. And turning to me with his face full of rage he said "I will follow you to the end of the world and as long as you live, I will denounce you to your government and in every newspaper in America." That relieved me considerably, and I said pleasantly, "Now it is Mr. Moreno in his own proper person that is speaking, and I am delighted to hear you."

He went back to the Palace infuriated.[60]

A few minutes later, Comly received a note from the king. It said, "Mr. Moreno has given his resignation and I have accepted it." The news was announced at the *haole* meeting and the crowd erupted into cheers.[61]

It may have been, as Alexander put it, that Moreno was "generally detested by the foreign community," but Comly's statement that he was "odious to the whole kingdom" revealed the ambassador's racist myopia. According to Fuchs, Moreno was a darling of the natives but "a real anathema" to the *haoles*.[62] Evidently, the native Hawaiians' meeting where they had denounced the *haole* meeting, condemned the ambassadors, and expressed their loyalty and love for the king, had escaped Comly's notice. *The Pacific Commercial Advertiser*, no friend of Moreno, wrote a satirical piece about the gathering: "No one spoke before Moreno arrived, and then nothing was said until a vote, by a show of hands, in favor of Moreno retaining his office. Wilcox and his followers raised their hands amid groans and hisses mingled with laughter."[63] Portrayed by *haole* contemporaries and historians as a demagogue stirring up racial hatred, Wilcox criticized "the interloping foreign element" in fiery words. He was also believed to be the author of a broadside posted in the streets of Honolulu, which read in part:

> We have with us one Celso Caesar Moreno, a true naturalized Hawaiian. His great wish is this country's prosperity, and the salvation of its people, by placing control of the government into Hawaiian hands. Moreno's great desire is to remove foreigners from official posts and to put true Hawaiians in their place, because the country belongs to them. . . . Moreno is the heart from which life will burst forth for the real Hawaiians.[64]

The next day, *Ko Hawaii Pae Aina*, Gibson's Hawaiian-language newspaper, described Moreno as a "martyr." In defense of the king's right to choose his cabinet, and denying that his decisions were open to criticism, it went on to warn the *haoles*: "Let the foreign element in these islands beware! They may not be able to quiet the storm they have raised."[65]

Such rhetoric revealed growing racial consciousness among the native Hawaiians as well as a deep and bitter sense of dispossession. In Andrade's words, the Moreno episode was "the first notable outburst of racial antagonism in politics" in the islands' history.[66]

Although the king threw Moreno to the wolves, he privately maintained close relations with him. Surely it was at Moreno's request that Kalākaua gave orders to recall the ambassadors who had offended him, among them Comly, because of their intervention in internal Hawaiian affairs.[67]

On August 30, 1880, five days after he was named prime minister, Moreno boarded the *Zealandia* bound for San Francisco. He carried a confidential document signed by the king that day that expressed "complete confidence in the integrity, talent, knowledge, and experience of our worthy subject C. C. Moreno, Knight Grand Cross of the Order of Kapiolani, as a statesman and diplomat."[68]

This royal document appointed him ambassador to Italy and special envoy with the authority to negotiate with representatives of the United States and European governments. It also empowered him to write and ratify treaties guaranteeing the Kingdom of Hawaii's neutrality. As further evidence of his trust, Kalākaua gave Moreno custody of three Hawaiian youths: Robert Boyd, James Booth, and the aforementioned Robert Wilcox. All *hapa haole*, they were sent abroad to complete their education in European military academics. The king would come to regret this act of faith that ensured Moreno's continued entanglement in Hawaiian affairs.[69]

Moreno sailed away from Hawaii not in sackcloth and ashes, but with elevated titles and power that assured him a privileged status in both the new and old worlds. What were the Italian adventurer's thoughts as he watched the golden sands of Hawaii recede on the horizon? Did he appreciate the importance of the dramatic events in which he had been a crucial figure? He had precipitated a constitutional crisis that challenged the king's absolute power and the limits imposed by legislative power. The crisis revealed the Hawaiian majority's latent hostility against the *haole* oligarchy and strengthened their determination to use the superiority of their "brains and money" to gain complete political control.

CHAPTER 6

Celso's Vendetta

During his weeklong voyage from Honolulu to San Francisco onboard the steamer *Zealandia*, Celso had time to brood over his defeat and humiliation at the hands of the "missionary element." Living up to his warning that "whosoever tries to play a mean dirty trick on me does so at his own peril,"[1] he plotted his revenge. Italy was his final destination, but first he had important business in the United States. He regarded General Comly as the chief architect of his downfall, and Moreno sought his removal as the U.S. ambassador to the Kingdom of Hawaii. He avoided acquaintances in San Francisco.[2] Instead, he headed directly for Ohio and sought an audience with president-elect James Garfield. The meeting, which took place in West Mentor, on the shores of Lake Erie, was not satisfying. Charles Foster, the governor of Ohio, who had known Moreno in Washington as "a pleasing and intelligent gentleman," attested that Moreno was acquainted with Garfield, as he had claimed.

Continuing on to Washington, Moreno secured a letter of introduction from Secretary of the Treasury John Sherman, another acquaintance, to Secretary of State William M. Evarts. After a "patient" wait of several days, Moreno, along with his "three young Hawaiian gentlemen," was admitted to speak to Evarts. Moreno asked that "the gross wrong done to me by Minister Comly be righted." Evarts knew that Kalākaua had rescinded Moreno's commission as envoy to the United States. He did not meet Moreno in the "diplomatic room" but in his private residence, and he declined to accept any official communication. Furthermore, Evarts claimed he was completely satisfied with Ambassador Comly's work. Moreno, however, did not leave Washington empty-handed. Relying on his talents as a publicist, he printed and distributed his own version of the "Moreno affair," finding a sympathetic ear in certain quarters.[3]

Moreno's party left for the French port of Cherbourg and there continued to Paris. He was charged with the education of the three Hawaiian students: Robert William Wilcox, twenty-five; Robert Napu'uako Boyd, sixteen; and James Kaneholo Booth, seventeen. Moreno seems to have taken the responsibility very seriously, behaving like "a conscientious travel guide" who introduced them to "some of the world's most celebrated leaders."[4] In Washington, they met with Carl Schurz, a German American statesman, and with Frederick Douglass. Their grand tour of European capitals began in early 1881 and was undertaken like a state visit. Moreno occupied himself with finding the best military academies for the youths and demonstrated a great attention to ceremony. Although William L. Green, the new Hawaiian Minister of Foreign Affairs, had tried to rescind his diplomatic credentials, Moreno displayed documents with the king's signature. The three "princes" (Moreno implied that they were the king's "natural sons," a "rumor" Kalākaua vigorously and repeatedly denied), proceeded undisturbed from one reception to another. The "three youths with bronzed faces and quick, white eyes like porcelain in a blackened pipe," as Faldella described them,[5] worked wonders to open the doors of Europe's palaces and salons. In Paris, the group met Léon Gambetta, the president of the French Chamber of Deputies; Victor Hugo, the author of *Les Misérables*; and Count Ferdinand de Lesseps, the architect of the Suez Canal.[6]

Kalākaua wrote to the emperor of Germany asking to enroll his students in Prussian military schools. He received an encouraging response, and the group headed to Berlin. Moreno thought about enrolling them in the military academy in Potsdam and the naval school at Kiel.[7] Once in Germany, however, Moreno realized that the youths were not "adequately prepared for the rigorous Prussian schools." Moreover, they would could do little in an environment in which they were obliged to know German, a language that none of them knew.[8]

Booth wrote a long letter to his father relating the complicated and vaguely Kafkaesque situation that was King Kalākaua's education abroad program, a program that King's governing circle firmly opposed. An incredible portrait emerges in which it seems the government's aim was to obstruct Moreno above all, even if it meant sinking the program. At this point, the young Hawaiians were clearly on the Italian's side. They testified to his commitment, showing that the Capitano Marittimo corresponded a great deal with several Hawaiian consular representatives in Europe while staying at Berlin's Central Hotel. He asked for financial assistance from the representatives in Bremen and Paris, since, as Booth wrote from Berlin on December 23, 1880, "we are now in a very critical position. Mr. Moreno has hardly any more money to finance us."

Help did not come. The consul in Bremen had not received instructions from Honolulu. The consul in Paris, William Martin, explained that he would be happy to use his influence with the consul in Bremen but that it was not possible to give him orders, since he was not his "subordinate." Writing to him again "would be like returning to talk about things that he already knows, and at that point he would have the right to tell me that I should mind my own business." Martin added that he had not received additional instructions from Honolulu. Booth's comment was terse: "This is our present condition: since we arrived here, we have not received a single cent."

Booth then focused on Moreno's attempts to surmount the difficulties of enrolling the youths in the German military academies. The long letter concluded with an outburst that provides an interesting insight into the climate in which the events unfolded. It demonstrates the frustration felt by the young *Ponoi* ("true sons of Hawaii"), who were certainly influenced by Moreno, over the drama that was developing at home:

> Since we left Honolulu on August 30, 1880 we have been kept at Mr. Moreno's expense. He has always treated us like a father. He has kept all the promises he made to the king, to whom he feels a boundless love. If Mr. Moreno was only half or an eighth as bad as Messrs. Parker, Waterhouse, Armstrong, and Brigham said on board the *Zealandia*, we would have left him a long time ago, but Mr. Moreno has behaved honorably and has kept his promise to the king to enroll us in school. Mr. Parker is a true scoundrel . . . like the rest of them. It is their fault that we have suffered so much, and they have created tensions between us and Mr. Moreno. . . . The missionaries are jealous of our journey of education, because they are afraid that we will learn more things than they know, and the government of Hawaii would fall into the hands of the true Ponoi. It is their intention to sabotage our education program . . . and all the consuls are on their side, all willing

> to fight against our Mr. Moreno who is a thousand times better and more noble than they. For my part I have real hope that he will crush all of them.[9]

The youths' attachment to Moreno persisted after the group left Prussia for Italy. First they went to Genoa, where the boys had the privilege of meeting the composer Giuseppe Verdi, whom they brought a letter signed by his great admirer "Kalākaua Rex." Then they went to Alassio for a private audience with Giuseppe Garibaldi, to whom King Kalākaua had also sent a message.[10] This last meeting made a profound impression on Wilcox, who noted the general's words in his diary: "Know and love your fellow man. Love your King and your country, and acquire wisdom to return to the governmental work of your wise King."[11] After his return to Hawaii, Wilcox would model his own political career on the great general's example.

Moreno was certainly the one who instilled a cult of the Hero of Two Worlds in his young disciples. Garibaldi died soon after, on June 2, 1882, in the Spartan simplicity of his retirement on the island of Caprera. It is not difficult to imagine the sincere grief of the "Moreno Group," supposedly stirred up by the arrival of a letter from Antonio Meucci. Meucci was the overlooked inventor of the telephone who Moreno had befriended in New York, where Meucci had hosted Garibaldi for two years following the adventure of the Roman Republic. Meucci mourned the great man's death from his humble cottage in Staten Island and declared unwavering loyalty to his memory:

> I see by the newspapers you send me that Prince Torlonia desires to purchase the red shirt of General Giuseppe Garibaldi. Many Americans and English have asked the same thing of me, not only concerning this, but all the other objects once belonging to the Hero which remain in my possession. But to all I answer No, as I will not make barter of such relics. I am extremely poor, but, come what may, I shall always religiously keep these souvenirs, so as to be sure that when I die they will not fall into untrustworthy hands.[12]

Moreno presented himself, as Faldella has written, as the ambassador of a "people, who in less than a century, passed from well-founded suspicions of cannibalism . . . from the certainty of gory barbarism to representative government with upper and lower houses, steamboats, a Ministry of Public Instruction and stamps."[13] Thanks to the influence of Prime Minister Benedetto Cairoli, who he claimed had been a schoolmate and fellow naval officer, Moreno obtained an audience with Umberto I, the king with the magnificent handlebar mustache, on March 23, 1881.[14] The king's unprecedented intervention facilitated the Hawaiian cadets' enrollment. The sovereign "showed great interest in those little people of the Pacific Ocean, already so far along on the path of civilization." He congratulated Moreno for inspiring King Kalākaua to send the three youths to Italy for their instruction, and he was pleased that an Italian had made his homeland better known and respected in foreign countries.[15]

Later, on February 22, 1881, the three Hawaiian youths addressed a letter from Rome to "the People of Hawaii." The letter of denunciation seems to have been inspired, if not written, by Moreno.

> Beloved countrymen,
>
> We three sons of Hawaii and young subjects of His Majesty, sent by the government of Hawaii and entrusted to Mr. C. C. Moreno, a good and honorable man with whom we are on the best terms, have decided to inform you that the ministers of His Majesty are behaving toward us in the most shameful way, leaving us without means of support in a foreign land. Mr. Moreno has been obligated to spend his own money to support us, while the state funds allocated by the last legislature lie unused in the government building in Honolulu. That of Mr. Moreno you can call an act of Christian charity, since he has no obligation to act has he does. We therefore ask His Majesty's ministers to immediately send us the sums of money payable according to the decisions of the last legislature.[16]

That did not happen during their time in Rome. After a final series of audiences with various authorities, including the ministers of war and of the navy, Moreno succeeded in enrolling the youths in three different military schools: Wilcox in Turin at the Royal Academy of Civil and Military Engineers, Boyd in Livorno at the Royal Naval Academy, and Booth in Naples at the Nunziatella Military Academy.

Boyd and Booth were with Moreno on June 30, 1881, when King Kalākaua arrived in Naples. The king came from Egypt as part of a voyage around the world. Though he sought to escape "the tedium of island life," he was also evaluating suitable immigrants in order to avoid additional Chinese coolies.[17] Some *haoles* were convinced that this tour masked a plot by the king and Moreno to sell Hawaii to the highest bidder. But others thought the trip would provide a welcome cooling-off period after the past few months of political agitation.

Fearing that the king would be an embarrassment, two companions—chaperones, really—were assigned to accompany him: William Nevins

Armstrong, now Royal Commissioner of Immigration, and the Court Chamberlin, Charles H. Judd. They were both sons of missionaries, but their puritanical rigidity was insufficient to restrain the irrepressible "merry monarch." Kalākaua continued to enjoy his whiskey, and his hosts poured it generously during the long tour. On one occasion, in his cups, he went on deck and sang Hawaiian songs to everyone's amusement—except Armstrong and Judd. In Vienna there were rumors about a dalliance between the king and a Scandinavian woman. Generally, however, Kalākaua knew how to behave as fit his rank, in a dignified and gracious manner that earned praise in the European press and charmed society in the capitals. Interestingly, on one occasion, the American press came to liken him to "an Italian, with rather heavy features . . . a black beard and mustache, and a very amiable expression."[18]

In nine months of traveling across Asia, the Middle East, and Europe, an unwanted and invisible companion plagued the king and his dignitaries. Moreno haunted them in the most unpredictable ways. In Japan, they remembered him as a nuisance and bearer of the evil eye. In China his reputation was even worse. As Armstrong wrote from Shanghai to the Hawaiian Foreign Office: "Everyone knows him here . . . and everyone called him a scamp." They said that he was a penniless swindler who did not pay his hotel bills and often appealed to the American consul for help through flattery and begging. To Moreno's misfortune, Ferdinando De Luca, the same Italian diplomat with whom he clashed in New York ten years prior, had been the Italian ambassador to China since 1878 and lived in Shanghai. Doubtless, De Luca happily told Kalākaua his own version of Moreno's defamation campaign against him. He evidently succeeded in convincing him of the duplicity of the ex–minister of foreign affairs and caused a rupture in their relations. In Vienna, the king met with Count Luigi Palma of Cesnola, director of the Metropolitan Museum of Art in New York. Cesnola had also had an encounter with the irascible "CC," and he gave the king "another chapter of Moreno's biography."[19]

Still, Armstrong feared that the king and his erstwhile Italian friend were planning to meet in order to carry out their nefarious schemes. It was clear to everyone, including journalists, that Kalākaua was still susceptible to Moreno's charms, despite everything, although the king refused to speak publicly about his ex-minister.[20]

Armstrong's worse nightmare materialized on a pier in the port of Naples. Neither Armstrong nor Judd spoke a word of Italian, and the Capitano Marittimo was well prepared, using the Italian press as the event's deus ex machina. The newspapers had announced the Hawaiian king's arrival several days earlier, news Moreno probably supplied himself. One newspaper even wrote that "friends of Moreno, who is favorably known in Asia and in America and who was in Egypt for a little while, decided to go all the way to Suez to meet King Kalākaua and commend and thank him for choosing an Italian as his prime minister and for having, deservedly, put his faith in him.[21]

When Kalākaua disembarked from the Rubattino Company's steamship *Asia*, the flags of Italy and Hawaii, the latter "made especially for the occasion,"[22] waved on the pier of the old Bourbon dockyard. Some journalists were present, including one destined for fame, then twenty-year-old Robert Bracco of the *Corriere del Mattino*. Inexplicably, the Neapolitan newspapers ignored the news. The most detailed account was written by Nicola Lazzaro for the *Gazzetta Piemontese*. He reported that Celso Moreno "had disclosed that in the two Colleges of the Navy and the Nunziatella were the son and nephew of King Kalākaua," that is Boyd and Booth. Lazzaro's description of the king seems to echo Faldella's as he talks at length about Kalākaua's "very bronzed hue," despite which "it is difficult to believe that he is descended from those famous savages that on February 24, 1778, massacred the renowned explorer and ate his raw flesh." The Turin newspaper correspondent added that Kalākaua had stayed at the Hotel Royal des Etrangers in Santa Lucia, "occupying a quarter of the second floor, composed of two parlors and three bedrooms. The three bedrooms are not for a potential harem, since the king is Christian, but for his ministers." Lazzaro noted that the king was rather sparing with his statements: "A bow, a greeting and a farewell . . . indeed the cold, glacial manner which he used with everyone hardly invited one to prolong the conversation."[23]

Perhaps such aloofness was the result of nervousness and irritation. We know from more confidential sources that Moreno took the situation in hand in a rather brusque manner: after making introductions, Moreno pushed Kalākaua into a carriage and left Armstrong and Judd behind, who were very angry. As soon as they recovered from the humiliation, they hired another carriage to pursue them.[24]

Later, when Umberto I and his wife received Kalākaua, Armstrong and Judd learned from Queen Margherita's sister that Moreno had spread the rumor that the three youths were the king's natural sons. Umberto, too, had been misled by this rumor, and Armstrong himself corrected him.[25] Consequently, the two dignitaries continued insisting that the king free himself from the Italian and entrust the youths' supervision to others. Kalākaua was persuaded, and during his brief trip to Naples, little more than two days, he conferred administration of the youths' finances to the banker Michele Cerulli, who would later be named Hawaiian consul in Naples at his suggestion.[26]

In a letter to the queen on June 30, 1881, the day he arrived, Kalākaua wrote that Moreno had met with Armstrong and Cerulli that afternoon with the aim of "settling the accounts" and ending his supervision. He added, "There has been a great fuss made about Moreno and his young men, and now that his mission has ended I feel a great sense of relief."[27] Armstrong described the meeting in his journal: "I found myself on a balcony overlooking the Gulf in a discussion with this sly Italian adventurer." It was a rather animated discussion, which gave him the impression that his adversary was "very clever." However when Kalākaua told King Umberto about his miserable experience, Armstrong noted with satisfaction: "I think that the Moreno question is definitively resolved."[28]

But things were much more complicated than they appeared on the surface. A passage in Kalākaua's letter to the queen showed it was all an act. The sovereign was very impressed by the welcome for him and his youths. King Umberto himself enrolled the young men in the military schools because they did not meet the necessary requirements to be admitted otherwise. Kalākaua seemed to understand the problems his Italian ex-minister posed, but he did not appear entirely convinced that Moreno should be blamed instead of a larger government "clique":

> The man is not such a "devil as he is painted," and I find the authorities look to him with a great deal of respect. Of course if the reports against his character is [*sic*] as he has been represented, not only he can be counted on the same category. Many others who are near me, and when put to the extreme of necessity would do anything. But the hostility of a certain clique was not aimed at him but to me, for Mr. Moreno only came to me some time after. The hostility had already commenced at the commencement of the Election in July and August, and Moreno arrived in October [*sic*: He actually arrived in November].[29]

But Armstrong's letters and book tell a very different story about that time. The king visited Pompeii and the military college at Nunziatella.[30] He exchanged messages with ex-Khedive of Egypt Ismail, who had been in Naples for two years with his forty wives. (From time to time, someone escaped from the great harem. One of the runaways married an Italian man in Naples.)[31] After receiving the news of the July 2 attack on President Garfield, he continued to Rome. Despite his pink slip, Moreno followed the royal court to Rome, where the pope received Kalākaua. In a July 18 letter, Armstrong said that the Italian king and members of his government knew that Moreno was only "an adventurer." He added that Moreno was trying to regain his grip on Kalākaua and that he was "desperate." In another letter to Green, the Hawaiian minister of foreign affairs, Armstrong recounted with relish how Moreno tried to get on the king's train car when he left Naples for Rome. He was rejected and had to sit in third class, which he managed to spin to the newspapers as the king's idea.[32]

But Moreno did not back down. In Rome, he once again tried slipping into the royal court. Again turned away, he succeeded in getting a note to the king at his hotel asking for immediate payment. He turned up at the king's departure for Paris with the pretext of greeting him. Moreno, wrote Armstrong, "expected to make a triumphal march through Italy" at the Hawaiian sovereign's side. So, though deprived of any official role, Moreno had been busy working surreptitiously. For example, in anticipation of the Hawaiian delegation's arrival, he made arrangements with Cardinal Jacobini for a papal audience. Armstrong also described how Moreno interrupted him in his hotel room with his usual request for immediate payment. Worried that the situation would escalate, Armstrong asked Green to find a solution to the problem.

Moreno's specter continued haunting Armstrong's correspondence while the king was in Paris. In an August 11 letter, Armstrong wrote that the Italian recognized that the Hawaiian youths were no longer under his guardianship. That letter and another from London on September 1, shed light on two important situations. The first was that Prussia had accepted the young Hawaiians into German military schools, creating an embarrassing situation. It would be a great insult to the Italian authorities, and to King Umberto in particular, if the youths were removed from Italian institutions and sent to Germany, as the government had always wanted to do. They knew, however, that Moreno had acted on his own and that, "having waited for some time in Germany, then because of the inclement weather and the delayed response to the application for entry, he had been forced to leave Germany and go to Italy."[33] The second issue was that the king had repeatedly talked with Moreno about his payment during his time in Italy, but he had never received a bill. Kalākaua told Cerulli that he would pay $1,200 of the requested $2,000 for Moreno's services, provided that all expenses were detailed in a report, but Moreno never produced one. In the absence of this, Kalākaua gave Cerulli additional instructions: "Do not pay him until the accounts are given to me with a final report."[34]

A few months later, the three young Hawaiians' school situation had resolved for the best. The press in Honolulu followed their progress. The *Pacific Commercial Advertiser*, which supported their education abroad, wrote an article full of interesting details, expressing its "pleasure" that it could publish such an "encouraging" report. The newspaper received an update from a letter from Boyd dated October 16, sent from Livorno via Naples: the young man had just returned from a long voyage onboard the frigate *Vittorio Emanuele*, and he had been "enchanted" by his treatment. His superiors were very pleased with him. Boyd had taken advantage of the stopover in Naples to spend several weeks there as the guest of Cerulli & Co., bankers. Regarding Wilcox, the newspaper said a letter from General Giannoti [*sic*], commander of the Military Academy in Turin, reported that "he is in excellent health and his conduct is equally good." He was making progress and he would be doing even better if he had more familiarity with the Italian language, which would come with time. General Briganti, the commander of the military college in Naples, was generous with details: Booth had become one of the best students in his class. His exam grades, on a scale of 20, spoke for themselves: 14 in math, 18 in Italian literature, 20 in French literature, 15 in geography, 18 in Greek history, 18 in Latin, 18 in military science, 10 in design and cartography, 14 in spelling, 13 in gymnastics, 19 in dance, 10 in fencing. With an average of 17.16, Booth was described as a person of robust physical condition, lively intelligence, dedicated to his studies, of an excellent character, frank, respectful, good-natured and honorable. His superiors' comments were enthusiastic, to say the least: "He is one of the best students in the college, and we are sure that when he has a complete mastery of the Italian language (which he will have soon, since he already speaks it very well), he will become the best." The article concluded, "We have been informed that Mr. Booth will soon be recommended to the Minister of War for the highest honor that the College can bestow, that is the right to wear on his left arm the royal initials topped by the crown."[35]

The next year, however, the picture began to change. Since his arrival in Naples, Kalākaua had expressed his "hope" that his minister of foreign affairs would promptly provide Cerulli with the necessary funds to support the youths. But it was clear that the mechanism had become stuck and the three youths, initially accustomed to certain niceties such as invitations to Naples during vacations,[36] began experiencing deprivations due to the constant shortage of money. Cerulli and another Neapolitan friend, Commendator Giustini, the British consul in Naples, were friendly and willing to host them as always, but they were stingy with any other kind of financial assistance. The issue was raised many times, and Cerulli's explanation was always the same: He had not received different instructions from Honolulu.

In the summer of 1882, Booth wrote a long letter to King Kalākaua. After explaining that he needed to move to Turin to continue his studies, he wrote about Moreno, this time very differently than he had in his letters to his father the previous year:

> Mr. Moreno has not yet given up, as he had promised, the authority conferred on him by the Hawaiian government. Who knows what other stupid claims he will be able to put forward about us, as he did some time ago when he wrote to our commander because Boyd and I were forbidden to go out with Giustini and Cerulli. It seems that he has become a deputy in the Italian Parliament. It is time to properly evaluate what this man is driving at. He is the only person known to the Minister [probably a reference to the Italian Minister of Foreign Affairs] as having a legal prerogative to us. Allow me, therefore, to insist to Your Majesty that the issue be carefully considered by our ministers and settled as soon as possible in a satisfactory manner in concert with the Italian government. No one knows this man better than us, after ten months of common experiences. We are dealing with a man as deadly at the Fates, and stubborn as a mule. Command your ministers to take care of this complicated affair and do not forget us.[37]

Around that time, the *Pacific Commercial Advertiser* continued its support for the education program abroad. It published a piece explaining its purpose and observed how "the development of these islands that the missionaries wanted failed to stimulate the people's industrious instinct. It is not enough to free a nation from the yoke of superstition if, after it has embraced Christianity, it is left to its imperfect customs." It emphasized the lack of institutions of technical education and lamented the fact that "able-bodied men and women do nothing but eat and sleep" while "the more than exploited Chinese fill their bags with dollars" after having cultivated the land and "even cooked food for the natives." Therefore the government sent young natives abroad because their education was "a patriotic duty" that could secure the people's independence from foreign aid. The newspaper examined the plans of seven youth who had just departed: three mechanical engineers for Scotland, two surgeons for America and England, two to the military academy in Woolwich. Meanwhile, those who were already abroad shined, particularly the three in Italy. (The highest praise was reserved for Booth.) The newspaper criticized the argument that the program was too costly, and it predicted that their return would be a great advantage for the kingdom. It argued that the program should not only continue but expand, for example by sending youths to Germany to study agriculture and botany.[38] The young men's studies abroad were clearly an issue of the greatest national interest, a situation that contrasted bizarrely with the continuation of much more mundane issues involving Moreno.

On May 12, 1883, Booth again wrote to the king about Moreno. Although the issue had been raised many times, he remained, incredibly, the only person whom the Italian Ministers of War and of the Navy recognized as the young Hawaiians' guardian. He claimed that "we cannot do anything without his permission," not even leave the school, as if, Booth noted bitterly, "we had come here to become monks." Moreno continued denying that Giustini and Cerulli could be considered "agents," while the commander of the Nunziatella informed the Minister of War that Commendator Giustini and Cerulli, who was now the Hawaiian consul in Naples, were the only ones to whom the young men were entrusted and the ones who provided their expenses. Therefore, there was an immediate need for clarification or, alternatively, a decision to entrust the young men directly to their commanders.

That same year, Colonel Curtis P. I'aukea, sent by the king to European courts, visited and reported finding "a tangle of unpaid bills the young men had incurred owing to the misleading advice of Moreno."[39] According to I'aukea, Moreno was still in contact with the students and encouraged them to spend without restraint. Therefore, he instructed Cerulli to set their personal allowances at 40 lire ($8) a month. The young Hawaiians rebelled against this new financial discipline. Wilcox wrote to the king in July 1884 and pointed out that the meager sum was even lower than that of the cadets "from Romania and Burma," which made them "laughing stocks" in the eyes of their classmates. He asked that they be freed from Cerulli's supervision. He did not have to wait long: A year later, the banker resigned as Hawaiian consul, having declared bankruptcy.[40]

In his open letter to King Kalākaua on March 7, 1884, Moreno, who had returned to America in the meantime, accused "the missionaries and Your Majesty's ministers" of being opposed to the young natives' right to a superior education, preferring to keep them in "ignorance and darkness." He reported a conversation in Naples in which Armstrong had supposedly said that "he thought the Hawaiians unfit and unworthy of education" and that "the white foreigners would not give their money for keeping the nigger Hawaiians in schools abroad."[41] We may doubt that Armstrong had spoken this way but, being a known racist, the sentiments expressed could very well have been his.

Moreno's accusations appeared well founded when King Kalākaua's program for education abroad was abruptly interrupted by the Bayonet Constitution, which reduced the king's authority and consolidated the *haoles*' power. The reformed government quickly called the students home. When he returned, Wilcox was accompanied by his new wife, the Turinese baroness Maria Carolina Isabella Luigia Sobrero, known as Gina. He had become the petrel of Hawaiian politics, soaked in revolutionary Garibaldian fantasies.[42] Over the course of a decade-long correspondence, he was the "deep throat" who informed Moreno about affairs on the island.

At this point, a more intimate chapter of Booth's time in Italy opens, and we are obliged to divert our attention from Moreno for a little while.

At the beginning of September 1883, Booth passed his exams at the Nunziatella. In October he was in Turin in the care of the Nigra brothers but still in contact with Cerulli, to whom he wrote, "Turin is a very elegant city, with beautiful streets that are straight and comfortable; but all this cannot make me forget Naples, which will always remain in my memory."[43] Booth would return to Naples during a holiday. Back in Turin at the beginning of 1884, the Nigras informed him that nothing beyond the costs of the Academy was provided for and that there were many accounts to settle. This was the theme of several letters to Cerulli.[44] Then the situation became more difficult. The Nigra brothers had problems and the commander of the academy got word that Booth was a spendthrift. (We learn about this from a letter from Cerulli dated May 9, 1884.) Among the requests he sent was the repayment of a debt contracted in Naples that Booth would not explain to the Nigra brothers. His superiors in Turin were inclined to believe it involved women. But Booth told Cerulli that the debt was due to the fact that he had to borrow money because Cerulli would not lend him any.

On June 7, 1884, Booth again wrote to Cerulli. He had taken his exams, so, as he informed the commander, nothing prevented him from leaving Turin and going to Naples for the vacation period. Booth asked for more money. What Cerulli had given him was a small sum for more than forty days of vacation, and Turin "is now full of amusements and you certainly would not want me to deprive myself," as he wrote on July 10, 1884.

Other letters also addressed Booth's (and Wilcox's) financial problems:

> From Turin my Correspondent sent me the protest made by Mr. James Booth on the 16th of this month, and the costs have also been revealed through a postal order. With great displeasure I have learned that there was a bit of an uproar in the Academy over this blessed protest,

> but blame should not be attributed to anyone, if not to the indifference of those gentlemen of Honolulu, who were abandoned by their subjects in Italy, without means or appropriate funds for which you are the Banker.
>
> My uncle . . . asked me about the account about whose repayment he already written and complained, and I reassured him based on your reputation, because as soon as the Hawaiian Government sends the funds, Booth's debt will be paid off, as you have already promised.
>
> Now, for my peace of mind, please tell me how I must continue to behave with my uncle, who constantly presses me for the sum Booth was graciously provided in a moment of absolute need, and without any interest.[45]

But now a more dangerous enemy than a money shortage was at the door: a cholera epidemic. In a letter from Turin dated August 4, 1884, Booth informed Cerulli that the reopening of the Academy had been delayed until September 15 because of the epidemic. In the meantime, the students would return home, and he intended to go to Naples. If Cerulli did not object, could he please write to the commander?

Booth died of cholera in Naples, where he was staying in the Pension d'Orient in the Piazza Vittoria. We learn about the circumstances of his death from Cerulli's report, reprinted in the press in Honolulu.[46] It was all the more unexpected because, as the consul explained with a series of statistics, Booth was staying in a neighborhood, Chiaia, which was among those least affected by the disease, and he was "in excellent condition" until the day before he was infected. On September 4, he went to bed after eating dinner, telling the waiter that he was not feeling well and would not go to a seaside concert at the Villa Comunale, which is what he normally did each night. Unfortunately, however, he decided to go out a little later, and he returned at 1:00 in the morning. A fever seized him three hours later. Soon doctors were called, among them Commendator di Martino, King Umberto's private doctor. Drastic treatments were administered, including hypodermoclysis, the "new method" of Professor Arnaldo Cantani, the celebrated specialist at the University of Naples. But everything was useless. On the fifth day of his illness, the young man died.[47]

On September 13, 1884, the commander of the Tenth Army Corps informed the Hawaiian consul that the funeral could not be held with proper military honors owing to "the city's exceptional health situation." Condolences from the minister of foreign affairs, Mancini, were sent to the Hawaiian government via the Italian consul in Honolulu, Schaefer.[48] Cerulli then busied himself with settling Booth's affairs, including his accounts in Turin, the problems caused by an unpaid loan from Giustini, and above all with the costs for his medical care in Naples.

At this point, there was an ugly legal dispute and a clash between Cerulli and Dr. Bernardino Perli, editor of the *International Journal of Medical Sciences*. Perli accused Cerulli of sending a message to the *Corriere della Sera* on September 16 in which he said that "the consul of the Sandwich Islands wanted the body of the king's son embalmed, but the treating physician," that is Perli, "was opposed, observing that the death could have been apparent, and that he did not want to expose himself to legal proceedings!" According to Perli, Cerulli had offered a paltry three pounds for the embalming, "what is customarily offered for a beetle or a canary." Perli was supposedly willing to write to the *Corriere della Sera* and other newspapers, including foreign ones, to explain the truth, and he accused Cerulli of abandoning Booth to his fate in the final moments.[49]

Booth was buried in the English Cemetery of Naples, in an area beyond the graves of the cholera victims to allow for an eventual exhumation. Thus definitively closed the Italian adventure of a young man loved by all, perhaps for his exotic charm, who in turn had loved Italy. All that remains is a poem written for him at the Nunziatella:

When time passes
the laughing pages will have yellowed
in this dear Album, and, that fleeting dream of beloved joy,
for you will have taken
many sweetnesses of the most beautiful age,
these old pages
will give you new life. Leafing through them you will see
your gay flowering youth again,
and to the memory of a desired love
memory will return . . .
Love for the Italic sky,
for its enchanted, blazing land,
where the senses quiver, and speak to the heart,
rich with a thousand images
and powerful rhyme,
a verse, forever noble, that exalts us.[50]

CHAPTER 7

Electoral Intermezzo

Intertwined with the lengthy affair of the three Hawaiian youths, Moreno's Italian pit stop in the early 1880s involved another matter of interest: Moreno's attempt to build a political career. His Roman acquaintances were essential for this purpose, and one in particular was Giovanni Faldella. They met in February 1881 at a banquet at Rome's Central Hotel organized by the *colonia mondovita*, people from the town of Mondovì in Piedmont. Moreno was a somewhat exotic attraction because of his recent exploits in Hawaii, and he was the object of toasts and compliments. Deputy Carlo Rolfi, a writer, journalist, and Faldella's close friend, was enthusiastic about Moreno. Rolfi had written about him in the *Gazzetta Piemontese* and spoken about him to Faldella. Faldella later described Moreno as tall and robust, clothed in black evening clothes but wearing the Asian-style shoes of a sugar planter, and speaking with disdainful authority about Hawaii in an English accent.[1]

Faldella confessed that at first glance the man, though he appeared a "charade" worthy of study, seemed "almost unpleasant." Never mind: Moreno won him over soon after, when he met him by chance in a modest trattoria behind the Chamber of Deputies, the Fiaschetteria Caselli, where the Captain "polished off a head of lettuce." Faldella admired his "disdain for useless social mores," "his emancipation from and disinterest in certain little social submissions," which was a sign of "robust self-confidence."[2]

Fostered by common memories of Piedmont, which Moreno recalled in his first known letter to Faldella, a friendship between the two men was born.[3] Faldella was from Saluggia, in the province of Novara, today Vercelli. He was born in 1846, and after working as a lawyer and magistrate, he launched a brilliant career as a journalist. In 1873, the Turin newspaper *Gazzetta Piemontese* sent him to Vienna to cover the Universal Exposition, where he wrote his first book, *A Vienna: Gita con il lapis*. This work soon established him as one of the most capricious and original voices of the moment, in the vein of the Scapigliatura literary movement. With time, Faldella intensified his political activity. In 1872, he was elected for the left to the provincial council of Novara, where he kept his seat until 1908. In 1881, he entered Parliament, in the Chamber of Deputies, replacing his colleague on the right, General Bertolé Viale, who, elected the year before, had subsequently been named a senator. Not reelected in 1882, Faldella then returned in 1886 and was elected three times. He was finally named a senator in 1896.

Faldella and Moreno seemed made for each other. Moreno was a perfect figure to stoke the writer's imagination. With his unique story of escorting the three exotic young Hawaiians, Moreno appeared, depending on the moment, as a mother hen with her chicks or a lioness with her cubs.[4] In the Capitano Marittimo, Faldella saw the triumph of a dynamic philosophy aimed at "banishing the sectarian and Mephistophelian no, always responding yes to every offer of employment, always undertaking and knowing how to do everything, especially when you do not know how to do it," which was the attitude of "an adventurous novelist of life," one who, like Casanova, "was busy making novels rather than writing them."[5]

They also shared a passionate anticlericalism, which Faldella displayed in the pages of his short-lived magazine *Il Velocipede*, founded in 1869. This was the mental state of many of the Risorgimento's protagonists, and it became a source of funny quips in conversations between Moreno and Faldella. In one, King Vittorio Emanuele II, excited by the Sumatra project, promised the Captain that his father-in-law, the sultan, would make him pope, thus guaranteeing him "spiritual power."

But there was more. Moreno most dramatically embodied the restless spirit of modernity, enamored with great projects that would change the face of the earth: cuts made through isthmuses, telegraph cables, navigation lines, fabulous markets. Moreno was someone who "trims the continents with scissors."[6] We must imagine the pair's meetings in Rome and their long conversations on various topics. We know that Faldella was not only inspired by Moreno's life for perhaps the most interesting chapter of his 1882 book *Roma borghese: Assaggiature*, but he had to convince himself that the Capitano Marittimo, a man filled with experience and new ideas, might have gambled on a seat in Parliament. The prospect evidently must have been tempting for Moreno, particularly because of the economic uncertainty in which he now found himself. In all likelihood, both the literary dimensions and the political perspective were at play. To be able to impose himself on the political scene of the "New Italy," Moreno needed to make a reputation for himself and become as famous and respected a personality as possible. The Captain was extraordinarily good at attracting the press's attention. Faldella offered him very important assistance at a fortuitous time.

He wrote "A Piedmontese Traveler" in the *Gazzetta Piemontese*, which recounted the Capitano Marittimo's amazing deeds. With a few cuts and many additions, it was included in *Roma borghese*, appearing in four installments on October 11–14, 1881. Moreno's name had often appeared in the Italian press, first for the campaign against child slavery and more recently in reference to the events in Hawaii and his relationship with King Kalākaua. However, he undoubtedly would never have gotten so much attention in Italy without Faldella. With exquisite journalistic flair, Faldella, whose writings we have often referred to in the preceding chapters, took care to portray Moreno in a light that rendered him absolutely out of the ordinary. But he also was "faithful" in conveying Moreno's foreign policy and economic views. His portrait, which can be called admiring and engrossing, is the portrait of a man who certainty deserved an honorable destiny.

The first hint of Moreno's possible political career can already be found at the end of "A Piedmontese Traveler," in which Faldella imagined Moreno in Parliament fighting for "an experimental colonial policy."[7] But this idea was present already in the series published a year earlier. There was enough time before the elections that, thanks to expanded suffrage in 1882, there was a possibility of a substantial change in representation in Parliament. Though Moreno was considered a sort of international celebrity, his best option would have been putting himself forward in districts where he could have moved with the greatest ease and possibilities of success: his native Piedmont and the maritime province of Liguria.

Moreno showed up in these areas with some frequency. By the beginning of August 1881, "S. E. Celso Cesare Moreno, minister of the King" was noted among the famous people on vacation at the baths in Acqui. He also returned to hometown of Dogliani for several days at the beginning of September. The welcome that he received, if we are to believe the anonymous correspondent for the *Gazzetta Piemontese*, established him as a truly important person who could eventually aspire to a position of consequence: "As soon as news of his arrival came, a great crowd hurried to him on the Via Mochiero-Dogliani. And the welcome for the esteemed countryman that followed was truly 'honest and happy.' Moreno felt a great emotion upon returning to his native soil." Truly special, this welcome: "One night a band, accompanied by a large number of people, went for a serenade under Moreno's windows: that night, as they played they alternated new cheers and mutual congratulations."[8]

He was considered a very distinguished person, not just because of his recent and much-publicized transoceanic travels, but even more so because he had shown his wisdom and his love for the most humble Italians in an arena, the legislature, which was the ideal terrain for political loyalty. On August 28, 1881, at a "lunch of honor" held in Dogliani's Leon d'Oro restaurant by seventy "magnates of the town," the celebratory toasts made this perspective stand out: "Cav. Servetti di Trinità recalled the law against the trafficking of Italian children which Moreno obtained from the United States Government, and which was called the Moreno bill."[9] Moreno began to play the game more openly. His presence in the press, which was always notable, shifted from reports of events that could enhance his reputation, such as the fact that Li Fang Pao, the new Chinese ambassador to Italy and Germany, greeted him with particular warmth in Rome in 1881,[10] to journalistic interventions in which Moreno took positions on the country's important social and economic issues. For example, in a letter first published in Naples' *Piccolo* and later in *Il Popolo Romano*, he argued that Naples was the ideal terminus for commercial traffic with the Far East.[11]

But the Captain obviously paid more attention to his natural constituency. Some evidence of this comes from letters between him and the minister of public works, Alfredo Baccarini, that were reprinted in the *Gazzetta Piemontese*. Moreno pushed for the construction of the Dogliani-Monchiero railway on the Bra-Savona line, and he championed the cause with passionate emotions:

> Dogliani, my town of birth, the center of the Langhe, well-populated, very industrious and with extensive and extremely fertile territory for the cultivation of mulberries and vines, renowned for its wines, fairs, and markets, with the benefit of this rail line, designed by my master engineer Scellino, will become more important and more prosperous.

> If on the contrary the construction of this line is not granted, my dear Dogliani will not only lose its ancient importance at the center of the Langhe, but in a short period of time, by the force of things, will become a forgotten and poor town, causing immense damage and discouragement not only to its hardworking, intelligent, and loyal population, but to the numerous surrounding towns in upper Piedmont.

Although the minister seemed to settle the question with some coldness ("I have the honor of informing you that the application for a Dogliani-Monchiero railway, the requested documents not yet being complete, the pertinent examination cannot be concluded"), in Moreno's request we may recognize a notably modern vision that certainly could have impressed the people of Dogliani.[12]

As the autumn's elections approached but the date to submit nominations for the XV Legislature had not yet been set, the newspapers began making predictions. The captain was seriously considering politics, and they knew it, albeit vaguely. Moreno's name circulated as a possible alternative to the outgoing lawyer Carlo Vayra in the Bra-Alba district, where there were stronger candidates in the reelection of Professor Michele Coppino, a highly respected Italianist from the University of Turin, former minister of public instruction (1884–1888), and father of the 1877 reforms that made elementary education free and obligatory; and the fat lawyer Felice Spantigati, whom Faldella ridiculed in "A Piedmontese Traveler," imagining his "historic appeal" for Moreno's young Hawaiians, who would revert to cannibalism at just the sight of him.[13]

The election would take place under a new electoral system, the so-called list ballot—a law of January 22, 1882—that Prime Minister Zanardelli considered an effective means of "purifying" Italian politics. But few held illusions about the reform. The Genoese newspaper *Corriere Mercantile* warned that "in many circumstances the outgoing deputies . . . joined together without taking the different political color into account," and it gave the example of the district of Trani, outside Bari, where there was an unspoken alliance between Baccarini, a minister of the king, and the lawyer Giovanni Bovio, a famous republican.[14] The deputies worked with great secrecy and energy to strategize and consolidate alliances. Under Coppino's influence, three outgoing deputies in Piedmont's Cuneo III district worked together with the goal of "removing any desire for Celso Cesare Moreno of Dogliani, who flatters himself to have Coppino's support to replace Vayra."[15] Then the picture changed a few days later. It was said that Moreno had obtained "promises of votes" from "influential" circles and that support for Vayra was declining "in Cherasco and in the other towns of Dogliani, Morra, Novello." According to correspondent da Alba from the *Gazzetta Piemontese*, Faldella's intervention had benefitted Moreno. In short, the situation was fluid: More candidates were coming forward in other towns, and by the time of the election "it could be that . . . we could become aware of some well-prepared game, very successful and unanticipated!"[16]

The game, at least for Moreno, seemed to work. On October 25, the candidates for the Cuneo III district, which had three deputies, were announced. In addition to the three outgoing deputies, all liberals, there were four other candidates: the lawyers Bernardo Casalis (liberal) and G. I. Armandi (constitutionalist), General Lanfranco Lunel of Cortemiglia (liberal), and Celso Cesare Moreno.[17]

Moreno was also a candidate in another district, Genoa I, where five deputies would be elected. In addition to the outgoing Lazzaro Gagliardo, Carlo Randaccio, Giovanni Argenti, Gian Nicola Goggi, and Andrea Podestà were new competitors. The Democratic-Radical Association put forward Federico Campanella, the lawyer Antonio Pellegrini, Federico Gattorno, and the worker Valentino Armirotti. The socialists added a single candidate, Amilcare Cipriani. The Progressive Association tried to split the lists with Randaccio and Gagliardo, Minister Alfredo Baccarini, and the aforementioned Armirotti. The Constitutional Association chose Podestà, Randaccio, Baccarini, and Argenti. There were also three independent candidates: the outgoing Goggi, Carlo De Amezaga (commander of a frigate supported by a group of dissidents from the constitutional front), and finally, put forward by the Society of Maritime Captains, Celso Cesare Moreno, "man of broad commercial knowledge and noted for his travels."[18]

During this time, the clerical Genoese newspaper *Il Cittadino* also reported some news that seemed to echo his American past. From his arrival in New York when he raised the alarm about the danger of child kidnapping, Moreno had already learned that he could not secure the right support, or at least, that the support he hoped for was really an illusion. This was evident in how Genoa's numerous and lively newspapers chose sides. The city's two principal newspapers, *Il Caffaro* and the *Corriere Mercantile*, did not mention him when they gave readers their voting recommendations. The first, politically radical, recommended voting for the Constitutional Progressive Association's ticket: Randaccio and Gagliardo, because they had proved successful in the previous legislature; Baccarini for his "tender gratitude"; and finally Armirotti, the worker from Sampierdarena, because "no one will forget, we hope, that feeling of solidarity that unites us with many sons of work, whom the new law has called to exercise the right to vote."[19] The second newspaper, of moderate orientation, recommended: Baccarini, whom it praised (after an initial coolness) for the interest he showed in problems at the port of Genoa; Commendator Randaccio, director general of the Merchant Marine, who was esteemed by the "maritime class"; Baron Podestà (who had given a large contribution to the town and who, in a few weeks would become mayor of Genoa); and the engineer Argenti. Its sister newspaper *Il Commercio-Gazzetta di Genova* made identical recommendations.[20]

The newspaper *Il Movimento* fell more or less along the same lines as *Il Caffaro*, which, however, only suggested three names: Baccarini, Gagliardo, and Randaccio. It excluded Armirotti and made it clear that the list was incomplete because of internal disagreements within the alliance between constitutionalists and progressives. On the democratic side, the newspaper *L'Epoca* supported Armirotti, Gagliardo, Pellegrini, and Randaccio.

Few mentioned Moreno. What was worse, no one supported his candidacy. *Il Gottardo*, another moderate newspaper that endorsed Gagliardo, Randaccio, Argenti, and Podestà, advised its readers against the "absolutely impossible" candidacies of De Amezaga, Goggi, and Moreno, "whose names, even if respectable, would not disturb the concord of the great liberal party . . . including the three aforementioned names on our own list, there would be a useless dispersion of votes, resulting in a miserable outcome, the triumph of our candidates being assured."[21]

The election was held on Sunday, October 29. It was an utter defeat for Moreno. In the district of Alba (Cuneo III), the winners, as predicted, were Coppino (6,969 votes), Spantigati (6,535), and Vayra (4,707). First among those not elected was Lunel (2,197 votes). The Capitano Marittimo was not even listed on the summary table prepared by the parliamentary service. He did appear on the list in the district of Genoa I, but in last place, where he managed to scrape together a paltry 189 votes, in contrast with Randaccio's 6,594 votes, Podestà's 6,427, Baccarini's 5,362, Gagliardo's 5,301, Argenti's 4,278. The first among those not elected was Armirotti, with 3,910 votes.[22] Some time later, the *Gazzetta Piemontese* commented on the election's outcome in rather literary terms, saying that Moreno "could count on but 300 friends, too few, even if they were valiant like the followers of Gideon, for a fight in which not valor but numbers won."[23]

There was no time for self-pity. Baccarini opted for the office he won in Ravenna, where he had also been a candidate. There would need to be a supplementary round of elections, which was set for January 7, 1883. For

Moreno, the game could reopen, perhaps with more possibilities than his first, hastily improvised candidacy: He could at least try to reach the runoff election.

Moreno's friend L. Levi, with whom Moreno was staying in Genoa, wrote a letter to Faldella on November 11, 1882, that showed how Moreno was preparing for the new endeavor. After some consoling remarks about Faldella's recent unsuccessful campaign, Levi switched to a different tone:

> I am writing to you from the printer of the newspaper *Il Popolo*, at the same table where my esteemed friend the illustrious traveler Celso Cesare Moreno is correcting some drafts in which his entire political program is laid out.
>
> It is what suits those who sincerely love their country. I read what you said about him in your *Assaggiature*, and I do not need to add a single word, because you so esteem his valuable talents.

Levi said that Moreno was "deeply saddened" by Faldella's electoral defeat, but now he hoped for "a showdown." He posed a question:

> Don't you believe that the Chamber lacks a man like Moreno? Would it not be good for him to sit there, when we did not want to behave like the English conquerors, it would certainly not be another Bay of Assab, the aim of his thoughts. You have been able to understand him, and you have admired his self-denial, sacrifice, adventurous life, but his mind is always, solely, firmly fixed on the prosperous future of our fatherland, Italy. If only everyone was ruled by such noble ambition, as he is, I would be the first to sing the praises of their ambition. Ambition united to self-sacrifice is a principle of martyrdom. You, my dear Giovanni, started your public life in Montecitorio with all of your energy. You brought to it the fire of your youth, your elegant speech, your entire self, and after the fatherland, you thought about your compatriots with your artist's heart. And what was the reward?

The letter included a postscript in Moreno's handwriting: "Don't lose courage. Obstacles and failures and adversity are the anvil upon which the stuff of the men who want to succeed in something outside the ordinary is pounded."[24] Who would know better than he?

Humbled by this experience of failure, Moreno immediately wanted to bolster himself with propaganda. Since he could not expect much help from existing newspapers, except for a little attention from *Il Popolo*, he decided to start his own newspaper. We do not know if he funded it partially or entirely by himself. The four-page, biweekly newspaper was directed by

Pietro Borghero and published its first issue on November 4, 1882. It was called *O Ficcanaso: Giornale locale da cianze e da rie* (*O Busybody: Local Newspaper for crying and laughing*). Written almost entirely in Genoese dialect, it came out on Wednesday and Saturday and was intended to advance Moreno's battles.

It immediately addressed the issue of the election from a curious angle: it claimed that if the newspaper had existed a few days earlier, its candidates would have been Gagliardo, Lazzaro Negrotto Cangiaxo (Cambiaso), Enrico Piaggio, and Cesare Celso Moreno. As for those who had been elected, it said, regarding Baccarini, that it was humiliating to take people from the government and catapult them into the district; Randaccio had undeniable merit but, being a government employee, had his hands tied. Moreover, how could he be in Genoa and Rome simultaneously? Argentini was dismissed with an eloquent "*libera nos domine*." Instead, the city needed to be represented by experienced men of business and the sea. Piaggio, the architect of the port's redesign, would have been perfect in this sense, as would Moreno: "The enterprising man, the intrepid traveler, with encyclopedic knowledge who knows by experience all the places where we could expand our commercial ties. He would be more useful than any other candidate." But Piaggio had not run, and Moreno had run "too late."[25]

The newspaper wrote about Moreno extensively in its second issue, saying that his experience in trade, navigation, and politics in the many countries in which he had lived were reason enough to support his candidacy, but now he had to publicize his platform. The newspaper had already become familiar with it through "that circular which sooner or later he had published" (perhaps Moreno had printed and distributed leaflets for the election). The newspaper approved of his platform because they thought he expressed practical principles that were well suited to expectations of Genoa's "greatness" and "commercial dominance."[26]

The readers of *Ficcanaso* did not have to wait long. The following issue opened with a great explanation of the Capitano Marittimo's electoral agenda. It was a clear and concise eleven-point plan. The first points were the following: Italian unity, individual liberty, freedom of association, freedom of work, "with the application of Habeas Corpus by means of proportional bail," "the law for compulsory education rigorously enforced," agricultural development and land reclamation, replacing progressive taxation with proportional taxation. The sixth point was particularly important to Moreno, in a much expanded way from before: "Serious and radical reforms of our diplomatic and consular staff abroad, which is of pressing need and obligation. Italy is badly represented, a principal cause of the decline of our interests and national prestige among foreign peoples. In this sad, damaging, and humiliating state of things there must be only one opinion."

He continued with an issue of "maximum concern" for the Italian navy as "standard-bearer of our power in foreign environs." From this seventh point he passed to the eighth point, in which Moreno promised ample assistance to the merchant marine "and in a special way to the steamship lines to Indochina, which will be conduits of work, commerce, and riches as well as a powerful vehicle for the exchange of ideas," as well as transatlantic lines, which would bring the nation riches. The ninth point called for the abandonment (if not the sale) of the national railroad to an Italian or foreign company. Tenth point: a greater push for relations with the other peoples of the planet. Finally, "a new foreign policy, not aggressive but serious, resolute, and dignified, immune from fluctuations in compliance and weaknesses. A true national politics that soon would erase the errors made and the humiliations and damages suffered."

Moreno felt the need to clarify this last point. At the end of the program he explained that thanks to the opening of the Suez Canal and the Gotthard Tunnel, Italy was preparing itself for a pivotal role between East and West. Therefore, "a vast outlet to Asia," the harbinger of "immense and inexhaustible" markets, would be enough to return Italian ports to the prosperity that had been taken from them by Vasco de Gama's discovery. All of this led to a grandiose finale, which Moreno intended to warm the hearts of his potential voters. He sketched for them the arc of Genoa's "manifest destiny" as "Italy's principle maritime metropolis."

> Trade is the life of Nations, the spirit of enterprise is its main artery, foresight, broad views, and strong will are the progress, the prosperity, and the liberty of a people. The best means of reaping all the benefits of our important geographic and maritime position assisted by the opening of the Gotthard Pass is to make Genoa the free port and clearing house of the Mediterranean, and thus offer this golden opportunity to the fatherland of Christopher Columbus in order to compete with Marseille, Liverpool, Hamburg, and Amsterdam in the exchange of goods between Asian and Europe, and thereafter supplant all of them. *Will is power.*

At the end of this text, which Moreno signed, *O Ficcanaso* included a document from the Genoese Chamber of Commerce (from the minutes of its April 20, 1866, meeting) to the Ministry of Commerce expressing its total support for his proposal about his project in Sumatra.[27]

All this was intended to communicate the idea of a person accustomed to thinking on a large, global scale, upon which his American experience had left unmistakable traces, and who would do anything but lower his horizons to local squabbles. It was a rather advanced political platform, positioned within the purview of the historic left and yet rather "reassuring" for the entrepreneurial middle class which Moreno considered his key constituency. It was certainly less radical than a program proposed by a fiercely anticlerical and republican newspaper like *Il Popolo Italiano*. In calling for the defense of liberties, Moreno did not go so far as to call for the freedom to strike, and he did not talk about limits on working hours, a minimum wage, women's emancipation, the abolition of prostitution, and so forth. Yet, a few days before the *Ficcanaso*, that paper had called Moreno's program "unique," considering it "the impetus of advantageous commercial reforms for Genoa's future," and it published the program in its entirety.[28]

The biweekly socialist newspaper *O Stafi*, published in dialect, did not think the same way. Perhaps the pompous airs of the statesman that Moreno often assumed annoyed the newspaper. It predicted an uncertain future for him and mocked his peasant origins. He, who deluded himself with obtaining heaven and earth, was in danger of ending up an ordinary sailor, or of returning to the village in Piedmont where he had been born "a germ of wheat."[29]

We do not know how many or what kind of commitments Moreno's campaign entailed. We can imagine rallies and lectures for a very select public, but what remains is only what was published in the newspapers, particularly in the *Ficcanaso*. It published an article, with ample evidence, which claimed Moreno was the first to propose cutting the isthmus of Malacca. It was at the time when he had proposed an Italian protectorate over the small state in which his father-in-law, "the Sultan of Acin" reigned. The idea now served to help him attack the moderates and their champion, ex–Minister of Foreign Affairs Visconti Venosta.[30]

As January 7, 1883, the date of the supplementary election, approached, *O Ficcanaso* painted a picture of the candidates. First were Goggi, Pellegrini, and Armirotti, then "four others whose number of votes obtained was not mentioned" (omitting the fact that Moreno could also be placed in this category). Then it introduced the new candidacy of the engineer Cesare Parodi as an example of a name imposed by the government and for whom the progressive constitutionalists would have to come together begrudgingly. Parodi, moreover, had too many commitments to be in Rome consistently. He was also the architect of a project for the port that, according to the *Ficcanaso*, humiliated Genoa in favor of Sampierdarena.

(At that time, Sampierdarena was a populous, independent town, although its annexation to Genoa was already being discussed and approved by *O Ficcanaso*; it would take place in 1926.) It was therefore necessary to oppose the liberal Parodi as well as the moderate Goggi.[31]

It was clear to everyone that Parodi, the former commissioner of public works, was the man to beat, although in theory Armirotti—supported by *L'Epoca* and the new democratic newspaper *Il Mare*—could count on a greater number of votes. For his part, Parodi had the *Corriere Mercantile*. Instead, *Il Movimento* preferred Piaggio, as did the *Caffaro*, maintaining that Parodi's candidacy was inconsistent with the intentions of those who had voted for Baccarini, Randaccio, Gagliardo, Argenti, and Podestà. It was essentially an expression of *trasformismo* that, in the election of 1882, had meant that the Right had been "thrown to the Left, leaping directly over the center, and making Stradella's program theirs" as set out by Prime Minister Depretis.[32]

As for our Capitano Marittimo, no one would have bet on his success. "It is doubtful that Moreno, a very great person with whose achievements we would never be displeased, has a large enough base," wrote the *Corriere Mercantile*.[33]

Moreno tried *in extremis*, we do not know with how much conviction, to harness the power of the press in a letter to Minister Baccarini published in *O Ficcanaso*. He called Parodi "a good man," although "too attached to the past to be able to adequately appreciate the present and anticipate the future." The man who would take the place that Baccarini left vacant had to be "familiar with the Sea and Trade," and "bold, with new ideas, of great vision with a good dose of entrepreneurial spirit, finally a man of vast experience in the affairs of the world." It was obviously his self-portrait.[34]

Of the twenty thousand men who had the right to vote, less than one-tenth of the area's population, few went to the polls on January 8 and 9: just 3,457, according to *Il Commercio-Gazzetta di Genova*, a result even lower than those previously obtained under more restricted suffrage. Parodi (3,102) and Armirotti (2,654) earned the greatest number of votes, followed by Piaggio (1,615) and Goggi (1,117). It is not known how many votes Moreno scraped together. His name did not figure in any recap, except in *Il Gottardo*, which had supported Goggi, which mentioned that 186 ballots were wasted "with the names of Moreno, Oberdank, and others."[35]

How did Moreno take this? To read *O Ficcanaso*, it almost seems that the Goggi fiasco and Piaggio's failure made him happier than his very modest performance upset him. Patience: Little by little Moreno would become known, and sooner or later he would have the opportunity to enter Parliament and support Genoa's cause. Now, however, it was time to express himself about the runoff voting. The analysis was that the city had voted for two opposite men: a clerical and moderate (Parodi) and a most extreme radical worker (Armirotti). Although the *Ficcanaso* claimed not to share the principles of the latter, it nonetheless chose him "if for no other reason than to see Zena represented by someone from the popular classes."[36]

A week later, Parodi prevailed slightly in the runoff, 5,374 votes to 4,993. If we are to believe the very disappointed *Mare*, which had initially predicted Armirotti's victory on the basis of the city's results alone, there had been "a thousand reasons for the invalidity of the elections."[37]

As for the *Ficcanaso*, it continued publishing until June of that year. It engaged in a campaign against the Marquis Marcello Staglieno and Cesare Imperiale of Sant'Angelo, which concluded with a famous trial in which the newspaper was accused along with others condemned as extortionists. The editor Borghero and his collaborators Luigi Vassallo and Giovanni Battista Giorni were arrested. Events took a tragic turn when Vassallo (the only namesake of the more famous Luigi Arnaldo, known as Gandolin, who became editor of Rome's *Messaggero* and then Genoa's *Secolo XIX*) began a hunger strike and died in prison in July. The trial concluded in December with Borghero sentenced to eight years in prison and three years of probation.[38]

No matter how hidden by his usual strength of spirit and a show of great nonchalance, regrets for the missed opportunity must long have troubled the Capitano Marittimo's heart. But there is no a trace of it in the historical record except for a single a postscript in a letter to Faldella a few years later. Moreno confessed: "Whenever I think about it I regret not having become the deputy when I had been in Italy for three months, and then as now, I am convinced that I would have made a talented service to my native country. I would have offered new things not known even nowadays by Italy's myopic ministers; nothing would have stopped me in my way, neither threats nor flattery."

As a member of Parliament, Moreno would have wanted to direct his energies toward rescuing Italy from the alliance with the British "shopkeepers." Not only that: "The bombardment of Alexandria would not have taken place and Assab would have been abandoned for better places." The failed election was therefore a true shame, brought about in Genoa by the prefect "on the orders of Minster Depretis." That is to say nothing of the district of Alba, "where they elected a mute man" like Vayra.[39]

CHAPTER 8
The New Italian America

Returning to the United States, Moreno resumed his now long-standing habits as a lobbyist in Washington, buzzing around the House of Representatives, the Senate, and the White House. In the White House garden he cut cinnamon and coffee leaves to send to Faldella and explained that he had collected the seeds of those plants in Sumatra and replanted them there in the past.[1] Newspapers remained an integral part of his world. Moreno continuously proposed articles and submitted letters to a number of Italian, Italian American, and American papers (above all the *Washington Post*, which became one of his regular outlets, although his pieces were submitted as letters to the editor). At the same time, he maintained, as was his custom, a robust correspondence with numerous personalities on both sides of the Atlantic. His disappointment over the failed election had to be strong, but the Capitano Marittimo—as we have often observed—was not the type to be discouraged: "There are injustices and misfortunes which make man superior. I am sorry that I have not yet received and endured enough!" he confided to Faldella.[2]

The America in which Moreno resumed his place was very different from the place he had left only four years earlier. Italian immigration was, numerically, relatively small during the "heroic" times of his first campaign against the exploitation of the "child slaves" but in the meantime it had transformed into a full river. In addition to the pioneering newspapers in New York and San Francisco, *L'Eco d'Italia* and *La Voce del Popolo*, there were numerous other newspapers for the many Italian communities now present in almost all the states of the union. On September 29, 1880, *Il Progresso Italo-Americano* began publication in New York. It was destined to become the most popular and longest-lived Italian newspaper in America, and its example encouraged the birth of others. Giovanni Francesco Secchi de Casali, Moreno's old friend turned bitter enemy, had transformed his *Eco d'Italia* into a daily, and in subsequent years other daily newspapers would emerge, from San Francisco's *L'Italia* (1886) to New York's *Cristoforo Colombo* (1887) and *L'Araldo Italiano* (1894), to Philadelphia's *La Voce del Popolo* (1893), as well as many periodicals, including Philadelphia's weekly *Il Vesuvio* and Chicago's *L'Italia*, both launched in 1886.

Moreno, who in some way belonged to the "aristocracy" of Italian pioneers in America (not a few of whom watched the spectacle of the new mass immigration with a certain unease, so miserable and different were they from the old exiles of the Risorgimento), did not hesitate to make contact with this new reality, soon becoming a sort of star in the Italian press, which was inclined to take an interest in a man who was always making news and who did not hesitate to use the pen as a hatchet. Moreno was able to inject himself into the new Italian American context as a kind of senior mediator between the American establishment and the immigrant "reality," an influential spokesman and a combative defender. In this capacity, as he attempted to write a new and updated chapter in his historic battle against "Italian slavery" in America, he began to take an active role in the initiatives and public demonstrations promoted by many emigrant associations.

Italian emigration was becoming an exodus of biblical proportions. The poorest of the Mezzogiorno swelled its ranks, with unprecedented waves of illiterate and very poor laborers, and ethnic prejudice grew around them. White, Anglo-Saxon, and Protestant America watched the new "wops" and "dagoes" with horror and an attitude very different from the warmth and sympathy with which they had viewed the arrival of the heroes of the Risorgimento. Moreno, the fortunate pioneer who was fated to have relationships with the most eminent American statesmen, had suddenly become a rather authoritative spokesman for a minority that disturbed the dreams of the conformists and occupied Protestant missionaries busy bringing the light of civilization to the fetid slums now called "Little Italy."

It was a world that needed to be led by the hand through the difficult process of Americanization.

An important test for Moreno presented itself almost immediately with the 1884 presidential campaign. The choice was between his friend James G. Blaine, a former speaker of the House of Representatives, senator, and secretary of state; and Grover Cleveland, the Democratic candidate who won the election, becoming the twenty-second president of the United States. Moreno presided over a meeting of five hundred naturalized Italians at the Fencing Academy on Baxter Street in New York. He explained, with his famous rhetorical fervor, that Blaine was a statesman. In the course of his career he had proved himself the "Demosthenes of both Houses," as well as "the Cavour of this Republic," illustrious precedents that would certainly have allowed him, once elected, "to immortalize" his administration. With his typical didactic tone, Moreno told his compatriots that the Democratic party was not what that adjective meant in Italy or in Europe, but that instead its leaders were all "well-known businessmen," which made them very different from the Republicans, whose party was "the advocate and protector of the worker" and, even more important, "of the Italian exiles." He called on them to take an active role in the politics of their adopted country, a call received with thunderous applause and bolstered by Moreno's election to the presidency of a new Italian American Republican association. Over the years, for reasons that we will see, the Captain would become an admirer of Cleveland, and he remained loyal to him even after his defeat by Benjamin Harrison. Moreno even predicted Cleveland's 1893 reelection and openly sided with the Democrats, accusing the Republicans of relying on a "terrible" Italian delegation to the national party committee.[3]

The Italian American arena was an interesting diversion, to be cultivated methodically and profitably. But there remained many other things for Moreno to do, and some of them, as we know, were particularly close to his heart. In Washington, the Captain waited while Congress debated "a subsidy of several million dollars for my Transpacific cable" to complete the concession already obtained.[4] The captain also said that he was grappling with a book that he also wanted to publish in Italy, perhaps with Sommaruga, which had published Faldella's *Roma borghese*. He also announced the American publication of another book "towards the end of November, at the opening of Congress."[5] He did not lose sight of the Hawaiian situation, and he followed developments in Italian politics with almost morbid interest. He felt the need to make his voice heard on one of the most sensational cases of the time, an incident which gripped Italy and elsewhere: the conviction of Professor Pietro Sbarbaro, a journalist and republican member of Parliament, for defamation. He expressed what he claimed was the opinion of an "eminent" American senator, namely that the Italian courts had behaved like their colleagues during the time of Savonarola.[6]

But overseas adventures were of even greater interest to him. He had much to say on the topic, and in August 1881 he sent his friend Faldella the draft of a document that he claimed would provide Luigi Roux's *Gazzetta Piemontese* with a tantalizing scoop about the behavior of the Minister of Foreign Affairs, Pasquale Stanislao Mancini. "To you, Mr. Faldella, my good *cannoniere* . . . I entrust this bomb. Shoot it from the cannon of Mr. Roux and others." However, we do not know what was in the news bomb, which would supposedly have revealed "governmental gangrene." The *Gazzetta* decided not to pounce on it. But Minister Mancini's profile was such that we can guess the issue of contention. Mancini was the architect of Italy's entrance into the Triple Alliance with Austria and Germany in 1882, an alliance that Moreno called "the hybrid alliance of the month of June with the month of January."[7] Mancini was also a staunch proponent of colonialism, which began that year with the occupation of the Eritrean port of Assab. He resigned in 1885, when he was unable to obtain a majority to support his policies in the Chamber of Deputies.

In Moreno's view, Italy, its ministers, and its diplomats cared little and poorly for foreign affairs. "Is it possible that as soon as they enter into the diplomatic corps these men become moles and rabbits if not puppets in the hands of the bureaucracy?" the Captain asked.[8] On another occasion he could not help but remark, "The ministers of Vittorio Emanuele let the great opportunity of Sumatra escape. Umberto paid too dear a price for the arid beaches of Africa. They do not realize that they are fighting the battles of the weak, perfidious, selfish, and greedy shopkeepers of England. O what blindness!"[9]

The subject was certainly not new. But in this new climate of mass emigration it took on a different dimension. Moreno, used to being a player, could not tolerate the fact that upstart emigrants, the so-called *prominenti*, could overshadow him, perhaps with the complicity of the diplomatic representatives, whom he resumed attacking with his usual contempt because he considered them "ignorant, incompetent, timid, and corrupt" to the point that "the prestige of the Italian name is going quickly into the Sun Set [*sic*]."[10] Now, however, the wrongdoings of these "ministers and consuls" were enough "to shame and make even the most skeptical blush." It foreshadowed the imminent resumption of his campaign against the "trafficking of young Italian slaves and adult men and women" and now even seemed to affect the Crown's behavior. Moreno wrote to Faldella that "recently the Queen of Italy wanted to mimic her husband's ministers and made the mistake of appointing four daughters of tavern keepers, shopkeepers, grocers, and butchers of America as ladies of her court, thus giving the women of Italy an inferiority complex. This is an undeserved and cruel insult."[11]

We do not know whom Moreno was specifically talking about. But he is clearly referencing the widespread custom among the Italian American *prominenti* and their family members of trying and often succeeding in obtaining absurd, impressive-sounding honorifics to solidify their new social status. These steps up the social ladder, which the immigrant press stressed emphatically and often with unintentional humor, harmed Italy's reputation and made "those abroad believe us a people in decline," unable to withstand competition from other nations.

It was in this context that he reached his decision to wage a new battle against the exploitation of Italians. It was no longer just the painful issue of the wandering children but a much larger problem involving tens of thousands of people and enormous economic interests that could unleash dangerous social and labor tensions against the newcomers. Italians were extremely low-priced labor at the mercy of their unscrupulous compatriot intermediaries, the bosses or *padroni* who easily recruited them from the multitudes of the new immigrants.

The Captain was alert, sniffing the wind. He had just returned to America when the columns of *Il Progresso* began to get worked up over the problem. In June 1884 he found a more effective platform in the *New York Herald*, which interviewed him on the tenth anniversary of the passing of the so-called Moreno Bill. Moreno said that between Mulberry and Baxter Street there were hundreds of "men, women, and children that are owned, body and soul, by men, some of whom are wealthy and go around the world with their head held high, with a great pretense of respectability."[12]

The 1874 law had some effect on preventing the false adoption of children, but now the situation was "worse than before," with cases of mistreatment comparable to those in the American South before the Civil War. Moreno spoke about poor people who arrived in America ignorant of everything and fell into the trap of the *padroni*. They signed illegal contracts believing that they were under the protection of generous compatriots who would protect them against Americans' hatred and contempt. In this way, the immigrants became heavily indebted to the *padroni* and this debt was the chain from which they could never free themselves. In the end, "instead of earning something to take back home, as everyone hoped when they came to America to 'make their fortune,' they were poorer than when they had arrived."[13]

In January 1885, Moreno raised his voice to denounce the existence of an organization that recruited Italian "slaves" in America on a vast scale. The occasion arose when the city of Washington, D.C., through Commissioner Lydecker, refused an offer from two Italian "businessmen," the owners of the firm Bertola, Gennaro & Co., who "promised to provide any number of Italian workers (read: slaves) for any work in Washington." Not content to stop there, they asked interested potential contractors to send them their address. Lydecker had detected the scam and avoided it. In a letter to the editor of the *Washington Post*, Moreno observed that it was certainly not the first time that someone tried to import "cheap slave labor" in the nation's capital as well as many other cities. He claimed to be well informed about trafficking by similar "crooked *padroni*" who formed a vast and multipronged organization with the support of "friends and accomplices" in all states. He recalled having already addressed the problem in 1873–74, at the time of the Moreno Bill, and hoped that Congress would again address it, perhaps passing a new law that would push the "infamous *padroni* and their equally infamous accomplices back into the sea."[14]

The timing of Moreno the lobbyist was admirable: Congress was working on an "imported contract labor bill" to suppress large-scale labor contracting like the *padrone* system in effect among Italian immigrants and others in America. Always in search of transatlantic support for his convoluted maneuvers, Moreno found it in one of the proponents of the *Patto di fratellanza*, the *operaista* (labor organizer) Antonio Maffi. He sent Maffi copious documentation about the problem of the *padroni* and their alleged accomplices whom he claimed were in the consulates. Maffi encouraged him to pursue the issue, offering to call the government's attention to this disgrace.[15]

Only those who remembered the "Moreno style" exhibited fifteen years earlier could have understood that behind those references to "friends" and "accomplices" gathered threatening storm clouds, and that before long the new campaign would erupt, recalling his memorable duel with Consul De Luca. Perhaps the first references to specific people were in a long article called "Italian Slavery" published on April 12, 1885, in the *Philadelphia Times*. Moreno, introduced as a former member of parliament who had "an important position among Europe's men of thought," accused Consul Arrigo Pignatelli of being the head *padrone* in Philadelphia, succeeding Count Galli in this position. He then proceeded to accuse several other people in various cities.[16]

After this sortie, the frequency of Moreno's denunciations became impressive. He was at the head of constant, obstinate journalistic activity in the newspapers, Italian American organizations, and important labor organizations like the Knights of Labor. On February 26, 1886, the Captain appeared in Washington in front of the House Labor Committee, presided over by Congressman Foran of Ohio, and testified in support of the law to abolish the *padrone* system.

Moreno dredged up the past, returning to his accusations against Consul De Luca, and claimed that at least eighty thousand Italian "slaves" had been transported to America. New York, Philadelphia, and Chicago, in that order, were the three cities most affected by the phenomenon. In Chicago, Moreno continued, the Italian consul (in reality a consular agent), Agostino Scuitti, was involved in trafficking. He was the "principal owner" of approximately five thousand slaves. In Philadelphia, Consul Galli and his assistants, Pignatelli, Scarlatti, and Rondinella, were involved; in Baltimore, Consul Barrilis; in Denver, Consul Cupelli; as well as the Consul of San Francisco. According to Moreno, the traffic was overseen in several places in New York, and the Captain provided the addresses: 85 Broadway, 15 Center Street, and a house on Mulberry Street, in the heart of Little Italy. Moreover, the trafficking "organ" was the newspaper *L'Eco d'Italia*, while the head of the New York *padroni* was Joseph Vallosio. (Moreno had argued with him in 1873 during the Associazione Donnarumma's annual picnic.) Moreno claimed that Vallosio was the "night watchman" of the Metropolitan Museum of Art and in cahoots with Luigi Palma di Cesnola, the museum's director. Another Italian of high reputation, Doctor Tullio de Suzzara Verdi, was supposedly the organization's head in Washington. Therefore, Moreno asked Congress to pass a law prohibiting the traffic and a resolution requiring the secretary of state to make the Italian government recall its "corrupt Italian consuls."[17]

When they published the news, the newspapers also included the perspectives of the accused. The *New York Times* interviewed Francesco Zanolini, one of the owners of *L'Eco d'Italia*, who called Moreno's accusations the ravings of an "agitator" who had previously attacked almost all the Italians of a certain rank living in the United States. They could trace his accusations against the newspaper to his years-long resentment over imaginary wrongs inflicted by its founder and former owner Giovanni Francesco Secchi de Casali. *L'Eco d'Italia* made a similar statement to the *Washington Post*: The editor said, "In Italy, we find better material with which to fill our papers." Giovan Barrista Raffo, the consul in Washington, called the accusations "absurd" and made by a person "unworthy of belief." His deputy said that Moreno was definitely crazy. American journalists asked their Italian American colleagues for insight. Moreno, the editors of *L'Eco* told them, "is always trying to make trouble. We do not consider him or his statements worthy of notice. He is simply a tramp, in one place today and another tomorrow, picking up a precarious living."

Italian American journalists could not find enslaved Italians, at least not in New York, where many immigrants were very poor and engaged in very hard labor. Perhaps many were also dirty and inclined to use a knife, but in no case could the picture Moreno painted be considered truthful.[18] The *Chicago Tribune* briefly spoke with Consul Scuitti, who, when the reporters informed him of the accusations that had been made, showed great astonishment and claimed to be completely uninvolved in the alleged activities. He added that he only knew Moreno by reputation and that he did not like him. Some time back, Moreno had claimed that there were three thousand enslaved Italian children in Chicago alone, and that news had proved completely false.

The next day, also pressed by reporters for the *Tribune*, Consul Scuitti gave an extended interview with was prominently published.[19] The reporter who visited Scuitti in his office wrote that the Genoese septuagenarian had quick black eyes, was "gray-headed, and with a bountiful beard, white and flowing "and was "sitting at his desk, with a trembling pen in his hand and old-fashioned, silver-rimmed spectacles near the tip of his nose." He looked like an old gentleman "without a moral or intellectual trait of the slave-driver or *padrone*." Scuitti asked how he could have been the owner of fifty thousand Italian slaves when all the Italians in Chicago added up to sixty thousand at most. And besides, there was no trace of slaves in Chicago. Scuitti had been at his post for ten years, since Consul General De Luca had appointed him in 1876,[20] and he did not have the slightest knowledge of the existence of a *padrone* system. He admitted, however, he had previously received some sign, though he claimed he had never been able to prove the validity of the accusations. Therefore, he believed that if something of the sort—particularly child slaves—existed, there was no one responsible for it in Chicago. Italian law, said Scuitti, would never have permitted anything like it:

> You cannot take Italian children here without the consent of their parents or guardians. If an Italian living in Chicago wanted to bring his wife or children here, he must come to me and obtain a certificate

> which says that he will be able to support them after their arrival and promise to send the children to school, and only on the basis of this statement will they get permission to emigrate from the Italian government. And then, in New York and elsewhere, there have been founded organizations to suppress any deal that favors the padroni. So you see how absurd and false Moreno's claims are.

The consul was adamant, but the unnamed reporter in front of him must have been a tough nut to crack. He abruptly shifted his questions from the children to the more general issue of Italian workers, abruptly asking him, "What do you think about the statement made to the commission by Congressman Lawler, alleging that he knew about hundreds of Italians working on the streets of Chicago for about 90 cents a day?"

Scuitti replied that he did not know anything about it. But if it was true, it meant that these poor people had been cheated because of their ignorance of the language and American customs. The interview ended shortly thereafter, but not the article, which continued with a detailed investigation into the phenomenon's past and present. The article recounted cases of children who had been exploited with the agreement of their parents or guardians. It went back over cases to 1870 and gathered opinions about Moreno's accusations. The general consensus was that, while they were not completely unfounded, the accusations at least seemed "exaggerated."[21]

On one side, there was an underestimation of the heavy exploitation of Italian labor that was very much present and constantly denounced. Adolfo Rossi, the first editor of *Il Progresso Italo-Americano*, who would later become the general commissioner for immigration in the first decade of the twentieth century and then the ambassador in Buenos Aires, agreed with Moreno and wrote that "our government . . . has never done anything to protect the wellbeing and morality of the Italian colonies in North America, and it is no wonder that there the mafia and camorra flourish as in the worst of Bourbon times and the Italian, illiterate, slasher, exploiter or exploited, is greater despised than the Irish or Chinese."

It was not an isolated accusation. Emilio Franzina, the most important scholar of Italian emigration, has argued that "there is no doubt about the negligence and arrogance with which the offices, whether staffed by professionals or the Minister of Foreign Affairs' appointees, operated, even in America."[22] On the other hand, Moreno's accusations seemed decidedly over the top. In many, if not all, cases, they seemed to be vendettas or uncalled-for provocations. Surely his attack on *L'Eco d'Italia* was inspired by old grudges. Moreno had a strange—and it would be tempting to say almost pathological—taste for revenge against guilty persons who enjoyed greater social respectability, as he did in the attacks he hurled at Cesnola and Suzzara Verdi.

The accusations against Cesnola and the Museum "provoke a smile of contempt," the editor of *Il Progresso Italo-Americano* told the *Washington Post*.[23] At that time, Cesnola was doubtlessly the most eminent Italian in the United States. From Rivarolo Canavese in Piedmont, he was a year younger than Moreno. He was a veteran of the war in Crimea as well as the Civil War, in which he had fought as colonel in the cavalry and earned a Medal of Honor. He had been the American consul in Cyprus. There, he undertook archeological excavations that produced a rich collection acquired by the Metropolitan Museum of Art, where he had served as its first director since 1879. His reputation established him in a sphere thousands of miles from the world into which Moreno wanted to drag him.

Similarly, Tullio de Suzzara Verdi, a political exile from Mantua who arrived in the United States in the middle of the century, had created an enviable position for himself. He had been the personal doctor to Secretary of State Steward, chairman of the District of Columbia Board of Health, a pioneer of homeopathy, and the author of numerous scientific publications. In 1894 he published a book on his experiences in the United States that was published in Italy as *Vita americana* (*American Life*). Widely respected, he was not a credible target. His biggest sin in Moreno's eyes—apart from having doubted Moreno's role in passing the 1874 law—was probably having lived for many years in the principal theater of Moreno's endeavors, Washington, while enjoying a much better reputation. He also had considerable wealth, enough to permit him and his family to frequent the best company, to participate in the society events that occupied the newspapers, to study in the best universities, and to take vacations in Europe. In 1891, one of Suzzara Verdi's daughters, Sophie, married Alfred Jerome Weston of New York, a contributor to *Scribner's Magazine* and later a contributor to the *Washington Post* on cultural topics. Francis Fava, the son of the Italian ambassador to the United States, had been the witness at their wedding.[24] That was perhaps enough to rouse the ire of Moreno, a man of talent who had never had the luck to be appreciated to that degree. Hence he had a real hatred, which was reciprocated, for that doctor of whom the Capitano Marittimo had on various occasions spoken very badly, and whose name he had enjoyed mangling in many ways, such as "De Stuffato" and "De Sozzura."[25] In the face of such indignant denials, Moreno, as usual, decided to return blow for blow. With the excuse of intervening in a debate over the celebration of Columbus Day, he repeated his accusations against *L'Eco*. He called the newspaper the "organ of the *padroni*" and claimed it was "associated with every shame, harm, and humiliation that the Italians and the prestige of their name had had to suffer in this country for more than a quarter century."[26]

The *padroni* system which Moreno had denounced in the 1870s for its abuse of children, and which he had tried to stop with the measures discussed in Chapter 4, was by no means extinct. Instead, it had evolved into a less primitive means of legally exploiting the growing masses of Italian immigrants. Scholars delineate a second phase of the phenomenon in which the *padroni* controlled the compensation of their slaves, who were employed in marginal occupations as newsboys, flower and fruit sellers, beggars, shoe shiners, and sometimes prostitutes. The *padroni* took their earnings and gave them back a modest stipend ("$40 a year was considered a fair salary").[27]

Now this relationship took on a new dimension. The *padroni* became mediators with absolute authority who, at their pleasure, decided the work to be done, the hours worked, the penalties inflicted, and, naturally, the wages. For the American employer, the *padrone* was the man who could guarantee the efficiency and reliability of his subjects in Little Italies. More than a few *banchisti* (the owners of agencies which provided various services to emigrants, including sending their remittances to Italy) acted as agents who acquired orders in various parts of the country. They relied on expert labor recruiters who could bring squads of Italian workers to construction sites while exercising iron control over them. All the money the workers earned ended up in their hands. The cost of room and board was deducted from these modest salaries, so the workers were completely at their recruiters' mercy and heavily indebted to them. The entire system was out of any labor union's regulatory control and undoubtedly an advantage for American industry during an era of enormous works and frenetic transformation.

The system was familiar to Italian immigrants. In fact, it was one of the most frequent themes in the popular theater produced in New York's Little Italy. In Bernardino Ciambelli's pioneering feuilleton *The Mysteries of Mulberry Street* (1893), the protagonist has a past as a *padrone*, and there were numerous references to the issue. The terminology used recalls Moreno's bitter polemics. In the novel's initial pages, Ciambelli, after having explained that the Civil War had freed an "immense mass of blacks, who for so long groaned under the baton of ferocious and cruel masters," turns to the present and shows how these inhuman times are far from over:

> It seemed that after so solemn an act was forever ended, the sad odyssey of men treated like beasts, oppressed by poorly paid work, always threatened, held on a leash like wild beasts. It seemed so, but it was not: because the slavery of blacks had been substituted by that of whites. Africa no longer sent its sons, but Europe sent hundreds of hundreds.
>
> Here it is not the novelist who speaks, but it is history, sad, true, nefarious, that unfolds day by day, hour by hour, for the workers, wronged by the villains, who had given themselves to the white slave trade.[28]

But there was more. Ciambelli, a journalist involved with various Italian American newspapers, discusses a case in his novel that Moreno himself, relying on the testimony of a man named Domenico Speroni, had raised on the pages of New York's *Cristoforo Colombo* on April 10, 1891. Violent and unscrupulous bosses had recruited Italian workers to go to South Carolina and "remove from the water, which he was in up to his knees, large shells." In the novel, the episode is set in a phosphate mine, still in South Carolina: "The phosphate is covered by water, and the workers must be in that water for hours, searching, rummaging in the sand in search of it." The entire chapter was punctuated with unmistakable references to Moreno's article.[29]

The Padrone Act (the law that our Capitano Marittimo was in the habit of calling the "Moreno Bill") had been passed in 1874 with the support of Senator Charles Sumner. Now it was followed by the Alien Contract Labor Law, also known as the Foran Act, encompassing the name of Ohio representative Martin Foran. Others, including the Knights of Labor, had called for it since 1883. The law was enacted on February 26, 1885, the first of a series of measures intended to eradicate the importation of foreign contract labor. The law levied heavy fines against the businessmen and captains of ships on which the laborers were found traveling. It gave American immigration inspectors the power to reject immigrants suspected of having obtained a labor contract before departure. For Terence V. Powderly, the head of the Knights of Labor and the future Commissioner General of Immigration, those workers represented a threat to the union as well as a weapon in the hands of employers anytime they needed to break a strike. Samuel Gompers's American Federation of Labor (AFL) had a similar perspective, sharing the tendency, widespread in those years, to support immigration restriction.

Moreno was obviously inclined to view the investigating commission's work as confirmation of the merits of his own long-standing insights. In the summer of 1888, he said he was ready to provide new testimony about the *padrone* system, and a few months later he denounced a merchant in San Francisco named Zabaldano. Moreno accused him of running a ranch in Cloverdale, California where a hundred Italians were imported in violation of the law and forced to work "eighteen hours a day for $20 a month, excluding room and board."[30] Moreno, who had written a letter to King Vittorio Emanuele I during the previous decade, now decided to write directly to the new king of Italy, his son Umberto I, to show him the gravity of the situation. Moreno reminded the king that if the Italian diplomatic service had listened to him since 1871 "the Italian name would not be so disparaged in America today." Moreno promised to continue his denunciations ("I will pursue the wrongdoers without pause") and repeated his usual accusations against the ambassadors and consuls, singling out the New York consulate as "the headquarters of the entire affair." Moreno knew about Italian Prime Minister Francesco Crispi's shakeup of the diplomatic corps, but, as he asked the king, "What is the sense in recalling the consul when the camorra of the consulate remains standing?"[31]

Between 1887 and 1891, there were new appointments, transfers, and promotions in the Italian diplomatic corps involving almost five hundred people, including consuls, vice consuls, and consular agents, mainly in Brazil and the United States. Consuls Raffi of New York and Lambertenghi of San Francisco were recalled and major changes affected the offices in Philadelphia, New Orleans, Chicago, Baltimore, and Boston.[32] Moreno was aware of this but still furious. In his letters to Faldella, he launched into obsessive, repetitive tirades against the diplomatic corps. Moreno had already begun fixating, though only in his private correspondence, upon his future (and fatal) "big target." The consuls had been recalled "although very late," "but Ambassador Fava in Washington, guilty as the rest of them, is left to dishonor the name of Italy in America."[33]

The consulates were dens of every vice, not only involved in the infamous traffic in human flesh, but they were also responsible, as he wrote to Faldella "for all the scams which harm Italian emigration" including "so many small and large inheritances of dead Italians which disappear in foreign lands to the detriment of their heirs in Italy." Revisiting his Hawaiian memories, Moreno told the story of a man from Genoa, Giovanni Appiani,

> the only Italian living in the Sandwich Islands after my departure, who died September 6, 1880 and with a false will dated the same month and year, that is two days after his death, a German shop boy from a small shop of beer, wine, gin, aquavit, and whiskey and the Royal Italian Consul by the name of A. Schaeffer came into possession of the will . . . he produced the false will and the lame hocus pocus that Appiani was married to a local woman with children in a country in which marriage does not exist he also produced a marriage certificate created by the owner of his shop the German Catholic missionary Herman: all this is possible in the legations and consulates of Italy abroad—they divide the spoils with their greatest and most guilty accomplice in the diplomatic corps the corrupt Peiroleri.[34]

The Capitano Marittimo was not aware that the powerful Augusto Peiroleri, his contemporary from Turin, had also fallen under the ax of Crispi's revolution in the diplomatic corps. But apart from that detail, Moreno was convinced of the fact that "any outrage can be done with impunity against Italians by foreigners in their country and abroad!!" Less than three years after the massacre in New Orleans (and five years before the massacre in Aigues-Mortes), that statement could have been viewed as a sinister prophecy. Moreno considered the tragedy in New Orleans as a direct consequence of the "trafficking in human flesh" that was "the cause of all the evils and the sum of all the shame and guilty not excluding that of New Orleans." That was what he wrote to Faldella, also sending him "a copy . . . of the arguments that the American Government will use in the judgment in New Orleans against the claims of the Italian Government."[35]

In 1889, both the Senate and the House of Representatives created committees to investigate immigration, and evidence emerged that agents and shipping companies had repeatedly violated the law. Moreno testified on March 20, 1890. He spoke on behalf of his fellow Italians but, as Keith Fitzgerald, a scholar of late nineteenth-century American identity, has observed, Moreno ended up conforming to the prevailing climate. He made a distinction between the "desirable" elements, in his view the Italians who "had fought for liberty," and the undesirables who the *padroni* subjugated likes slaves.[36]

In his statement in front of the House Committee on Immigration and Naturalization, Moreno resumed his usual accusations against a long line of diplomatic representatives. He elaborated on a theme that he had previously raised in front of the House of Representatives' Committee on Labor presided over by Congressman Foran on February 26, 1886: Moreno stated that if the 750,000 Italians currently residing in the United States were freed, it would be "an excellent acquisition for this country," and could make it "fertile like Italy from the Hudson to the Mississippi." Unfortunately, tens of thousands of Italians were "held in the most abject slavery by cruel *padroni* and their shameless accomplices." While Italians' conditions were good or acceptable in California, the heart of the problem was cities on the East Coast, particularly New York, where most Italian immigrants worked for the *padroni*.

Moreno had an exchange with Representative Covert about the 1874 law's efficacy. Moreno said that it was a good law but it was not "enforced" as it should have been. Each time that they had tried to enforce it, the consuls claimed that the alleged "slaves" were children or relatives of the *padroni*. Therefore, there needed to be a new, "more restrictive" provision to prevent the *padroni* from taking hold of immigrants in Castle Garden and sending them across the country. Moreno, responding to Covert, said that he was against the admission of lunatics and those unable to work. Criminals—among whom he claimed were many *padroni* who had escaped Italy's prisons or justice more generally—would never become good citizens. Moreno added, "Those who were brought by the *padroni* are undesirable because they are slaves and are inclined to resort to desperation because of the *padroni*'s cruelty." When the representatives asked how so many people believed the promises of the *padroni* and accepted their tyranny, Moreno said that consular officials were able to take advantage of their total ignorance "of the laws, customs, and language of this republican nation."[37]

In a climate of mounting restrictionist sentiment, an Immigration Act was passed in 1891 that strengthened controls but did not yet restrict arrivals. Italians were the most discussed immigrants. The 1890s, which began with the horrific lynching in New Orleans, would be among the most incredible of their American story.

Now Moreno had advanced far forward in his battle, utilizing, as usual, the press, particularly the immigrant press. Though it was surely an optimistic idea, he believed that at his side to defeat the "nefarious traffic in Italian slaves" were all the most important Italian American newspapers, scattered from the Atlantic to the Pacific and directed by "gentlemen, scholars, thinks, and patriots" (including those, such as *L'Eco*, that had ridiculed him for his recent attacks) who "have taken to heart the mission of journalism, which is to tell the truth, to educate, and to elevate the people."[38]

Only one target remained: Baron Francesco Saverio Fava, the Kingdom of Italy's first ambassador to Washington. When the Captain made his distinction between the Italians who had fought for liberty and those who had not, he had Fava in mind. Before Fava, who was originally from Salerno, had passed into the service of the house of Savoy, he had been a diplomat for the Kingdom of the Two Sicilies. Fava had served in Algiers, Genoa, Trieste, Marseille, Malta, and Smyrna. He was transferred to Monaco shortly before the fall of the Bourbons. Suspended from service in 1862, at the age of thirty, he was readmitted into the profession for the new Kingdom. He was first sent to Bern, then to The Hague, Constantinople, Bucharest, and Buenos Aires. In 1881, Fava was appointed ambassador to Washington, which was then considered a second-rank position. He remained there, feeling sometimes as though he was in exile, until 1901 when, retired, he was appointed senator.[39]

Those crucial twenty years were the years in which the United States emerged as a great world power. It was not by chance that the Italian legation was elevated to an embassy in 1893. Fava, occupied with many pressing issues, must have felt on his neck the breath of his implacable tormentor: Celso Cesare Moreno.

The first face-off between the two took place on June 6, 1890. Moreno told the *San Francisco Chronicle* that he had confidential information from Italy, and he spread the rumor that the Italian government considered recalling Fava, who Moreno had already accused of supporting the traffic in slaves in defiance of the 1874 law. Now Moreno added another accusation: Fava and Consul General Riva had appropriated a considerable sum of money and bought 11,000 quintals of tobacco from a business in Kentucky on behalf of the Italian state, paying a price considerably above market value. According to Moreno, the Italian government had ordered an investigation into the case. Riva had already been recalled and Fava would be soon, to be substituted by the Marquis Dall'Ungaro. The news was false, and Fava's friends condemned it. Tullio de Suzzara Verdi, for example, knowing who the source was, called it "the ravings of a madman" and "the invention of a scoundrel."[40]

In the meantime, Moreno had failed to bring the campaign to Italy, either through the media or politics. The newspapers were not the problem. Moreno inundated them with letters, articles, and complaints, almost all written in the form of "circulars" but with such strong tones that he almost always succeeded in whetting a correspondent's appetite for the news. In a piece in Florence's *L'Elettrico* (July 18, 1890) he accused the ministers and consuls of complicity in the "traffic of Italian slaves," with only minor variations from his articles in the American press. He was also mentioned in the influential Jesuit magazine *La Civiltà Cattolica*, which, albeit with some caution, wanted to use the report as a tool in its own campaign against the liberal Italian state. In light of Pope Pius IX's famous *Non possumus*, which rejected the privileges that the Kingdom of Italy offered him under the 1871 Law of Guarantees, the magazine reaffirmed "the absurdity of the Pope, his liberty guaranteed by those who hold him prisoner" and brandished a religious message for the purposes of colonialism from Asia to Africa and Oceania. The magazine, referring to the newspaper article, remarked: "We refrain from any comment. . . . But we ask if it would be possible, that people and states would resign themselves to see the influence of the Papacy exploited by a Government that can be gravely branded in this manner by its former diplomat or servant."[41]

Perhaps not even Moreno, the anticlerical who passed himself off as the nephew of a bishop, could have imagined being able to take so much credit in the most illiberal of Catholic publications. But, as he wrote to Faldella, he "surpass[ed] the Jesuits in influence."[42]

Politics also served him. By December 1888, he had succeeded in having his complaint heard in the Chamber of Deputies. The issue was raised by a deputy of the historic left, Michele Ungaro, based on an article by Moreno in *Il Progresso Italo-Americano*.[43] Moreno now turned to Ruggero Bonghi, a moderate Neapolitan deputy, former Minister of Education, and friend and confidant of Alessandro Manzoni. Moreno sent him newspaper clippings documenting the conditions of Italians in America and a letter written on letterhead from the U.S. House of Representatives. "The Italian slaves" the Captain wrote to his illustrious correspondent, "are bought and sold, rented and beaten like beasts of burden and worse than black slaves in the southern states before the Civil War." Moreno reminded him how it was "an anomaly that Italy sent its delegates to the Congress of Brussels for the purpose of abolishing the black slave trade in Africa while it permitted thousands of free Italians to leave Italy's shores and swell the already great number of Italian slaves in America." All this happened, of course, "with the complicity of the Ministers and Consuls of Italy." According to Moreno, Crispi was "misinformed" about the problem because of the diplomatic corps' intrigues.[44]

Moreno chose Bonghi to bring an echo of his American campaign to Parliament because Bonghi was Crispi's long-time adversary. ("In the twenty-seven years that we have been together in the Chamber, I believe over a hundred votes, in ninety-nine we have found ourselves against each other," Bonghi reminded Crispi on May 3, 1888, during a lively debate in the Chamber about the complicated African situation.)[45] Bonghi took the bait, making an inquiry to the prime minister and interim minister of foreign affairs, "to know if he has knowledge of the accusations made in the congressional commission in Washington on Italian immigration in the United States against our consuls and ministers, and if he intends to find out whether they are true or false, according to the case, or punish the guilty or protest against the accusers."

Bonghi received an irritated response from Crispi during a session of the Chamber of Deputies on January 29, 1891:

> Not only do I know about the unjust accusations made against our consul in New York and our minister in Washington by Mr. Celso Cesare Moreno, but I have acted because they have asked for a strict account of them, and so that this cruel slander might obtain the consequences it deserves.
>
> It is enough to know who Cesare Moreni is, who changed his name to Celso Cesare Moreno, trying to make us believe that he is the nephew of the bishop of Ivrea. From investigations made, we have proof that the charges made by this individual have no foundation whatsoever.

Not content with mocking him, Crispi, amidst the deputies' laughter (indicated in the stenographic report of his speech), added new blows to the definitive demolition of the accuser's credibility:

> Mr. Celso Cesare Moreno, the new edition [*laughter*] was in the *bersaglieri*, but was not reenlisted because of his misconduct. He runs around the entire world; was in Peking, the United States, and then in the Hawaiian Islands, where the good prince made him minister of foreign affairs, but after a week had to dismiss him because he learned that he was an adventurer.

Such a person could not be considered credible: his were only "lies." Moreover, "after the latest law it is not possible that the trafficking in children that occurred before is taking place."

But the combative Bonghi did not give up. He interjected loudly: "A word for the consul!" And Crispi did not make him ask:

> I can assure you . . . that Mr. Celso Cesare Moreno, with his stories, only intends to seek revenge upon our consul and our minister, who have made very grave reports about him, in keeping with what has already learned about him from Peking and other places.
>
> Now he is in the United States of America; he has its citizenship . . . and from his new position he tries to revile our representatives abroad in every way.

At that point, Bonghi appeared convinced. He thanked Crispi, and told him "the reputation of our representatives in America is itself enough to convince me and everyone else that all of the accusations made were false." Moreover, Bonghi said that Baron Fava was universally recognized for his honesty, most recently in a letter from Blaine, which was "full of confidence and praise." But all this did not invalidate the need to be vigilant about the condition of Italian emigration in America, which was now "broken," and ran the risk of further damaging "the reputation of the Italian name in those lands."[46]

American and Italian American newspapers, particularly *Il Progresso Italo-Americano* on January 20, 1891, also followed the parliamentary investigation, encouraged by Moreno. Moreno wrote to Bonghi, not yet over the disappointing outcome of the investigation:

> Various newspaper correspondents and reporters went to the boarding house where Fava lives for news of the question and its proponent, and since Minister Fava does not know how to speak English he responded through an interpreter, a former barber by the name of Verdi with various aliases, who is the de facto minister of Italy while Fava and the ex-barber are the objects of public ridicule and public scorn in Washington.

Here we outline Moreno's accusations against Baron Fava. Important parts of the picture are that the ambassador did not know English, he lived in a boarding house without the least regard for the national honor, and he kept company with people of dubious reputation, or at least individuals considered as such by Moreno, since in this case he was referencing the aforementioned Doctor Tullio de Suzzara Verdi. With diabolical irreverence, Moreno told Bonghi that Fava, speaking with a journalist, "had painted the honorable Bonghi in quite gloomy colors" also depicting Moreno "as a brigand from Calabria escaped from the galleys of Italy." In short, Moreno was enjoying himself in addition to being indignant. After all, "calling me a fugitive brigand is not a new thing, ministers Corti and Blanc [Italian diplomats in the United States] said that before, Fava and minister De Luca said it in Peking in 1879 when I was there in China, and the Italian consul in Honolulu in the Sandwich Islands said it in 1880, this Italian consul is a German . . . professional waiter and spirit-seller who many times served me at table with an apron on his stomach."

To bolster his credibility even further, Moreno enclosed two clippings: one from an American newspaper and the other probably taken from the

Italian American newspaper *Cristoforo Colombo* (a newspaper which was opposed to Fava). The articles, which drew upon the *New York World* of January 15, 1891, related a curious episode that happened on January 14 at the Metropolitan Club of Washington. A young naval officer, who had gone to the Italian legation several times to speak with Fava about certain issues without ever finding him, met him by chance at the Club. When Fava gave him a business card to direct him to the legation's secretary, he had thrown it in Fava's face. The episode had only avoided a violent outcome thanks to the intervention of third parties. Moreno remarked that "this affront is a result of the traffic in Italian honors carried out by Fava and Riva."[47]

At that point, as we have seen, Bonghi had decided to abandon an issue that seemed not to lead anywhere. Moreno expressed his regret for this decision, reminding him in a letter how "instead of continuing on the straight path of his inquiry against Fava and other terrible representatives of Italy abroad, he passed arms and information to the opposing camp."[48] Above all, Moreno immediately wanted to retaliate against Crispi, and he did so in an article in Genoa's *L'Epoca* at the end of February 1891. Moreno called Crispi "the pontiff of official disgrace," and predictably took advantage of the opportunity to repeat his accusations against the entire diplomatic corps. He wanted to drag two other figures into the supposed tobacco scandal ("the swindled government of Italy paid enormously and the Italian people smoked badly"): the Florentine-American banker Egisto Fabbri and Adriano Lemmi, a grandmaster of Italian freemasonry and Crispi's old friend.[49]

Crispi referred to him as "a certain Moreno," and we can imagine with what sense of liberation the Captain greeted the kingdom's new prime minister, Rudinì, in 1891. Moreno dedicated an essay to him in the *Washington Post*, praising his intelligence, firmness, and courage, but also warning him: "Hopefully, for the good and prestige of Italy, prime minister Rudinì will not allow himself, as did his predecessor, to be erroneously informed by minister and consuls supported by the ministry's bureaucracy, on the true state of men and Italian affairs in foreign lands."[50]

Moreno's obsession remained the same: attacking Ambassador Fava. This "priority" occupied a position of dramatic prominence in Moreno's life alongside the Hawaiian question. (Not being equipped with the Captain's ability to play on multiple tables, we are obliged to examine these two trajectories separately.) Soon the (false) news of Ambassador Fava's recall to Italy would prove almost a prophecy. In April 1891 Fava was officially recalled—not because of scandals or embezzlement, but because of the lynching in New Orleans. On March 14, 1891, eleven Sicilians were taken from a courtroom where they had just been acquitted for insufficient evidence on charges that they had murdered the local police chief. An angry mob murdered them in the street. The relationship between Italy and the United States entered a critical phase. Italy demanded an immediate trial of the perpetrators of the massacre, but the United States responded that federal authorities could not interfere in individual states' judicial affairs. Fava held repeated meetings with Secretary of State Blaine, and on March 31, having been recalled by Rome, he took his leave.[51]

The controversy reached a boiling point. Other lynchings followed in Denver (1893, one victim), Boone, Kentucky (1894, one victim), Huerfano County, Colorado (1895, three victims), Spring Valley, Illinois (1895, one victim), Hahnville, Louisiana (1896, three victims), and finally Tallulah, Louisiana, where five Italians were murdered on July 19, 1899.[52] Even among American observers, the federal government's Pilate-like position raised more than a scandalized doubt about how New Orleans had conducted the investigation into the tragic episode. As an important Italian American journalist wrote thirty years later:

> it was denounced to the civilized world—and it had to make America burn with shame—along with the Grand Jury called to investigate, since it welcomed the assassins, those who lynched the Italians, to its breast, and the *New York Herald*, in its May 12, 1892 edition, recounted the horrific circumstances in these words: "the Grand Jury maintained a stony silence when a witness, asked if he could identify another of the lynchers, responded by immediately pointing his finger at a member of the jury."[53]

Moreno decided to take advantage of Fava's absence and spew a torrent of jokes, insults, and insinuations against him. He blabbed a series of private facts about the ambassador to the newspapers, portraying him as a "windbag": "He wears a monocle, spats, a big cane, and has the manners of an aged dandy. He loves high society and spends most of his time in an exclusive circle. He accepts all invitations to dinner because it is more enjoyable than dining at home, and also cheaper."

It was said that a decade earlier Fava was rich, thanks to his wife's patrimony, but that, after a stormy marriage, she left him and went to live in Paris, where his son lived too, a respected engineer who had broken ties with his father. It was also said that, reduced to living on his meager salary, he had tried to make his fortune in the stock market and had lost everything, and that things had not improved with real estate speculation.[54]

Moreno added additional details to this unflattering portrait. He revealed that Fava had used the $5,000 that the government gave him annually to rent a respectable residence for completely different purposes, and he lived in a little room inside a building on Connecticut Avenue in Washington, where there was a black barbershop and an Italian bakery on the corner. Moreno claimed that he had learned that the ambassador paid an average of $14 per month to rent space for the Italian legation, and he claimed to have documented the scam, even sending a series of photograph to Prime Minister Rudinì.[55]

The Captain, as he already had with Bonghi, sent his dossier to Matteo Renato Imbriani, a patriot and deputy of the historic left, and to Felice Cavallotti, a far-left deputy famous for his duels. Two new parliamentary questions were born. Prime Minister Rudinì, decidedly embarrassed, had not responded to Cavallotti's inquiry with Crispi's passion. He declared that, until proven otherwise, he kept his faith in official sources.[56] After an absence of more than a year, during which the crisis between the United States and Italy passed from collective hysteria, including fears that the powerful Italian navy would attack the American coast, to a contentious solution that provided compensation for the families of the lynching victims, Fava, welcomed by the immigrant community, resumed his post in Washington on May 16, 1892, "without any serious satisfaction having been given to Italy."[57] The ambassador continued supporting the Italian cause for a long time, and he tried to get the lynching cases heard in federal court. This, however, was impossible, as we have observed, because of congressional opposition from southern segregationists. (African Americans were far more numerous victims of lynchings.)[58]

Moreno, though distracted by events in Hawaii, did not back down. Through *L'Eco d'Italia*, he resumed calling for the ambassador's immediate removal because of a supposed rivalry between him and Riva, the consul in New York. It was an old story dating back to 1889. There were a variety of views about the construction of an "Italian institute" that would be the most effective instrument for fighting against the abuses of the *padroni*. Since 1883, as he himself would later recall, Fava adopted the same point of view as Moreno. He worked for the creation of an office to rescue Italians who had just landed "from the rapaciousness of greedy speculators, mostly Italians, accustomed to exploiting them into extreme poverty." He tried, with little success, to divert new immigrants to destinations other than metropolitan areas where they could be employed in agriculture.[59]

It was clear to everyone, especially journalists in the nation's capital for whom Moreno was a familiar figure, that the Captain had "one absorbing object in life, which is the political destruction of the Italian Ambassador," which was almost a "monomania." Fava, when asked why he did not respond to Moreno's attacks with legal action, preferred to shrug and say, "Oh, it keeps him employed, and it does not hurt me." The gossip about the ambassador's marriage was also invented. The *New York Times* contacted Fava's son, Francis, an American citizen and professor of civil engineering at Columbia College. He denied everything.[60]

The question finally seemed to lose steam. Occasionally, however, Moreno sent ambiguous messages that sounded like allusions to complicity between crime and the consular services. In September 1893, for example, "Don Caesar," as journalists sometimes called him, claimed that an unknown man had confronted him in the Pension Français restaurant on Pennsylvania Avenue in Washington. The man said that he was the son of the chancellor of the Italian legation, and he threatened to stab Moreno if he did not stop his defamatory articles. The man escaped before the police could intervene.[61] A year later, Moreno reported that a man stopped him on the corner of Fourteenth Street and threatened his life because the Captain had called the Immigration Bureau's Superintendent Stump an importer of Italian contract labor. "We are two brothers: one or the other, or both together, will blow off your head and we have good and influential friends who will stand by us," the big man had yelled. Moreno had maintained a perfect calm and explained that it was the authorities, and not him, who demanded respect for the law Congress approved on February 23, 1887. He then tried to get the man to tell him his name, but in vain. He commented theatrically, "If my head is going to be blown off, I should like to know who is going to do it."[62]

But Moreno was not mollified at all. He entrusted the pages of the African American newspaper *The Colored American* with his most violent attack against the ambassador and his gang, a choice that does not seem accidental in that climate of xenophobia and racism.[63] The article, with the usual formulas, accused "Don Basilio" Fava (as Moreno had taken to calling him, alluding, with in a reversal of roles, to the character in the *Barber of Seville* who sang the famous aria "La calunnia è un venticello") of collusion with the *padroni*. The Ellis Island office had been entrusted to Alessandro Oldrini, but Moreno considered Dr. Onofrio Abruzzo, a respected doctor from Brooklyn engaged in a dispute with the *padroni*, better for the position.[64] Oldrini allegedly had no other purpose than to "deceive, trick, and dupe the police, as he deceived the immigration commissioners."

On this occasion, Moreno also displayed the anti-Semitism that he sometimes unleashed. He called Fava a Jew in whom all the race's shortcomings appeared in the highest degree, "like stinginess, greed, thirst for profit, and avarice." The attack was perhaps based on the fact that during more than a decade of service in Bucharest, the ambassador had repeatedly supported the rights of the large Jewish community. The community was subjected to abuse and violence, especially in Moldavia. The Italian government, at Fava's urging, took the stance that the Jewish community should be protected and naturalized. By the early 1870s, the Italian government was one of the most active supporters of this position, alongside the United States.[65]

Fava again refused to file a libel suit, but in July 1895, in "an unprecedented action," the U.S. Attorney issued a grand jury indictment against Moreno for libel. As proof of Fava's innocence, the case files cited 1884 correspondence between the ambassador and Secretary of the Treasury Carlisle on the need to suppress the *padroni*. For this purpose, Fava appointed Oldrini (the "self-styled Professor, Count Oldrini") to the Ellis Island office that aided Italian emigrants in order to "promote their welfare and give information to the officials of the [U.S.] Government of any violation of the immigration or contract labor laws."[66] Oldrini, Moreno alleged, hid the illegal traffic from American authorities as the office's head.

An arrest warrant was issued for Moreno and a subpoena for Fava. The Ambassador never showed up. As one scholar has written, Fava probably feared that so much publicity would damage him. Deputy Sheriffs Wilkinson and Hempstead arrested Moreno on the morning of July 12 while he was at the Tremont House hotel restaurant. Accompanied by the lawyers John B. and Eugene J. O'Neill, Moreno was taken to the Second Criminal Court in front of Judge Cole. The judge set bail at $1,000, which was paid by a guarantor, Thomas E. Kirby, and Moreno was released pending a trial date set for October.[67]

At this point, an explanation of the much-contested Italian office at Ellis Island is needed. During his time in Washington, Fava repeatedly raised the issue of providing more rational outlets for the flood of Italian emigration. He tried redirecting a portion of it toward agriculture and the southern United States, particularly Arkansas, where a model agricultural colony had been created. Fava was convinced that "the best safeguard for adult immigrants was to separate them from the *padroni* upon their arrival on Ellis Island." To do this, the ambassador worked with the American Secretary of the Treasury to open an office on Ellis Island where there would also be an office of the Bank of Italy to protect emigrants' savings. The idea was to collaborate closely with American authorities and provide new arrivals with the assistance necessary to avoid the negative influence of labor brokers as well as the so-called *banchisti* who were often their principal allies. Fava obtained Secretary Carlisle's approval in 1894. At that time, no other European nation had a similar organization.[68]

Moreno's specter even haunted the office's organizing phase. At one point, Fava asked the Department of the Treasury if Moreno had a job with the Bureau of Immigration. The Department responded negatively. Moreno noted that Fava's request for information "had not originated from the best motives or from the kindest sentiments toward me." In a letter, Moreno told Carlisle that he had had a meeting, followed by a letter, with Superintendent of Immigration Herman Stump, but he had never tried to obtain such employment.[69]

In August, there was a brief exchange of letters and a conversation between Moreno and Stump. The superintendent had asked him to put into writing "your opinions about the most suitable instructions" for the suppression of the *padrone* system, and Moreno had done so. Despite this, as Teresa Fava Thomas notes, "Stump generally maintained a good relationship with the Italian Bureau even praising them in one of his Washington reports."[70]

As he waited for his trial, the Captain made a show of optimism. A *New York Times* reporter wrote, "Mr. Moreno rejoices in the opportunity thus given him of airing his visionary theories, and announces that his prosecution affords him an opportunity he long has been waiting for." The American government's good intentions risked producing an undesired effect. The trial had every appearance of becoming a powerful megaphone for Moreno's accusations, which the newspaper believed unfounded, but they could still cause "considerable personal annoyance to the amiable Italian Ambassador." In fact, Moreno was preparing something like a nightmare for Fava. Moreno announced that he would represent himself and that he would question Fava for a week. Considering the Capitano Marittimo's incredible capacity for histrionics and the stir the case was already making in the press, a truly spectacular event loomed.[71]

A hearing took place in front of Judge Cole in criminal court in the District of Columbia. Fava was absent, and the court police declared him unreachable. It was the morning of the August 10. To open, District Attorney Birney said that for the first time in the history of the United States they were judging a person for defaming a diplomatic representative of a "friendly power" in the press and that perhaps a degree of "scandal" could be glimpsed in the affair. Colonel W. A. Cook, assisted by his colleague J. B. O'Neill, handled Moreno's defense. Cook immediately asked for a postponement, claiming that there had not been enough time to prepare a defense. Birney replied that there had been sufficient time since July 11. After a "notable quibble," the court ordered that they proceed.

Birney exhibited the incriminating article and the correspondence between Fava (absent due to commitments in New York) and secretaries Gresham and Carlisle in order to show that the ambassador had maintained a firm position against the *padrone* system. At that point, Cook asked that Fava be heard, and he tried to argue that Fava's absence was a valid reason for a new trial, insinuating that he, and not the government, initiated the case. Cook added that if the request was accepted, they would need to prove how the Ambassador was "in complete sympathy with the *padroni*." The witnesses were called, first James E. Cooper, the editor of a newspaper in which the defamatory article appeared. He confirmed that Moreno was its author. Then Detective Mattingly was called, who declared under oath that Moreno had showed him the article and said that he had written it. Alessandro Oldrini, the Italian official at Ellis Island, was also called, and finally Moreno himself. Moreno repeated his accusation that the ambassador not only knew about the *padrone* system but that he was also its accomplice. An obvious objection was raised: Moreno had to prove this, and if he could not, he would have had to refrain from making this claim. The parties having been heard, Judge Cole formally turned the case over to the jury, which retired at 2:15 p.m. and returned with a guilty verdict eight minutes later. Colonel Cook asked that Moreno's bail be set at the same amount as before, since a request for a new trial was pending. But Judge Cole, at Birney's suggestion, raised the bail to $3,000. This time Kirby did not come forward to pay it. The wait for a guarantor dragged on until late afternoon, when Moreno finally realized that he had to prepare for jail.[72]

Things had gotten ugly for "Don" Celso. He had been arrested while waiting for Judge Cole to sentence him. Word spread that he had taken more moderate advice and was preparing to withdraw his request for a new trial. Instead, he would rely on the mercy of the court so that he could receive a financial penalty, rather than a prison sentence.[73] On Monday, November 11, Moreno's lawyer withdrew the request. The Captain gave a defense of himself in which he talked about his arrival in the United States, how he had become a citizen, and his dedication to combatting the shame of the *padrone* system. What he had published had been for that purpose and if, in the heat of the moment, he had done something against the law, he was sorry, but he had no regrets. Judge Cole interrupted him: "I have no doubt that the system exists in this country as you have portrayed it in the objectionable article." Moreno, perhaps emboldened by the statement, insisted: "I think it an outrage that a man should be tried and convicted for doing good." But Cole reminded him that defamation was a serious crime that could not be escaped by paying a small fine. It was afternoon when Cole issued his verdict: "I feel compelled, against my personal inclination, to impose imprisonment." He sentenced Moreno to ninety days in the district prison. A reporter noted that the Captain, although upset that he had not escaped with only a fine, gathered his papers without showing any emotion and prepared to return to the prison where he had been since the end of the trial.[74]

Another reporter who despised Baron Fava was convinced that Moreno's fate was the result of the Italian legation's intimidation of the poor witnesses who were needed to confirm the Captain's accusations but who instead had not shown up. The reporter recalled that moment years later: "It was a pitiful sight to see Moreno . . . who responded to an accusation of libel, agony evident on his face that neither pen nor brush could have sketched it in the moment in which it appeared clear that the poor Italians for whom he had done his best would not dare to show up at the trial to support his accusations."[75]

The crime for which he had been sentenced was not insignificant. Moreno was no longer young and he decided to play the last card he held, asking President Cleveland for a pardon. In the newspapers he circulated the rumor that Fava had signed a petition to that effect or made a personal appeal to the president—in vain.[76]

Since Moreno was still an interesting character, journalists did not forget about him after his imprisonment. Some wanted to visit him to see how he was doing, and it was not a bad idea. On Sunday, November 17, a journalist from the *Washington Post* went to the district prison and approached a series of inmates, including the Capitano Marittimo. Moreno, while rattling off a list of wrongs endured that needed redress, was mindful of how Faldella had depicted him. He told the reporter how, that day, he had prepared his "Italian salad." The reporter noted the aristocratic behavior of a diplomat, his beard and his silvery white hair, his full cheeks and healthy coloring. Moreno's manners were "exquisite," as he recounted "with a softly modulated accent all his own" the story of his troubles and a conviction that he believed unjust.

> I am very glad that you have come to me, more glad than I can tell you. For I want the world to know about my case. To-morrow, or perhaps the next day, I will lay the facts before your honorable President, and ask him to take me out of this place. I hope to be pardoned. Why, I am known and very well known. See! Here are the certified copies from the files in the State Department! And see! That certificate is

signed by Mr. Bayard, who was then Secretary of State! Please, publish this, so that the world may know.

At that point, Moreno had pulled out a letter, yellowed with age, that bore the stamp of the Department of State. It was a letter of recommendation, dated May 4, 1868, that the American ambassador in Paris, John A. Dix, had given Moreno to show William Seward when he arrived in the United States. The Captain was proud of it, and he considered the memento proof of his respectability. He told the reporter that whatever he wrote in Italy or America he had been for the sole purpose of ending the shady trafficking of the *padroni* that kept their poor compatriots in slavery.[77]

During his imprisonment, Moreno made his voice heard again. He wrote to the *Washington Post* to commemorate his "discovery" of the island of Pulau Weh, where, he had recently read, Russia intended to build a refueling station for its fleet so that it would no longer have to depend on British or Japanese stations. The Captain recalled offering the island to the United States, saying that he still had the June 11, 1868, document in which he offered it to Congress for $750,000. The newspaper added that Moreno was well and that he passed his time reading newspapers and chatting in the prison's "big rotunda" with everyone who stopped him. Above all, he wrote.[78]

As if the sentence had not been enough, as soon as Moreno was out of jail he published a new collection with his usual stubbornness. The pamphlet was bilingual (Italian and English) and contained clippings and various documents about his campaign against the *padroni*. It was published on February 21, 1896, less than a month after the Captain had finished his sentence. It was titled *History of a Great Wrong: Italian Slavery in America/ Storia di un gran male: Schiavitù italiana in America*. An excessively long subtitle called for the attention of *The representatives of the King of Italy, Ambassadors Corti, Blanc, and Fava; the past and present Consuls, the padroni, their accomplices, and the Agents/Brokers. The horrors, miseries, cruelties, atrocities, thefts, disappointments, tears, desolation, sorrows, crimes, punishments, demoralization, tormented, and tormentors*. The only Italian section, which began on page 30 of 53, began with a title page that included the following: "Celso Cesare Moreno, the well-known gentleman and Italian patriot, tells the truth about the infamous Italian padroni, the ignorant, corrupt, despised, and ridiculed Ambassador Don Basilio Fava, the consuls of the King of Italy and the unhappy Italian slaves in America."

The English part opened with a preface (pages 1–8) titled "A Deplorable Error" in which a rather combative Moreno lamented that he had been denied "man's most sacred right," that is, "to defend himself when he is certain he is right." While the court allowed the reading of Fava's messages to American authorities about the creation of the Ellis Island office for the protection of Italian immigrants, it had not permitted a public reading of the Captain's materials. In court, Moreno had recalled the words of the Irish patriot Robert Emmett, who had exclaimed before his English judges: "I was condemned before being judged." Moreno claimed to have put great faith in the judicial process to order to raise his voice even louder against the "great evil" of the *padroni*.

Moreno criticized the ratio that his American judge had supposedly employed, "the greater the truth, the great the defamation," an idea that seemed to him not just unfair but "un-American." Thirty-five years after the abolition of slavery, it must have been disgusting for Americans to see their court take the side of the Italian *padroni* and punish the man who had fought them for twenty-six years. He had been denied freedom of thought and of the press. Moreover, history was repeating itself. Moreno had touched the same violent destiny that had already touched Charles Sumner, John Brown, and President Lincoln. He only hoped that Judge Cole and District Attorney Birney would one day recognize their error.

Moreno reiterated that he had never met Fava nor desired to meet him. In a strange assertion for the man who bragged about his American citizenship, he added, "I pay taxes in Italy, so I contribute to his annual salary of $16,000, and for this I have the right and the duty to object to his base and shameful manner of representing the great Italian nation." Moreno returned to his usual arguments that the embassy was housed in a third-rate pension and that the ambassador had lunch with anyone "like a wandering beggar" between Washington and New York, New London and Newport, Lenox, Boston, and Bar Harbor, for the sole purpose of profiting from the funds that Rome allotted for his food.

Moreno also resumed his anti-Semitic insults and connected them to his attacks on the false nobility:

> Fava is a name of a bean that is given in Italy to horses, mules, and donkeys, like in America you give them oats. Fava means this, and does not refer to any noble or feudal title; it follows that the title of Baron and Baroness de Fava is simply ridiculous and vacuous, and similarly are the titles of count given to the barbers Verdi and Oldrini in Washington, and to L. P. Cesnola in New York, friends and advisers to Fava. Moreover, there is in Italy no hereditary noble title among Jews, who are not lords nor have ancestors.

In a crescendo of fury, he also described former Prime Minister Crispi and Minister of Foreign Affairs Blanc as "two of the most immoral, corrupt, mercenary, and despised charlatans of Italian politics," and insulted their wives Lina Barbagallo and Therry Blanc. In the Italian pages of his pamphlet, he heavily insinuated that the latter had been a prostitute.[79] He maintained that Crispi and Blanc, fearing that the trial might pose a danger, had interfered with it, pouring 50,000 lire, taxpayers' money, into it for a good outcome. The *padroni* contributed $10,000 for the same purpose. Moreno was very vague on the details, and he did not say if this money was used to soften some official. Nevertheless, he spewed bile against Fava, who was always "deaf, blind, and dumb" with the *padroni*. He claimed that it "is not a myth, but a fact" that appointing Oldrini to the Italian Office had perpetuated the desires of the *padroni*. Moreno then made a (wrong) prediction: that on March 5, with the opening of the Italian Parliament and the fall of the current cabinet, the diplomatic corps would also collapse.

Moreno also cast suspicion on the agricultural colony in Sunnyside, Arkansas, and on the nature of its labor contracts, which, as an exception to the rule, had recruited seven hundred Italian laborers through an agreement negotiated between Austin Corbin and the mayor of Rome, Prince Ruspoli. Sunnyside's vast cotton plantations represented the possibility of realizing Fava's dream to send the best Italian laborers to the United States. Between 1895 and 1897, a sizeable contingent of workers had arrived with a guarantee of fair economic treatment and the possibility of owning their own homes in the future. Corbin's death in 1896 and various difficulties ultimately caused the project to fail, but at the time of Moreno's publication, there was still some reason for hope. But the Capitano Marittimo was unable to restrain himself, and he alleged, among other things, that Fava's son was the owner of some lands involved in the operation.

The History of a Great Wrong (which in Italy received the honor of a favorable review by the great Luigi Einaudi of Dogliani)[80] was a comprehensive collection of articles. The first was the article from *Colored America* that had sparked the legal action. Others were connected to the first, successful campaign in defense of the child slaves, a problem that Moreno could say that he had fought against for some time. He launched "a crusade" to rekindle the theme in 1885, asking Senator Blair of New Hampshire and a delegation from the American Federation of Labor to propose a law forbidding the importation of Italian contract labor. The following year he repeated the request to Representatives Martin Foran of Ohio and Lowering of Massachusetts (page 9–17). The articles from the 1880s discussed measures to be adopted on the theme of "imported contract labor." There was also Senator Blair's speech from the debate over law 2550, printed in the *Congressional Record* on February 18, 1885, in which Blair read an open letter from Moreno.

In many of the documents, the Captain repeated his assessment that complicity in the trafficking of workers was an expression of organized crime, often called "camorra," sometimes "mafia": "an association or gang . . . of criminals that have ramifications in all the cities, towns, villages, and rural districts in this vast continent and even in Washington under the eyes of the Goddess of Liberty."[81]

In the long run, this focus on organizations that broke the law made an impression on America, practically becoming the cornerstone of anti-Italian prejudice during the severe economic crisis of the 1890s, a time when many people called for the doors of immigration to be closed. In one of the most recent studies of the Moreno case, Teresa Fava Thomas argues that the Captain's long campaign against Fava, although apparently fruitless, should be considered one of the impetuses behind that closure. We can ask ourselves if Moreno was aware of this. Did he know, as he was denouncing the dubious collusion between the *padroni* and diplomats, that he was in the service of anti-Italian, and more generally, xenophobic, designs?

We tend to doubt this, but there are certainly some moments from that campaign that elicit questions, and some positions that lend themselves to ambiguous interpretations. Perhaps the Captain did not realize that, at a certain point, there were those who thought to take advantage of him. Or perhaps he did have doubts, but, seized by his irrepressible desire for self-aggrandizement, he did not understand the full meaning of what was happening.

Among the many materials in *History of a Great Wrong* was an article from Washington's *Daily Critic* on November 1, 1890. The article reported that in New Orleans, where there was an ongoing investigation into events that would lead to the lynching of eleven Sicilians the following year, "a frightening Italian secret society, the Mafia" had called for the death of Hennessy, the chief of police. That "trail" led directly to Moreno's testimony in front of the Senate immigration committee the previous March 20. He spoke about the Camorra and the Mafia, which was received as indirect confirmation of Italians' guilt. In fact, the mayor of New Orleans sent Moreno a message praising him for "his statements made to the Senate commission," which seemed to mirror the situation in New Orleans.[82] As Fava Thomas noted, "While Moreno denounces lynching he earns praise from Mayor Shakespeare who helped shield the lynchers." She also suggested an interesting comparison. Moreno's obsessively repeated accusations resembled the anticommunist tirades of Joseph McCarthy, with whom Moreno also shared insufficient evidence and numbers that were always contradictory.

According to Fava Thomas, however, under the new McKinley administration (1896) Moreno's accusations ended up dealing a great blow to the project for the expansion of the Italian Bureau of Ellis Island. The meeting of two technically opposed points of view produced insurmountable obstacles for the Italian office that Fava wanted. The first was the position of mayors who feared that immigration would steal work from Americans and allow dangerous people into the country at a time when the anarchist threat was acute. The second was supporters of a politics of power whose position would be boosted by war in 1898. The two viewpoints were embodied by Terence Powderly, the grand master of the Knights of Labor and the superintendent of immigration after succeeding Stump in 1897; and the Republican senator from Massachusetts, Henry Cabot Lodge, who became the voice of the Immigration Restriction League, which was particularly opposed to Italian immigrants.

Moreno influenced both Powderly and Lodge. In 1899, Powderly was called to testify in front of the U.S. Industrial Commission about the status of labor. He said that not only did Italians fail to respect the Alien Contract Labor Law, but the Italian Office, which he had already had tried to abolish the year prior, helped them do this. He identified Moreno as his source: "I have heard him say that the Bureau is only an agency of the *padroni*." The accusation provoked astonishment in Rome because it was based on the fantasies of an ex-convict. There was even more astonishment and protests from Fava when the Commission interrogated the head of the Italian Bureau, Egisto Rossi, demonstrating considerable preconceptions about the Office's activities. It ultimately had to close.

CHAPTER 9

The Destiny of Hawaii

In the spring of 1887, Moreno published a new pamphlet, *The Position of Men and Affairs in Hawaii*, a long "Open Letter to His Majesty King Kalākaua," dated Washington, August 7, 1886.

From the first lines there was a new request for reimbursement of the expenses that Moreno incurred for the maintenance of Wilcox, Booth, and Boyd. The bill should have been settled at least six years earlier, but the king had remained deaf and blind "at the instigation of your Guizot, the Mormon criminal Walter Murray Gibson," forgetting "your duty as an honest man, friend, and king." Since July 1882, Kalākaua had made it known on many occasions that if Moreno contacted Gibson, he would be paid soon. But Moreno had not done so because, as he wrote, "I do not wish to dishonor myself by entering into a correspondence with a Mormon convict and fugitive, whose position should be in the barrier reef [the state prison in Honolulu] for life and not in the government." To Moreno, Gibson was nothing but a permanent insult to decency and morality who would ultimately foment the people's hatred against the king.

Gibson was a very ambiguous character indeed. After the adventures that we related in Chapter 5, he purchased the Honolulu newspaper *Pacific*

Commercial Advertiser in 1880. He had endured defeat, while Moreno, in no time, had supplanted him in Kalākaua's heart. But then Gibson eclipsed the Captain's star in 1882, when the king appointed him minister of foreign affairs. In 1886, Kalākaua promoted him to prime minister.

In his new pamphlet, Moreno called Gibson a reborn Judas Iscariot in search of the protection needed to free himself from his uncomfortable past as an escaped convict from a Dutch prison. Gibson, he said, had not hesitated to devise a plan to either dethrone his benefactor Kalākaua or force him to abdicate. Moreno lamented the fact that John E. Bush had decided to admit Gibson "as a member of the special council."

In Gibson's luck, Moreno saw the signs of an elaborate plot. All his enemies from his Hawaiian period played some part in it:

> All the stupid rumors, lies, slander, intimidation, and quixotic boasting of the so-called "great American general, statesman, and journalist" namely that trombone by the name of Comly from Toledo, Ohio, and his absolute *padroni* Clauss Spreckles [*sic*] and the pusillanimous Christian missionaries (who are very rich and pay their servile tools well), in the months of August and September 1880, they did well by their religious rival, the Mormon missionary W.M. Gibson, who is the living antithesis of their beliefs, of their customs, of their trafficking.[1]

Gibson, according to Moreno, had no qualifications for the role of prime minister. He was nothing but "an ordinary crook, a shameless charlatan of low rank, a slimy, callous, and superficial politician" who was seriously undermining the Kingdom, and who would bring Kalākaua to the same humiliating exile that had already happened to Ismail Pasha, the Khedive of Egypt: "A similar crisis is rapidly approaching Hawaii, whether because of the exasperation of the natives and resident foreigners or foreign interference, and he who does not see it is blind."[2]

Moreno positioned his Hawaiian misadventures within a wider geopolitical framework. It was no accident that he was "the projector" of the transpacific cable, and Cyrus W. Field was "the opposer." It was he who sent "the hypocrite son of a missionary 'General' Armstrong" to Hawaii in 1880 to plot against the project and against Moreno with the assistance of Comly and another suitable accomplice, the Italian consul Schaefer, who had been "appointed without even being known to the Italian Minister of Foreign Affairs." Moreno, as usual, dedicated numerous poisonous passages to Schaefer in his pamphlet. He had sent Rome a series of "false" reports against Moreno and against the king himself in 1880 and 1881.

Moreno claimed that he had read three confidential reports about the Reciprocity Treaty, and advised that it was intended to make Kalākaua a second-rate figure, handing the real power to Gibson and Spreckels. They were laughing about Kalākaua in public, in San Francisco, Washington, Philadelphia, and New York. Therefore the king should get rid of such a dangerous entourage as soon as possible and recover the dignity of his predecessor, Kamehameha V.

In Moreno's view, the treaty was a very good thing, as long as the king removed Gibson's gang, which comprised "men who monopolize it for their own interests and to the detriment of American taxpayers, who no longer receive cheap sugar, and of the excellent natives, who deserve a better fate and a king with greater firmness and most correct judgment." The king should also free himself from Carter and Mott Smith, the two missionaries in Washington.[3] Then Moreno took on "Niven Armstrong" and "Kalabash Judd," calling one "a blabbermouth barber" and the other "a vulgar butcher" who had accompanied the king on his "voyage fiasco" around the world. There had to be a total house cleaning: Moreno accused the king of trusting whomever he had spoken with last—a fault which others had often observed in the old friendship between Moreno and Kalākaua.

To make an impression upon the American reader, Moreno compared Gibson to the "jackal of New York finance" or "the infamous boss W. M. Tweed." The notorious politician, who had accumulated many public positions and appointments at the top of various companies, had been the "Grand Sachem" of Tammany Hall, the control center of the New York Democratic Party. In 1871, Tweed was arrested and convicted of stealing millions of dollars in public funds. Moreno launched a vigorous tirade against the Dutchman Spreckels (who was an immigrant and neither Dutch nor Jewish) as "the Jewish fruit seller," and as "de facto king," whom Moreno accused of "wolfish rapaciousness" and other monstrous inclinations. Between these two monsters, Kalākaua was only "the fat and timid lamb."

To conclude, his "immutable friend" Moreno repeated his "peremptory demand" to the king for the refund owed him. According to Moreno, the Hawaiian legislature had appropriated $15,000 for him in 1880 and another $30,000 in 1882.

He attached an extensive postscript dated April 7, 1887. Again Moreno brought up the reimbursement and reminded the king that he had received assurances from him on July 1 and 2, 1881, in the Hotel Royal des Etrangers in Naples, and again on July 4 at the Hotel du Quirinal in Rome. Then Moreno repeated his accusations against Gibson and an alliance formed at the very moment that "Government, Congress, and public opinion in America are determined to put an end to the scandal of Mormonism . . . suppressing it in Salt Lake City and in the entire Utah territory." It was a real insult to progress, in particular to the "gentle sex," and the destruction of more than a half century of good work accomplished by Christian nations in Hawaii: "The Mormons are an immoral remnant of paganism and barbarism." In this way, relations between Hawaii and the United States were ruined, since the misdeeds of the Mormon bandit were well known in the archives in Washington. One thing, Moreno added, must be clear:

> President Cleveland, Secretary of State Bayard, and Deputy Secretary Porter decided not to allow the present geographic and political situation of the Hawaiian and Samoan islands to be changed for the benefit of any European or Asian nation, even if this must involve all the power of the United States; they will not also allow any foreign influence to prevail in these islands, nor that trespassing or transfer of territory occur. The unalterable status quo of Polynesia is the short-term policy of the United States.[4]

According to Moreno, the modern and enlightened proved less wise than savage King Malietoa Laupepa of Samoa, who had refused the king's protection. Moreno said that a German copy of the document in which Malietoa declined the offer had arrived in Washington. The document said that the king of Hawaii "does not know how to protect himself and offers to others what he does not possess and which he would have great need of for himself and his race." In Apia, "grocers, Mormons, and convicts do not govern, but must stay in their place."[5]

Here Moreno referred to the complex oceanic cases of 1866. While Samoa experienced an ongoing revolt led by the tribal leader Tamasese, supported by the Germans, against King Malietoa, Hawaii decided to send an ambassador to Apia, John E. Bush. Bush, whose diplomatic responsibilities also included Tonga, left Honolulu on the steamer *Zealandia* (the same one on which Moreno had sailed) on December 26, 1886. The (secret) idea of Kalākaua and Prime Minister Gibson was a federation under the guidance of the only constitutional kingdom in Oceania, which could include Samoa as well as Tonga, the Cook Islands, and perhaps the Gilbert Islands (to their great advantage, as Kalākaua had pointed out in a public speech in March 1886). The Hawaiian proposal generated enough enthusiasm in Apia that Malietoa signed the agreement on February 17, 1887. It was celebrated with a party that Robert Louis Stevenson described in *A Footnote to History*. A month later, Kalākaua approved the agreement, although with the stipulation that Malietoa had to meet his agreements with foreign powers.

The situation in Samoa was very complicated. That year, it was the subject of an international conference in Washington among the United States, Great Britain, and Germany. The Hawaii–Samoa accord was received very badly as undue interference. The Germans saw it as a worthless initiative, since Malietoa was not recognized as the sovereign by a majority of his people, and Germany threatened to declare war against Hawaii.[6] At that time, the future was already clear to the Western powers: Samoa would go to Germany, Tonga to Great Britain, and Hawaii to the United States. By June 1887, hope for the oceanic federation had already collapsed. Bush was recalled to Hawaii on the steamer *Kaimiloa*, a Hawaiian ship armed with six cannons that had been sent to Apia for the purpose, more symbolic than anything else, of protecting King Malietoa during the tribal conflict. Soon after, the "Bayonet Constitution" ended Hawaiian imperial ambitions.[7]

A resumption of the projects that Moreno had supported in the Pacific was recognizable during the final phase of Gibson's time in government. In his pamphlet, released shortly after the Samoa–Hawaii agreement, Moreno claimed he had discussed the project with Kalākaua since November 26, 1879. Then he and Governor Dominis, another "Italian" from Hawaii, the son of a man from Trieste, had discussed some projects related to a Chinese shipping company and the transpacific cable. Moreno said that if Kalākaua truly intended to follow the example of King Vittorio Emanuele II and unify the entire Polynesian race under his rule, making Honolulu "a royal Washington," he needed advisers up to the task, and Moreno gave the example of Camillo Benso, Count of Cavour. He reminded the king:

> The first step I proposed to achieve the union of all the Polynesian islands into one kingdom was to take immediate possession of the Ocean Islands, which I passed through on the steamship that took me from Canton to Honolulu at the beginning of November 1879 and then, gratefully, group after group, to annex all the other islands, naturally with the approval (plebiscite) of the leaders and people.[8]

But now the project was destined to end badly, Moreno said, because of Gibson, who Kalākaua himself had spoken badly of "dozens of times." Kalākaua had changed and he believed his bad advisors' slander against his real friends. He even believed Ferdinando De Luca, the "scoundrel" who, after Moreno's crusade against child trafficking, had wound up in Shanghai, where he met Kalākaua during his trip around the world. He told

Kalākaua lies about Moreno that "you took as true and that caused you to shut yourself away from all sympathy, respect, and honor when you arrived in Rome, because of your impolite behavior unworthy of a king surrounded by bad company, after the great reception which I had obtained for you in Naples when you landed on the classic shores of Italy."[9]

Moreno was obsessed. The king had "disgusted" the islands' best men, "the pillars of the nation," and mentioned, among the others, the banker and philanthropist Charles R. Bishop; the wealthy ship owner and former interior minister (dismissed at the time of the "Moreno episode") Samuel Gardner Wilder; the businessman, very close to the Hawaiian monarchy, James Isaac Dowsett; the annexationist doctor John Strayer McGrew; the future president of the short-lived Republic of Hawaii and then governor and federal judge Sanford B. Dole; and Judge Alfred S. Hartwell. He was offering the world "a very miserable spectacle of instability, incompetence, insincerity, ingratitude, and wicked subordination to the two bosses Gibson and Spreckels." All this made Kalākaua "the most miserable mortal in Polynesia," a man Malietoa could have offered protection, instead of receiving it from him. "Long live Malietola and down with the servants and cowards."

The Captain then told the ugly story of a $70,000 bribe by a Chinese company in 1886. The company sought a law to obtain a license for manufacturing and selling opium in Hawaii. The reference was to the "Opium Act" that sought to legalize the sale and production of opium with appropriate taxation and the exclusion of native Hawaiians from the trade. Though many of the leaders of the archipelago officially condemned it, they were supposedly engaged in this business for profit. The king and the government issued two licenses a year with a starting bid of $40,000. A Chinese merchant and sugar planter, Tong Kee, alias Aki, offered Kalākaua a gift of $75,000 to secure the license. The king accepted $71,000 in advance, and was to receive the other $4,000 when the license had been granted. But another Chinese man, Chun Lung, won the bidding for a reported $80,000. The scandal broke at the end of May 1887. Aki died, perhaps poisoned, on the eve of his deposition in which Kalākaua expected to be exonerated. Overwhelmed by approximately a quarter million dollar in debts, Kalākaua gave a trust the responsibility of paying the creditors. This excluded the Aki case from his more urgent obligations, and the king was met with a lawsuit. In September 1888, the king was ordered to compensate Aki's heirs.[10]

Along with the missteps in Samoa, this scandal inspired the Hawaiian League to impose the "Bayonet Constitution" with the cancellation of the Opium Act. Paradoxically, the proponents of the new Hawaiian order were also in the opium business. In 1892, a new Opium Act was approved, and it was one of the strongest justifications for the overthrow of Queen Lili'uokalani.

According to Moreno, the affair was well known in the United States and viewed very negatively. Similarly, the loan of $2 million guaranteed by the London bankers Skinner, Mathieson, and Hoffnung (the Hawaiian chargés d'affaires in London)

> is believed to have been used to replenish an empty Hawaiian Treasury, arising from the misappropriation of an enormous sum of money since May 1882, that is from the beginning of the Mormon, criminal, and monopoly form of government, and not for the development of the country, that is to build streets, docks, telegraphs, nor to ensure that Hawaii is in suitable condition to obtain the benefits that it should derive from them, for its strategic geographic position it occupies in the Pacific from the opening of the canals in Panama and Nicaragua.[11]

According to Moreno, the Hawaiian deficit, whose size was not yet clear, was large enough to cause financial collapse. It was necessary for a supervisory committee presided over by the "honorable and fearless Sanford Dole" to immediately go to work and identify the damages and punish the guilty—who were obviously, as Moreno repeated for the umpteenth time, "the Mormon Gibson and the Jew Spreckels."

Moreno's final point was that a "Christian, moral, and civil" nation could not enter into a reciprocity treaty with nations that did not meet a similar standard. But Hawaii was governed by a man, Gibson, who in that kind of nation "would have been deprived of civil and political rights, and thrown into jail for life." The treaty risked being monopolized "by three foreign pagans," meaning Spreckels, Gibson, and the Chinese Buddhist Ah Fong: "A very funny trio."[12]

Moreno formulated his sinister prophesy: "The unfortunate King Kalākaua is so involved in the Gibson-Spreckels web that he is obligated to swim with them, until the two scoundrels will have no more need of him, and they will let him sink—*abyssus abyssum invocat.*" He concluded with a return to the issue of the king's debts to Moreno: "As soon as Your Majesty pays his debts to me, so much the better will it be for everyone. A rapid agreement will not only save further accumulation of interest, but also the heavy expenses of recovering the claim." And a final threat: "To be continued."[13]

Moreno's grim predictions seemed to come true on June 30, 1887. An assembly of Hawaiian residents, convened by Sanford B. Dole and including the Honolulu Rifles militia, asked King Kalākaua to dismiss Gibson's government and promulgate a new constitution. The Honolulu Rifles arrested Gibson the next day under the pretext that a secret cache of weapons had been discovered—they were actually pistols used by farmers to drive birds away from their fields. The king asked for the assistance of the American ambassador George W. Merrill and other representatives from Great Britain, France, Portugal, and Japan. He was advised to agree to the requests, and so Lawrence Thurston became minister of the interior and William L. Green became prime minister as well as minister of finance. Kalākaua signed the new constitution—called the Bayonet Constitution for the manner in which it had been obtained—on July 6. A group of lawyers had drawn it up, including Thurston, Dole, William Ansel Kinney, William Owen Smith, Edward Griffin Hitchcock, and George Norton Wilcox (Robert's cousin). It was an influential lobby that favored the end of the Kingdom of Hawaii and its annexation to the United States. Gibson escaped the archipelago, where he now feared for his life. He took refuge in San Francisco, where, reduced to poverty, he died on January 21, 1888.

Kalākaua became a constitutional monarch. The legislature and the government held most of the power. The king was no longer above the law, as he had been under the 1864 constitution. He lost the greater share of his authority, particularly his veto power, which could now be circumvented with the approval of two-thirds of the legislature. The upper house, the House of Nobles, was no longer made up of individuals appointed by the king but instead of elected representatives. In practice, this put the legislature in the hands of the richest landowners, the only ones who could exercise the vote either actively or passively.

The Reciprocity Treaty of 1875 was renewed for an additional seven years. The United States secured exclusive navigation rights to the bay of the Pearl River, on the island of Oahu, and the maintenance of a refueling and repair station at Pearl Harbor. In his first speech to the Hawaiian legislature in 1887, King Kalākaua reported that the treaty had been renewed under the same terms as 1875, "with the addition of a clause that guarantees United States vessels the exclusive right to enter Pearl River Harbor and to establish in that place a recoaling and repair station." The clause had been added after lengthy consideration and with explicit instructions that it would not involve ceding any territory, sovereignty, or jurisdiction. Secretary of State Bayard reaffirmed this interpretation on December 8, 1887, "as simply presented in good faith and accepted with doubt or hesitation."

There was a showdown in the Pacific, with the Western powers making the rules. Moreno called the 1887 revolt "an armed tyranny," supported by the Honolulu Rifle Volunteers, which he characterized as a foreign legion.[14] But grave upheavals, all negative for the indigenous population, were not limited to Hawaii. Malietoa Laupepa, the old king of Samoa, had to bend his head to his new German masters, who had dethroned him and put Tamasese in his place. After seizing him, they imprisoned him in Africa for seven months and then for a year in the Jaluit Atoll, in the Marshall Islands. There he was subjected to such cruelty that during the voyage from Jaluit to Samoa, where he had been brought back at the time of the Conference of Berlin to be nominally restored as king, he had attempted suicide by jumping overboard. According to Moreno, a similar fate was not difficult to imagine for Hawaii and Kalākaua, so powerful were the appetites of the European nations, particularly England and Germany, and soon Japan and China, if the United States did not step forward to stop them.[15]

At this point the oldest and most brilliant of the three young Hawaiians whose education the Capitano Marittimo had overseen returns to our story: Robert Wilcox. In December 1885, he completed his studies at the military academy in Turin, obtaining the rank of lieutenant, and he entered the artillery school. In that period he had also met the Baroness Maria Carolina Isabella Luigia (Gina) Sobrero, the daughter of Lorenzo, a Piedmontese army colonel and father-in-law of the future Prime Minister Giovanni Giolitti, and the Neapolitan noblewoman Vittoria Colonna di Stigliano. He married her on June 15, 1887. The new Hawaiian political order established by the Bayonet Constitution and the Reform Party's seizure of power ended Kalākaua's education program. In October 1887, Wilcox received orders to return home.[16]

After an initial and quickly abandoned position obtained for him by Superintendent of the Water Works Charles B. Wilson, Wilcox was convinced that Kalākaua no longer had the power to protect the Hawaiian people. Along with Wilson and Sam Nowlein, a colonel in Kalākaua's royal guard and the father of Maile Nowlein, the only woman included in the king's study-abroad program (she was sent to study art and music in Turin and Florence), Wilcox conceived of a coup d'état to replace Kalākaua with his sister Lili'uokalani. But it came to nothing, and in February 1888 Wilcox left Hawaii for Italy with his wife. Moving to San Francisco, California, he worked as a surveyor for the Spring Valley Water Company while his wife gave Italian and French lessons. But when Wilcox decided to return to the archipelago in the spring of 1889, the couple finally separated. Gina returned to Italy with their daughter, who died shortly thereafter, while Wilcox began the "heroic" phase of his revolutionary activity. It lasted until his death in 1903 and saw him on the front lines as a politician, a columnist for a bilingual newspaper that he founded and edited, and a rather controversial figure, accused of adopting lost causes and being a turncoat, but always inspired, even if in contradictory ways, by a sincere Hawaiian patriotism.

Back in Hawaii and in close contact with Lili'uokalani (he stayed in a house on her property), Wilcox organized an uprising on the night of July 30, 1889. It was a very strange undertaking whose components are difficult to understand, in particular the roles played by the king and his sister.[17] He tried to impose a new constitution, similar to the 1864 constitution, and to restore the recently checked royal powers. The rebels, led by Wilcox and Robert Boyd, another of the former "Moreno boys," included just over a hundred men who wore Garibaldian red shirts. They occupied the outskirts of the royal palace in Honolulu, but government forces overwhelmed them over the course of several hours, leaving seven dead and a dozen wounded, including Boyd. The soldiers of the American ship *Adams* soon restored order.[18]

Arrested for treason, Wilcox was tried in October but managed to avoid a conviction for conspiracy thanks to a jury of native Hawaiians. The opposite fate befell his young Chinese accomplice, Ho Fon, who was found guilty by a *haole* jury. While the newspapers of the Hawaiian establishment leveled harsh accusations at him, Wilcox enjoyed broad popular support. People lined up outside the prison to pay tribute to a man who was among the very few leaders capable of opposing the Reform Party's dominance.[19] Wilcox formed the new National Reform Party, whose objective was the restoration of the sovereign's power. In 1890, he was reelected to the legislature in a campaign based on clear racial opposition to *haole* claims; he had already been elected in 1880–81, before his studies in Italy began.[20]

On January 20, 1891, King Kalākaua died in the Palace Hotel in San Francisco. He had been in California for two months seeking medical treatment. His sister, Lili'uokalani, succeeded him. She fit the image of a sovereign of refined culture and was a skilled musician. It was not an easy time. There was an economic crisis due to the reduction in the sugar import duty set by the McKinley tariff. It brought the planters to their knees and they lost their old privileges under the Reciprocity Treaty. The possibility of enjoying the same treatment reserved for American producers encouraged those favorable to annexation. The gap was clearly destined to widen between the American and European profiteer oligarchy and the queen, who drew her support from the natives and the Asians cut off from privilege by the Bayonet Constitution.

At this point Moreno appeared as an "agent of the National Party of Hawaii," which shows him in perfect, or pretend, agreement with his old pupil Wilcox. He warned U.S. President Harrison about British machinations to take possession of the islands with the queen's consent. The Hawaiian consul in San Francisco, D. A. McKinley, was careful to immediately deny the existence of the English plan.[21]

"I will be more damaged than anyone," said Moreno, "for the reason that the English government will not recognize the law that the U.S. Congress passed on August 15, 1876, which gave me and my associates the right and the charter to lay the cable . . . between the United States, the Hawaiian islands, Japan, Korea, China, and Siam." He concluded: "The revolution, which will be the fruit of the discontent produced by greed, intense selfishness, intrigues, and also by the arrogance of the English, is imminent and will be full of significance." Bush and Wilcox, individuals "ready for the present situation" would lead it.[22]

Hawaii now faced an additional challenge to its form of government. Wilcox, who was also accused of maintaining a "subversive correspondence" with Moreno, now believed that it was necessary to shift from a monarchy to a republic since such a negative situation persisted in Hawaii. The problem was that the United States was going to permanently establish itself in Puloa (Pearl Harbor) with Lili'uokalani's approval. Therefore, a move toward a republic could encourage annexation.[23] In the summer of 1892, Moreno raised the specter of British greed in the Pacific, and he put it on a collision course with American interests, even as the possible cause of an armed conflict.[24]

His correspondence with Wilcox became more frequent during this period. Moreno regularly sent the letters that he received from Honolulu to American newspapers. The situation deteriorated and he feared a rupture in the fragile agreements with the United States. The kingdom reported a series of government crises. Wilcox was very pessimistic about the future of Queen Lili'uokalani. His political speeches increasingly touched on the possibility of Hawaii's becoming a republic, and he told Moreno about the Hawaiian intention to send a commission to Washington and ascertain the state of what he called the "gold mine" of Hawaii, Pearl Harbor.[25]

In this phase, Moreno took on the role of mediator. At the same time, he portrayed himself as the most trustworthy friend of the Hawaiian natives, who demanded, to quote Wilcox, "a representative government and not a personal executive led by favorites."[26] He also represented himself as a patriot committed to promoting the interests of the United States.

The situation in Hawaii worsened. Embroiled in an exhausting struggle with the Legislature, Queen Lili'uokalani suspended the legislature in January 1893. She proposed a new constitution intended to restore the crown's prerogatives, practically dusting off the ideals of the 1889 insurrection. The government was opposed. On January 17, the royal palace of 'Iolani was taken by a committee of public health led by Lorrin A. Thurston, a member of the business community tied to the Reform Party, with the support of the Honolulu Rifles and the U.S. Marines, whose intervention was requested by the American ambassador, John L. Stevens, to protect the interests of American noncombatants. The queen asked Wilcox to command the troops loyal to her. Perhaps, as Andrade suggested, Wilcox's loyalty was not particularly certain, since soon thereafter, to avoid unnecessary bloodshed, the queen was arrested and confined to house arrest in her palace.

She appealed to the constitution and the United States government to declare the interim government in Honolulu illegal and reinstate her on the throne, noting Stevens's abuse. Wilcox's newspaper, *The Liberal*—whose party, with the motto "Hawaii for the Hawaiians," was called the National Liberal Party—resumed publication at the end of January. On January 25, it published an article in which the "Garibaldi of Hawaii," in an unforeseen move, declared that the monarchy had committed suicide because of its own inability to resolve a crisis that it had created. At the same time, Wilcox began a discussion about the island's future as one of the United States or even as part of the state of California. That position, however, conflicted with that of the large landowners, who were instead interested in the status of a U.S. territory. As such, American labor laws would not be introduced, and they could perpetuate a policy of cheap labor. Wilcox's presence at a meeting sponsored by the Annexation Club made a stir, and what he said, even more so: "the era of Hawaiian independence was over and the best way that the natives had to ensure their freedom was to support annexation."[27]

In March, President Cleveland established a commission to investigate the situation in Honolulu after Lili'uokalani's appeal. He condemned the American intervention and spoke out against annexation. The Hawaiian interim government had sent a draft treaty to his Republican predecessor, Benjamin Harrison, who brought it to the Senate for ratification on February 15. The Democrat Cleveland, who became president on March 4, withdrew the treaty as one of his first acts. Moreno celebrated his decision, again playing the fatherly mediator. Addressing a letter to the Honolulu newspaper *Hawaii Kolomua* (and reprinting it in the *Washington Post*), he hoped that in the archipelago would warmly welcome the U.S. envoy,

Commissioner J. H. Blount. He had to ascertain the situation there, and Moreno depicted Blount as "an erudite person, just, human, a philosopher and metaphysician, perfectly adequate for dealing with a primitive, honest, warm, and friendly race, which you Hawaiians have been in the past, are in the present, and will be in the future, when these qualities are innate in you." He recommended that his beloved Hawaiians welcome the envoy of the "great and good American nation" without suspicion. He was a "powerful friend," who "will not do you any wrong nor permit others to do any," as was demonstrated by President Cleveland's decision to remove the annexation treaty from the Senate.[28]

To Moreno's satisfaction, Blount had sent Cleveland a clear picture by July. On this basis, Ambassador Stevens was removed and there were discussions with the provisional government about the restoration of Lili'uokalani. At the same time, Moreno sent John Edward Bush, a former minister and Kalākaua's envoy in the unfortunate Samoan mission, useful information to publish in the opposition newspaper *Ka Leo*, which was printed in Hawaiian. He also sent the American press letters and articles favorable to the queen's cause to counter the interim government's abundant journalistic output.[29]

Wilcox, after his brief flirtation with the provisional government, again changed camps; according to Andrade, he realized that he would never have obtained any compensation worthy of consideration from it.[30] He proved optimistic and combative, especially after the nomination of a new American ambassador, Albert S. Willis. In a letter to Moreno, he made a "caustic" critique of William DeWitt Alexander's book on the history of Hawaii. Wilcox hoped that Willis would receive full authority as soon as possible "to restore the queen's government, unjustly overthrown by Stevens in the most dishonorable way."[31] In a subsequent letter, he ridiculed the absurd sham that was the provisional government. In order to impress Willis, it had barricaded the palace with sandbags. He boasted, "I could get them out in a few hours with a hundred men of the queen's old guard. . . . A little cannon fire would annihilate them forever." Even this topic had a notable political implication. Moreno raised it a few days later to show how the provisional government's armed forces had only one native Hawaiian soldier, the others being a collection of mercenaries that comprised "the dregs of all nations," put together by "pious missionaries for the purpose of defending themselves and intimidating the natives and other peaceful residents."[32]

Ambassador Willis pushed for the queen to be restored to her throne alongside an amnesty for those responsible for the putsch. Lili'uokalani agreed in December. Willis confronted Dole and ordered him to disband the provisional government, but they refused outright. Cleveland, however, had already sent a message to Congress calling the Hawaiian revolution "improper." In response, the Senate, which was unhappy with the nomination of Blount, whom Cleveland had chosen without consultation, charged its Foreign Relations Committee, presided over by a Democratic senator from Alabama, John Tyler Morgan, to collect statements about the Hawaiian question.

In January 1894, Moreno worked feverishly on a sequel to his 1887 pamphlet: *The Hawaiian Question, or the Position of Men and Affairs in Hawaii*. The cover bore a portrait of Queen Lili'uokalani, "the most gracious queen of Hawaii." He presented it to the Senate and the House of Representatives at the beginning of February.[33] The pamphlet was a collection of his newspaper articles about the issue (we have already referenced many in these pages), accompanied by a "Conclusion" that he finished on January 31 and signed "Celso Caesar Moreno of Dogliani, Projector of the Trans-Pacific Cable." It stated that, until that moment, the only true information Congress had received on the complex Hawaiian question came from Blount's report and Ambassador Willis's correspondence. In his usual aggressive style, Moreno added, "I believe that the mission of the missionaries from Hawaii in Washington representing the so-called provisional government and wanting to testify before the Senate's investigating committee is nothing but the means of a deceptive, gossiping, slanderous, and arrogant venture intended to squander the finances of the Kanaka."

He directed a *captatio benevolentiae* toward Senator Morgan, whom he called "the Cato and Demosthenes of the American Senate," and whom Moreno admired for his patience in confronting the trite lies of the missionary clique, which was "a calamity worse than leprosy" for Hawaii and something comparable to the Spanish Inquisition. In a frenzied crescendo of accusations, Moreno called the Hawaiian missionaries, who were "despised and feared by the natives" as well as the Chinese, Japanese, Portuguese, and Polynesian communities, "uncivilized, without shame, decency or honor; arrogant, greedy, cruel, absolute egoists, insulting to men and women, mentally weak, incapable of speech, of lewd habits, immoral thieves, drunkards, polygamists, outlaws, capable of every trick and crime, moneylenders and shopkeepers, heartless usurers, worse than the Jews of the Bowery in New York and D Street in Washington."

It is perhaps superfluous to observe that this distinguished company of authentic scoundrels now included various personalities that Moreno had called "pillars of the nation" in his open letter to Kalākaua. Though Moreno usually spoke this away about Italian diplomats in America, according to him the Hawaiian missionaries behaved like them, without even disdaining the traffic in human flesh, "transporting to the sugar plantations, for so much per capita, Chinese, Japanese, Portuguese workers, from the islands of the South, or almost any other unlucky human being." They had only three rights: to work for eighteen hours a day, to die, or to be killed by ferocious overseers. Moreno, the anticlerical, curiously felt the need to point out "an honorable exception" to the cruelty of missionaries: the Catholic missionaries. They were the only ones who continued to worship "the God of Heaven and not Mammon" and did not support the idea of annexation, which was only intended as real estate speculation.

Though Moreno asked to be heard by Morgan, he had received no response up until then. Moreno also declared his profound admiration for President Cleveland, whom he had known personally since May 1885. Congress must follow his example and recognize that a diabolical plot had developed behind the backs of the queen and the Hawaiian people with the support of Stevens, who had acted "for profit and not for the prestige of the United States." Lili'uokalani's restoration to the throne was therefore the only way forward.

Indefatigable, the Captain continued taking loud initiatives, like addressing an open letter to the emperor of Japan that rattled off all of Moreno's accusations about the turmoil in Hawaii,[34] and producing other no less bizarre material for the press. Among these were letters from Wilcox and others who, expressing their deep gratitude to President Cleveland, refuted "the accusations and insinuations against Lili'uokalani's private character . . . so diligently propagated by ex-Minister Stevens and by friends in the provisional government." They were written in the hope that the Senate committee would not overturn the outcome of Blount's report and risk inciting the people to insurrection.[35]

Moreno succeeded in mobilizing his friend Frederick Douglass on the Hawaiian issue, appealing to him to raise his voice "in defense of the good and primitive Hawaiian race" and its dethroned queen. Douglass's response again was swift. He said he was certain that "if it was not for the unacceptable interference of our countrymen, Queen Lili'uokalani would be on her throne." And, with his typical references to the Bible, he added, "We are the Jews of modern times and when we want the lands of other people, such people are guilty of every species of abomination and are not fit to live. In our conduct to-day we are but repeating our treatment toward Mexico in the case of Texas."[36]

The comparison was not arbitrary. In the middle of the nineteenth century, American colonists in Texas had initially decided on succession and then annexation. But Douglass's remarks did not find the support that he expected. Another newspaper reproached him for having forgotten two things: that the queen wanted to repeal the constitution, and that she did not spare the lives of the conspirators.[37]

Unfortunately for Moreno, Wilcox, and the other Hawaiian patriots, the Senate, through the commission presided over by Morgan—a full-blown segregationist who was also said to have been "grand dragon" of the Ku Klux Klan—had already issued a report by the end of February. Its conclusion was the opposite of Blount's. The commission found Stevens and the other people involved in the events in Honolulu not guilty, with the exception of the queen. Cleveland would have to deal with the new order that had been established in the archipelago.

On May 31, 1894, the U.S. Senate passed the Turpie Resolution, named for David Turpie, a Democratic senator from Indiana, which recognized the Hawaiian people's exclusive right to decide their own form of government. It was a tombstone on Lili'uokalani's hopes, and that was how the provisional government interpreted it. On July 4—a date that was anything but random—a "bow in the direction of the United States" proclaimed the Republic of Hawaii.[38]

Even before that date, tensions in Honolulu had risen to alarming levels. Wilcox, in several letters that Moreno made public, put forth a proposal to "protect the queen." In one letter, he had maintained that "a bloody revolution will break out," adding that, whatever the Senate's verdict, "I will very soon do my duty for my country."[39]

Soon, confirming Wilcox's prophecy, the winds of counterrevolution began to blow. The loyalists, led among others by the aforementioned Sam Nowlein, needed a military leader and asked the untarnished Wilcox to assume the rule. The armed confrontation between republicans and monarchists took place on January 6, 7, and 9, 1895. There was only one victim, but it was a disaster for the monarchists. In the middle of January, they were all arrested, including Wilcox. The *New York Times* called him "nothing more than a crack-brained adventurer," inconsistent and untrustworthy, lost in smoky projects like—as he wrote in a letter to Moreno—China, which seemed to him "just now open for me to make a splendid career." The association between these two characters, with Moreno who, according to Wilcox, was in the thoughts of the deposed queen as a last resort to revive the fortunes of the Kingdom of Hawaii, was something strange and picturesque. The newspaper did not say it openly, but it was obvious that if they deemed Wilcox as a deranged adventurer, Moreno would not have enjoyed greater consideration.[40]

Wilcox was tried for high treason and condemned to death, a sentence later commuted to thirty-five years in prison. On January 1, 1898, he was pardoned thanks to President of the Republic Sanford B. Dole. He had pressed Lili'uokalani, who had also been arrested, and asked her to abdicate in exchange for the lives of Wilcox and five others. The queen accepted.

On the heels of the new imperialist drive inaugurated with American victory in the war with Spain, Hawaii was annexed as a U.S. territory on July 4, 1898, and Dole was named governor. In 1900 it was decided that the territory needed its own representative to Congress, and Wilcox, formally opposed to annexation, ran in the election. He represented a new Hawaiian independence party, called the Home Rule Party of Hawaii. Wilcox portrayed himself as the natives' unyielding champion, and he easily won the election. He remained in Congress until 1903. But all this would happen much later.

We may ask what Moreno could have gained from buzzing around the Hawaiian question, and perhaps there are several answers considering the complexity of the situation and the importance of some of its actors: Chinese businessmen, the Hawaiian royal family, and the lobby of many Pacific interests. From the autumn of 1894, however, the Capitano Marittimo's major energy and concern had shifted from Pacific geopolitics and returned to the United States where, as we have seen in the preceding chapter, dragged by his uncontrollable polemical passions, he had reached the most difficult period of his life.

CHAPTER 10

The Sunset Road

After his outburst in *History of a Great Wrong* and the battle for Hawaii, Celso Caesar Moreno ended up on the margins of the public life that had absorbed him for so long. Hard blows had been inflicted upon his credibility. The old Captain, however bold and self-confident, had to retreat to a more subdued existence. This did not stop him from continuing to frequent places of power with a certain assiduity. A newspaper reported how the untiring figure of the "habitual visitor" was perpetually in the corridors of the Capitol during the sessions of Congress. He was busy chatting up politicians whenever the occasion presented itself, but "nobody has ever learned what object he has in view."[1]

To give an idea of how far Moreno had fallen into disgrace, a 1896 article published in the *Los Angeles Times* recounted the Washington misadventures of an amusing Italian character, Stephen Nicoletti, who had been arrested following a scuffle on Pennsylvania Avenue. Nicoletti was blocking the street with a cart laden with freshly printed copies of an essay whose titled may sound quite familiar to our ears: *A Gold Conspiracy: Or, The Worst Financial System in the World, How the Bankers Get Rich, and All the Others Get Poor*. "Nice-a book, nice-a book! fifta cent; vera cheap; I write-a myself-a," Nicoletti yelled in his heavy Italian accent. The newspaper, considering his origins, ironically deemed him one of the two most illustrious representatives of the Italian community from California to New York, the other being Celso Caesar Moreno, "already Prime Minister of the King, a position he held for twenty-four hours," just out of prison for defaming Baron Fava.[2]

Moreno therefore remained a known character, a figure whose sanity some doubted. From time to time, the newspapers continued to pay attention to him. A weekly African American newspaper dedicated two almost identical covers to him a few months apart, complete with a portrait. The first time, it sketched an enthusiastic hagiography that concluded with the hope that Italy would make him its ambassador. The second time, it referred to him, from the title, as "the next Italian ambassador."[3] The newspaper had previously celebrated Moreno's love of liberty when he endorsed a resolution supporting the Republic of San Marino, introduced in Congress by New York Republican Representative Mahany following rumors that its ancient independence was in danger.[4] Moreno's "heroic" period was decidedly behind him. New leaders were emerging in the Italian community. The only remaining possibility for members of the old guard like him was playing the role of expert tutor for the latest arrivals.

Both before and after the battle with Fava, Moreno had always known how to find time to deal with many other issues. The great geopolitical game remained his most important topic, even if he now had to settle for more modest audiences. The *Gazzetta di Dogliani* happily considered him its correspondent in the United States. It printed three of his long pieces about the Anglo-American controversy over seal hunting in the Bering Sea. An Italian arbiter was involved, and the Captain took the opportunity to harshly criticize the Kingdom's foreign policy. In the same newspaper, Moreno published an expansive and pretentious article on the "social question," now the order of the day in Italy. It was dotted with solemn considerations ("The time will come when ignorance will be the worst offense and the ignorant man will be the worst delinquent"). Above all, Moreno intended to demonstrate the evolution of his political convictions, previously ascribed to the historic left, toward socialist sympathies: "Who is not a socialist in our day? He is to be considered a hundred times an ass he who, with his hand over his heart, he will dare say: I am not."[5]

There were also much smaller issues, and even these Moreno never disdained. He suggested that the city of Washington issue an identification badge to all authorized fruit sellers. He wrote articles about the flu, the "fashionable disease" that had arrived in New York from Europe, in order to praise the knowledge of renowned Italian specialists, like Senator Borelli and Professor Luigi Gori, who had faced it. Moreno participated in the movement for the erection of monuments to Christopher Columbus on the eve of the four hundredth anniversary of the discovery of America. Moreno even sent newspapers a letter from the mayor of Genoa, Baron Andrea Podestà, who had run alongside him in the 1882 elections.[6]

Toward the end of his life, Moreno often lent his assistance to the Italian American community, in which he always remained a leader and a broker who could help in dealings with American authorities. He became "the protector of the banana men."[7] Some traces of this activity remain in newspaper collections. For example, he defended Michael Cuneo, who was pursued by authorities in Washington for selling liquor without a license. Moreno spoke before city officials responsible for this and other routine issues. He became "the only thing that succeeded in interrupting the tedium of the proceedings" by giving a passionate argument in favor of his client, who came from the land of the "great and glorious Christopher Columbus." But "the idea that a man could have a license to sell liquor only because he was from the country that had given birth to Columbus struck all present as a pretty good joke, and even the commission could not prevent a smile, as a reporter noted."[8]

His incredible graphomania was exercised in disparate ways. For example, he wrote a long letter to Judge Kimball of the Washington Police Court to point out the error that they, in good faith, had made by entrusting a boy of eleven, Tony Tomasola, to social services in order to remove him from the particularly severe punishments his father gave him because of the boy's habit of disobeying him and returning home after midnight. Moreno reminded the judge that Tony had three uncles in the city, three good persons who would have been better and more natural foster parents, without counting another Italian who was about to leave for Italy and could have accompanied Tony to his poor mother in San Fele, in the province of Potenza. Even though he included a polemical line ("Italy in Washington is represented most miserably and there is need for radical personnel reform"), this time Moreno's prose took a decidedly heartbreaking tone: "Italian mothers love their sons, above all the boys, with a poetic love and ardent affection. . . . Tony's mother could not survive such a cruel outrage as being deprived of her only son who, in his piety and devotion to the Catholic religion, intends to become a priest. The Italian mothers believe that God has given them their sons, and that no mortal could take them away from their affection and their care."[9]

Diana Romi's case was similar. The young daughter of a "prosperous peanut seller," she, along with her mother, left her father's house because he used to beat her and accuse her of immoral conduct. Moreno served as the interpreter for her father, Joseph Romi, in court, but despite his eloquence the judge ruled in favor of the two women.[10]

Used to dealing with kings and heads of state, rich businessmen and prominent intellectuals, the Captain now worked with people of much more modest extraction, or with pasts more problematic than his. A defrocked monk, Raffaele Parlanti, was arrested because he went around carrying a sign that said that he was deaf. For that reason no one would give him work, and he was condemned to six months of forced labor because he was a beggar. Moreno informed the authorities that he was only a madman and that it would have been better to send him to an asylum.[11] It was a record of cases, in short, that said a lot about the grave problems that plagued the Italian immigrants of the time. Moreno fought in vain against the ban on itinerant fruit sellers on Pennsylvania and Louisiana Avenues and against the harassment that Italian workers in Washington endured, especially "the organ grinders and fruit sellers" who were forced to put up with harassment from "badly behaved white and black boys." Moreno called for a bigger police commitment to remedy this.[12]

The Captain's decline as a public personality and as a champion of Italians in America is also visible in his absence as a fiery orator at meetings in the emigrant community. For example, there was a meeting convened by the Italian Benevolent Society of Washington to protest against the statements of District Commissioner John B. Wight, who had said that the Italian residents were "a disgrace for the capital." On that occasion, Moreno had no official role but was only registered as among those present.[13]

The Captain could console himself by evoking his shining memories in Italian newspapers. In this phase, he returned to his collaboration with Genoa's *Il Giornale*, on whose pages he published three long pieces about international political issues. The first, on China, began with a spectacular opening

> I knew the old Celestial Empire in which I have traveled far and wide by land and navigated its rivers. . . . I was the first maritime captain from Europe or America who led with full success a fleet of ships, under the flag of the Chinese Empire with the mythological dragon in the center, through the Pacific from Canton to Manila in the Philip-

pines, to Honolulu in the Hawaiian Islands and to San Francisco in California. That was in the year 1879.[14]

Comparing himself to Marco Polo and Matteo Ricci, Moreno produced a description of customs and curiosities. He also made some corrections, such as those related to the figure of Confucius, or *Kong-fue-tze*: "that means the wisest man of his age, and not Confucius as foreigners have translated and conveyed. Kong-fue-tze is not a name but rather a title of veneration. The real name of the man of antiquity who was considered the wisest man among his contemporaries was Menciu-Lama-Woo-san-Ta-Yean, great man, pope, and prophet of the Buddhist religion."

China, led by Viceroy Li Hongzhang (who had quelled the Taiping Rebellion, and whom Moreno considered "the Napoleon and the Cavour" of his country), was portrayed as a subject of great fascination. It remained "the treasure of the world," even if England had plundered it after 1842, "when the ports of the South were opened with violence to the demoralizing opium trade." The Boxer Rebellion would soon erupt. Italy would participate with an expeditionary force to suppress it and obtain the commercial concession of Tientsin in 1902. Moreno's intervention therefore appeared very timely. China was on the front page of all the newspapers, and would remain there until the assassination of King Umberto I.

His second article came out while the Boxer Rebellion was already in progress. Moreno offered a close examination of Chinese military power, which had increased thanks to Western instructors for the navy and army. The Captain then discussed the foreign commerce of the Far East, which "approaches nowadays the magnificent total of a billion dollars, that is five billion Italian lire." Italy had only tasted the crumbs of this cake, although it allowed itself "the luxury of a well-paid and useless minister in Peking and an equally well-paid and useless minister in Shanghai." An old song: "It is the squandering of taxpayer's money in China as in other places." Moreno followed with a condemnation of Italian foreign policy, calling it a diplomacy that was "the antithesis of Machiavelli and too far beneath contemporary Italian civilization," which was ineptly represented by "the Lilliputians of the diplomatic corps" particularly Minister Visconti Venosta who "in the presence of Li Hongzhang . . . seemed a helpless chick against an eagle. I have known them both personally for over thirty years."[15]

In his third article, the Captain gave strategic advice about the Italian expeditionary forces, extensively citing historic precedents, particularly direct evidence from someone like him ("I have seen and not read"). He argued that the Italian unit in the Yellow Sea was not in any way an "auxiliary" of England. The risk was, as always, politicians' ineptitude: Crispi, who "is nothing but a verbose ineptitude, an Orlando Furioso and windbag;" Blanc, who "is not even that;" Visconti Venosta, who "has cold fish blood in his veins." With a sudden swerve, the article ended with the subject of Italy's energy resources as a final example of political incompetence.[16]

Pressed by financial problems, Moreno agreed to provide a testimonial in an ad campaign for a pharmaceutical company, the Peruna Medicine Company of Columbus, Ohio, which manufactured a remedy for catarrh. "I don't know of another tonic that strengthens a person as well as Peruna," Moreno wrote in a letter printed under his picture and titled "The former prime minister of Hawaii recommends Peruna to his friends as an effective remedy against catarrh." The ad was published in numerous small newspapers. Although his enemies in Hawaii held him up for public ridicule—"Don Celso at His Best" was the title of a biting commentary in a Honolulu newspaper—even this was ultimately proof of the "modernity" of a man who had explained the power of advertising in newspapers to his friends in Piedmont. He even sent the *Gazzetta di Dogliani* Hawaiian-language clippings from Honolulu's *Ka Nupepa Elele* as an interesting curiosity.[17]

It was also evidence of a renewed vitality. Suddenly Moreno's name again appeared in the press with notably frequency after he appeared before the House Committee on Territories in January 1899. He testified about the issue of Hawaii's "Crown lands," more than seven thousand square kilometers of land that had been the property of the monarchy since the time of Kamehameha III. The lands had been taken from the crown after the 1893 putsch. Moreno, back to his usual talking points about abuses by the "missionaries," stated solemnly in a letter to the president of the committee, W. S. Knox: "It seems that my destiny is that of the prophet, and also to be the source of the disappointments of great men who do not adequately appreciate my prophetic suggestions."

Moreno believed that the missionaries, in addition to seizing the crown jewels, had also taken the crown lands from their legitimate heirs. But who were these legitimate heirs? The "wily Don" had his answer for a question that, even today, remains debated in Hawaii. According to Moreno, the former queen, Lili'uokalani, could not lay claim to the lands because she did not descend from Kamehameha's house but from a black "barber" named Blossom who came to Hawaii as a coolie from Cape Verde. The lands, however, could not be considered public lands because they had belonged to King Kamehameha III's private estate. And who were his only living heirs? Simple: the princess Elizabeth Kekaaniau and her niece, Teresa Owana Ka'ohelelani, Wilcox's wife. It was a hypothesis that in

Honolulu could have been read only one way: It was the return of an old partnership.[18]

The alliance between Moreno and Wilcox soon appeared to target a series of very practical objectives. Wilcox, as the republican Honolulu newspaper *The Hawaiian Star* wrote, was aiming to be governor of Hawaii. Another Honolulu newspaper, *The Hawaiian Gazette*, tried to sum up the operation's potential benefits for Moreno. It concluded that Moreno, while "profoundly impressed by our Bob's merits as a statesman," was "incidentally" also interested in his prospects as the owner of the lands. Therefore, "the two Hawaiian-Italians leave their macaroni refuges and confront the lion of Congress in his den."

The Honolulu newspapers were at least correct about his willingness to confront Congress. Wilcox, the "Hawaiian Garibaldi," was in Washington—where deposed Queen Lili'uokalani was also visiting and protesting the Annexation Treaty that President McKinley had signed on July 7, 1898—trying to put pressure on the House Committee on Territories as it prepared the "Hawaiian Bill," or "Organic Act" that would make the archipelago a U.S. territory. Moreno was his guide through the corridors of power. In fact, as the Captain later revealed, Wilcox had gone immediately to his home. Moreno introduced Wilcox to Knox, the president of the Committee, and to other members of the Democratic Party. On January 22 and 24, the two men, accompanied by a Hawaiian lawyer, Edgar Caypless, asked for an audience, and Moreno recommended Wilcox as "the most suitable man for governor of Hawaii."[19]

Moreno also used his connections in the press. His African American friends at the *Washington Bee* put a photo of Wilcox, wearing his handsome Italian uniform, on its cover with the caption "the first governor of Hawaii." Inside, Moreno unleashed his usual attacks, promising that the Hawaiian Territory Bill represented the liberation of the defenseless natives from the missionaries' clutches. He concluded his tirade with the motto "Hawaii for the Hawaiians, *et delenda* missionaries [*sic*]."[20]

The debate in the Committee was punctuated by disputes between Republicans and Democrats. In this context, Moreno's maneuverings appear to have been effective. With Moreno, Wilcox made the rounds of all the editorial offices, and he abandoned his dreams of reinstating the monarchy. His passionate argument against restrictions on voting made an impression on the Committee. Finally John Moon, a Republican representative from Tennessee, introduced an ad hoc resolution, and the only remaining restriction limited the vote to those who knew how to write, either in Hawaiian or in English. The Hawaiian Organic Act was passed on

April 30. It created the position of a congressional delegate for the new Territory of Hawaii. Wilcox returned to Honolulu at the end of May, traveling with the deposed queen, with whom he had often spoken in Washington and perhaps had devised a political strategy. In June, his electoral machine was on its feet: an independent and nationalist party, the future Home Rule Party of Hawaii. It was based on the idea that the existing American political dynamic, that is the usual contest between Democrats and Republicans, could not represent the Hawaiian people's particular interests.[21]

Sanford Dole, as if to prolong his role as president of the Hawaiian Republic, was appointed governor by President McKinley on June 14, 1900. Wilcox spent the summer in a particularly intense election campaign. He was an independent candidate and faced Samuel Parker, a Republican, and Prince David Kawānanakoa, a Democrat. The former enjoyed considerably more support. Moreno supported Wilcox from Washington and arranged to have American newspapers print the letters that he sent them. Hawaiian newspapers often reprinted these articles, as happened when Wilcox declared his intension to fight for the crown lands.[22]

As the date of the elections approached, set for the beginning of November, Wilcox's adversaries redoubled their efforts to discourage the electorate, which they knew had grown to frightening dimensions. The *Hawaiian Star* wrote that it did not make sense to elect an independent candidate, particularly one like Wilcox: A piece of wood would serve better than he, and Wilcox was only "a pawn in the hands of Don Celso."[23] But not even the most fantastic theater director could have predicted the dramatic twist that was in store. On the eve of the elections, like a bolt of lightning through a clear sky, Moreno announced his break from Wilcox. Such a step could not be taken without attracting attention, and the Captain chose to do it in the most dramatic way possible. A letter from "Don Celso" was read at a large Republican meeting at the Orpheum in Honolulu. Its opening words, "Better late than never," were an entire program. It had taken him twenty years, Moreno wrote, to discover that Wilcox was "hypocrisy, mendacity, deceit, and instability personified," and that he "had all the vices of the Hawaiians and none of their virtues." What had happened? "I learned that the Hawaiians had sent him a lot of money, and that he used it only to strut around Washington as a Hawaiian prince, as he had done in Italy," Moreno declared, and that was enough for one of the leaders of the Republican assemblies of Honolulu to proclaim that Wilcox was not "a man of steel," but "a man of steals."[24]

Moreno's financial situation must have been quite ugly at the time. Wilcox had promised to pay Moreno a fee for his services as soon as he had the chance, and the Captain learned that Wilcox was funded from Hawaii by George Markham, his comrade in the 1889 revolt. Moreno went to the hotel where Wilcox was staying and asked him if he had received money. Wilcox denied having any or knowing Markham. Moreno, as he explained a few months later, was furious: "It was too much. I knew that he was lying, and from that time I no longer wanted anything to do with him, and on the contrary I have done everything possible to denounce him."

Mundane financial reasons, and not politics, were behind the rupture of the old friendship. With devilish malice, Moreno sent the newspapers a stream of information portraying Wilcox in a bad light, who at the time of his Italian education "immediately began telling nonsense to anyone with whom he came in contact. Everywhere he passed himself off as a prince and thanks to these performances he could enter into houses from which he would now be thrown out."[25]

Even allowing for Moreno's urgent financial need and the possibility of a conflict with Wilcox over money, it still remains doubtful that Moreno was telling the entire truth. There is no evidence that the Captain would volunteer for such a political maneuver, but one gets the impression that his distance from Wilcox was a step suggested, and perhaps funded, by the Democratic Party, at whose service the Captain, the former admirer of the Republican Secretary of State Blaine, now found himself. There is a clue in a curious October 1900 article published in a small Pennsylvania newspaper, the *Scranton Tribune*, which supported the Republican McKinley-Roosevelt ticket. According to the paper, Moreno, "a sixty-something man with white hair, beard, and mustache, 1.80 meters tall, of stocky build, dark eyes, who appears the classic *opera buffa* villain," had been traveling around Scranton and Lackawanna County for two or three weeks. There were sizeable Italian communities in the area, and he spent the majority of his time in long conversations with Italian fruit sellers. And what was he talking about? "His mission in Scranton . . . is to work Connell's defeat in his election campaign and to get Conry elected. Naturally, the national Democratic commission pays the bills for services rendered by Mr. Moreno."[26]

Connell was the Republican candidate for Lackawanna County, and Conry was his Democratic adversary. It is hard to believe that such an about-face would have been caused by such tiny motives. It was also in apparent contrast with the fact that a Republican Representative, Cyrus A. Sulloway of New Hampshire, was the last sponsor of a bill that reauthorized Moreno's transpacific cable in December 1899. Regardless, it was a difficult time for the Captain.

Despite the tempest Moreno unleashed, Wilcox won his election. On November 6, he was proclaimed the winner and became the Hawaiian representative to Congress. He had obtained a little more than 4,000 votes, less than the 5,500 that Parker and the Prince earned combined, but enough to win. Wilcox celebrated his victory with a great luau that the ex-queen also attended. His opponents immediately began plotting their revenge. On November 20, two lawyers, A. B. Loebenstein and A. N. Kepoikai, asked Congress to investigate his political and personal qualifications for the office. While some of the press in Honolulu urged neutrality, and though Governor Dole had ratified the election without delay, the defamation machine had been put into motion.[27]

Moreno was its most powerful operator. He accused Wilcox of posing as an aristocrat. Perhaps he was not entirely wrong, even if it had been Moreno who spread the first rumors in Italy in the 1880s that the young men he chauffeured around the country were "three princes of royal Hawaiian blood." Now Moreno claimed that Wilcox had only succeeded in winning the heart of his Italian wife and her family because of his noble charade. Moreno also alleged that he had received complaints from Italy for years from many people to whom he had introduced Wilcox. But the question of Wilcox's alleged princely origins was not news. Several months before Moreno's revelations about the rupture, the newspapers had reported that while Wilcox was in Turin at the time of his "romantic affair" with Gina Sobrero (and therefore far from Moreno and anyone else who could have exposed him), he succeeded in his deception. He added to his notable qualities—strength and youth, which made him a perfect gentleman—the only one that was missing: "He could have been a prince! A royal scion of Hawaii! . . . Who could ever doubt the word of an official?" The inspiration behind the articles was obviously the Captain, who "however strangely," as the newspapers noted, was not aware of it "except when the court had ruled that Wilcox had married the princess under false pretenses and subsequently had committed bigamy," that "Wilcox had deceived the people making them believe he was a prince." "It took me twenty years to understand that man," Moreno admitted: "I, who boasted of my judgment, was deceived."[28]

The Captain did everything possible to discredit the Hawaiian delegate. The issue of the contested marriage seemed an effective weapon, since in 1898 a Mormon, Brigham H. Roberts, was elected representative from

Utah and denied his seat because of his polygamy. The idea was to give the unlucky Wilcox a hard time since, as the press noted, it was unlikely that the accusations could have translated into legal action.[29]

The issue of Wilcox's "bigamy" dominated the conversation for a while. The troubled relationship between Moreno's ex-pupil and his Italian wife, although covered by a veil of discretion (Wilcox's full name was never revealed), was at the center of the memoir, almost a feminist text, that the baroness had published in Italy in 1908, five years after Wilcox's death: *Espatriata: Da Torino a Honolulu* (*Expatriate: From Turin to Honolulu*). In August 1892, Wilcox married his second wife, Theresa Owana Ka'ohelelani, a descendant of King Kamehameha the Great, thus of true royal lineage. With her, he had a son in 1893 named Robert Garibaldi Kalani-kupuapai Kalani-nui Keoua, and later two daughters.

It is not clear if Gina and Wilcox had divorced in San Francisco in 1889. As Ombretta Frau explained, "The annulment from Sacra Rota arrived only in 1895 and the one from the Court of Appeals of Turin on June 5, 1900." That was enough to make his adversaries claim that he had remarried before the divorce from his Italian wife was approved, although Wilcox maintained that he had notified the Italian consul in Honolulu before his second marriage, the start of the civil procedure for separation in Italy. Moreno claimed that "an examination of the procedural documents in Italy will show that the divorce had been refused and Wilcox had committed bigamy in the Hawaiian Islands." Moreno told the newspaper that he believed Wilcox had learned "all of the Italians' vices and none of their virtues."[30]

Various newspapers, from the *Philadelphia Times* to the *San Francisco Call*, circulated the rumor that Gina Sobrero was the one who inspired the campaign to deprive Wilcox of his seat and that the baroness intended to come to the United States for this purpose. Passages, supposedly from a letter to a friend in San Francisco, were published in which the reserved Gina had claimed: "I could never forgive a man who ruined my young life and convinced me to marry him with false stories of our future in Hawaii."[31]

Wilcox's alleged "betrayal" was in fact part of a larger smear campaign conceived in Honolulu in environments as much Republican as Democratic.[32] As Andrade wrote, George D. Gear, who orchestrated the plot, also tried undermining Wilcox's election by accusing him of high treason on the basis of an exchange of letters with Emilio Aguinaldo, the leader of the rebellion against the United States in the Philippines, taken from Spain after the 1898 war. Wilcox defended himself by saying that he was not sure if the letters were exact transcriptions of the originals and called Moreno, who he believed was the person corresponding with the Filipinos, a "useful ally for the cause of the Philippines." All these accusations, along with that of bigamy, were presented to Congress and the electoral commission but had no effect.[33] The most moderate of Wilcox's Hawaiian adversaries had expected that Congress would not listen to Moreno's shouting or to his ex-wife's wishes, since the will of the people could not be annulled on a whim, and in any case it was not worth turning Wilcox into a victim.[34]

Wilcox decided to respond to the attacks. He wrote to Honolulu's *The Independent* saying that the schemes set up by Gear, Moreno, and company were nothing but "petty blackmail" and that the Captain, in particular, was a "miserable old imposter." Moreno had accused him ferociously in the *Washington Bee*, his favorite platform during that period, but then, Wilcox noted, when he had been elected, Moreno had changed his tone—perhaps because he thought he could obtain some advantage from Wilcox—and had claimed the attacks on his old pupil were inspired by the *haoles*' racist beliefs. Wilcox perhaps underestimated the intentions of Moreno, who now had decided to go to extremes in his attempt to take his seat from him. On January 24, 1901, he told the congressional committee that perhaps what he was doing was not "generous," but it was "appropriate, just, and patriotic."[35]

One may wonder about the ultimate purpose of Moreno's ambiguous "crusade." Certainly, it seems unlikely that the Captain took issue with the morality of Wilcox's private behavior. Above all, it appears out of character to involve himself in an issue with clear racist undertones. Wilcox's election had caused great embarrassment, a discomfort that translated into disturbed thinking, like that in the columns of the *San Francisco Call.* It was argued that the disgraceful approval that native Hawaiians gave Wilcox demonstrated that they were "unfit for universal suffrage," a contradictory observation because a few lines later the same newspaper claimed that many of the natives had not voted for Wilcox, and that he had only won by a slim majority.[36]

The Captain would soon definitively leave the scene. Death caught him shortly after midnight on Sunday, March 10, in Providence Hospital in Washington. He had been taken there following a stroke the previous Friday while he was walking the streets of the capital. He had fallen to the ground, paralyzed and incapable of speech. Rescuers initially brought him to his apartment in the Anderson Building, at the corner of John Marshall Place and C Street.

The newspapers did not fail to tell the story of that singular character who had crossed half the world, taken on important positions, and who in his last years had led "a rather precarious existence" in the federal capital.[37] On March 14, Moreno was buried in the Catholic cemetery of the church of St. Mary. Because of the "strong individuality, wide culture, and interesting personality of the deceased," who over the course of time had acquired "a large circle of friends," many wanted to pay their respects to the corpse, which was displayed in a funeral home until shortly before the funeral. The service, officiated by Father Currier, who had donated the plot in which the Captain was buried, was attended by a large crowd including various important people and even some ladies "in addition to the compatriots of the deceased." The newspapers highlighted how the funeral expenses for a man who had married the daughter of a sultan, was the prime minister of a kingdom, and had negotiated concessions between major powers were paid thanks to a subscription among the Italians of Washington. It was promoted by Francesco Sanfilippo (whose name was mangled as "Francisco San Felipo," "Frank Philippo," and "Sanfellipo,"), president of the Unione Fratellanza Italiana; by Angelo Chica, president of the Victor Emanuel Society; and by Marco Lorenzi, Scipio Buonini, and Ignatius Graci. Moreno had no relatives in America, so a message was sent through consular channels to his brother, an officer in the Italian navy.[38]

Moreno died but his legend remained, or rather the enigma that even twenty years earlier had crossed Faldella's mind: "What is the secret, the recipe by which a man ambles through, navigates the world, can make himself seen by everyone, can pose to the press of the United States of America and to his countrymen the question is he serious or crazy? 'Is it true glory, or Pagliano syrup?'"[39]

Many newspapers remembered this exceptional adventurer. A Canadian newspaper, at the end of a rather informative article, called him "an extinct volcano."[40] Another newspaper noted that even if he had plummeted down the social ladder in recent years, he had never lost, not even for a moment, "the refined bearing and aristocratic manners that were typical of him" and that matched his courtesy and good character.[41]

Moreno's death unleashed several Hawaiian journalists. Though the *Hawaiian Gazette* warned "*de mortuis nil nisi bonum*," that is, speak nothing but good of the dead, it wrote that "he was a land pirate" and "a revolutionary wherever a revolution could pay him." In another article it equated him with his bitter enemy Walter Murray Gibson, calling him a "carpetbagger." Other newspapers focused on the adventurous aspects of his biography. The *Hawaiian Star* called his an "extraordinary life," although punctuated by "some very dark passages." Moreno "was plausible, loquacious, and knew how to wrap a certain type of person around his finger when he decided to do so." The *Honolulu Republican* stated, "Moreno's experiences could form, if collected, one of the most compelling real-life novels ever published." The newspaper tried to summarize them and said, with something like regret, "if he had only been a little more even-tempered he could have become one of the most remarkable men of his time." *The Independent* wrote that, now that Moreno had died, "another landmark has been removed from our archives."[42]

The man who had been portrayed as "a second Anastasius" because he embodied all the adventurous qualities of the eponymous protagonist of the Thomas Hope novel had been able to enchant America with his singular and fascinating ways. Among the many who bore witness to him, perhaps with the intention of criticizing him, were the country's greatest newspapers and hundreds of papers from small-town America. The latter included the *Daily Yellowstone Journal* of Miles City, Montana, whose editor had met the Captain in Washington and found him "a rather pleasing gentleman," one who seemed made for high society: "His mission is to laugh in ladies' salons . . . He is famous in society for his laugh, which is really remarkable, musical, and cheerful, but this is all that is good in him, apart from his linguistic skills."

Alongside this inclination to laugh, Moreno's strong suit was his invective, exhibited in the newspapers "through his truly excellent English and elegance of style" and yet with such harshness as to make "cutthroats" of all those who occasionally found themselves blocking his way, and who were in reality only "good citizens." The observation was a reference to his long campaign against Italian slavery, an issue the newspaper's editor still regarded with insurmountable doubts. In his opinion, "the sophisticated and eloquent gentleman from Rome" was nothing more than "the self-appointed successor of Cervantes' great hero."[43]

For more than thirty years, the United States had heard Moreno's voice. It was literally bewitched, especially at the beginning. The continuity of his presence on the pages of the country's newspapers and the caliber of his associations is really remarkable. Therefore, we cannot help but point out his "modernity" with regard to this formidable capacity to mobilize the press and to use it to stay on center stage. Moreno enjoyed considerable esteem in the African American press, which, as we have seen, came to his aid even in his most difficult moments. Moreno's "modernity" is moreover reaffirmed by the enthusiasm with which he had adhered to all the visionary projects of the era. In this, he was truly a man of his time, who embraced a romantic taste for adventure alongside a confidence in technological achievements. Moreno had been a true citizen of the world, in his always contradictory and ambiguous way: He claimed his Italianness or Americanness or Hawaiianness according to the occasion. He foresaw the extraordinary future that destiny had in store for China and as well as the inevitable decline of British hegemony in a world with new protagonists, chief among them the victorious United States.

Now dead, it was likely that he very much enjoyed the rumors that his mystery could still provoke, and he permitted himself one of his thunderous laughs.

NOTES

PREFACE

1. *Unione Italiana* (Chicago), August 5, 9, and 19, 1868. Emphasis in original.

2. Scrapbooks, William Nevins Armstrong Papers, 1869–1929, Yale University Library. Hereafter WNAP.

INTRODUCTION

1. "Anti-Social Personality Disorder," Mayo Clinic: http://www.mayoclinic.org/diseases-conditions/antisocial-personality-disorder/basics/symptoms/con-20027920. Accessed June 9, 2015.

2. William Dalrymple, "The East India Company: The Original Corporate Raiders," *The Guardian*, March 4, 2015.

1. THE TRAVELER'S SPIRIT

1. Libro dei Battesimi (Book of Baptisms), 9, faldone 2. Archivio della Parrocchia di San Quirico e Paolo, Dogliani (hereafter cited as *APQP*).

2. Casalis 1840, 95. Information about Dogliani in this chapter also comes from Conterno 1986.

3. Abba 1913, 4.

4. Casalis 1840, 95; Moreno to Angelo De Gubernatis, 20 March 1879, Collezione Autografi, Cassetta 83, n. 31, Biblioteca Nazionale di Firenze.

5. Einaudi 1894.

6. Ignazio Giuseppe Maria Vassallo di Castiglione Falletto, *Circostanze critiche nelle quali si trovò Dogliani* (1799), cited in Conterno 1986, 367–373.

7. *Stato delle Anime*, 1847, Archivio Storico del Comune di Dogliani (hereafter ASCD). Moreno is listed as a soldier. His wound was reported in Carlo Dondero (n.d.). Dondero knew Moreno in California. Andrew Canepa made his unedited manuscript available.

8. "Parlano i vecchi," in Abba 1996, 307.

9. *Libro dei Battesimi*, 1831, APQP.

10. See "Stato della Popolazione" and "Anagrafe," ASCD.

11. "Catasto di trasporti, 1793–1818, 1823–1855, 1855–1880"; "Imposta sui fabbricati, 1854," ASCD.

12. Moreno, *American Interests in Asia* (*AIA*), 24.

13. Abba 1992, 4.

14. The *Times* (Washington, DC, March 13, 1901) says twenty-five languages and eight dialects. The *New Orleans Crescent* (February 9, 1868) says forty-two.

15. Faldella 1962, 134.

16. Moreno to Arcangelo Ghisleri, September 23, 1893, Carte Ghisleri, B 111 b.43/1, Domus Mazziniana di Pisa. On Abba and Buffa, see Tognoli 1971. There are no documents that show Abba and Moreno were schoolmates.

17. See, for example, Faldella 1962, 127, 133.

18. The biographies of Luigi Moreno (Bettazzi 1989, Cerri 1878) make no reference to Celso Cesare Moreno. Research in the bishop's personal papers (Monsignor Luigi Moreno, Corrispondenza privata, Archivio Storico Diocesano di Ivrea) has not produced evidence of their connection, unsurprising given the ecclesiastical theme of his correspondence.

19. "Lista alfabetica della Comunità di Dogliani, Classe dell'anno 1831," "Liste di leva," ASCD; "Celso Moreno," Fondo Università di Genova, Registri dei Matricolati, Archivio di Stato, Genoa.

20. Faldella 1862, 143.

21. *La Gazzetta di Dogliani*, November 12, 1892. This weekly newspaper was published for five years, from 1890 to 1894.

22. Moreno, *AIA*, 23.

23. Ibid., 23, 40.

24. Faldella 1962, 134.

25. "Lista alfabetica della Comunità di Dogliani, Classe dell'Anno 1831, Liste di leva," ASCD.

26. "Inventario della Scuola di Nautica. Regolamento," B. 36, 1853, "Camera di Commercio di Genova," Archivio di Stato, Genoa, B. 36. No similar reference was found in the archives of the Royal Naval Academy of Genoa.

27. See "Sugar and Sandwich," *Brooklyn Daily Eagle*, February 24, 1884. All the details of the story are in *Martin Koszta—Correspondence etc.*, 1854.

28. "Intendenza Generale d'Armata, Campagna 1855–1856," Archivio di Stato di Torino. Research in this vast archive, which includes lists of officers and troop embarkation and disembarkation records ("Spedizione in Oriente, Indice degli Ufficiali Impiegati," "Registri degli Sbarchi nel Porto di Balaklava"; "Elenco nominativo degli individui che presero parte al Corpo di Spedizione in Oriente") did not produce Moreno's name. On the Kingdom of

Sardinia's participation in the war, see Degli Alberti 1910 and Lebrun 1889. On the use of mercenaries, see Bayley 1977.

29. "Registri dei Matricolati," Fondo Università di Genova, Archivio di Stato di Genova. This file also contains a practice exercise Moreno did for the final exam.

30. On November 18, 2006, Riccardo Moreni, the only resident of Dogliani with that surname, told Durante this story, which Moreni heard from his father, who claimed to have heard it from his grandfather. The story, passed from generation to generation for 150 years, can be considered more as fable than oral history. However, it may contain a grain of truth.

31. Abba 1983. On Bixio, see also Ferrari 1987.

32. Faldella 1962, 132–134.

33. Ibid. Tarchetti (1839–69) was from Monferrato, and he concocted an exotic island for his short story "King for Twenty-Four Hours," included in his *Racconti umoristici* (1869). Tarchetti also wrote a violent antiwar novel, *Una nobile follia (Drammi della vita militare)*. It was published serially in newspapers in 1866–67 and then revised and edited into a single volume in 1869. It recounts the horrors of the Crimean War, including the Battle of the Chernaya, in great detail.

2. THE TREASURES OF ASIA

1. Moreno did not hesitate to put himself in this illustrious company. Only three Italians, he said, knew the Chinese emperor and the rest of Asia: Marco Polo, Matteo Ricci, and Celso Cesare Moreno of Dogliani. "The names of these three bold travelers, he claimed, are favorably known, honored, and respected on all the islands and throughout the continent of Asia." Faldella 1962, 125.

2. Iannettone 1984, 84. Although an examination of the ships registers and captains leaving Genoa (Ministero della Marina, Archivio di Stato di Genova) produced no mention of Moreno, it did reveal a significant number of voyages to the Far East.

3. Faldella 1962, 122. His activities in the Red Sea were mentioned in various articles, particularly "His Dream Not Realized," *The Times* (Washington, DC), March 13, 1901.

4. Iannettone 1984, 109–167.

5. On Bruno, see Solero n.d., 20–22.

6. Iannettone 1984, 215.

7. Casella to the Minister of Foreign Affairs, Calcutta, 8 June 1860, *Le scritture del Regno di Sardegna*, B. 253, *Consolato di Calcutta*, 1859–60, Archivio Storico del Ministero degli Affari esteri (hereafter ASMAE).

8. Moreno, *AIA*, 38–39.

9. Yriarte 1867. The story also appeared in the *Christian Recorder* of Philadelphia, which said it came from the Parisian *Le Siècle*, with the title "A Curious Story—Fact or Fiction," 14 December 1867; and in the *New Orleans Crescent*. See Gupta 1963; Misra 1961; Shastitko 1980. None of the stories about the Sepoy revolt or the biographies of Nana Sahib consulted contain any reference to Moreno.

10. *Hawaiian Gazette* (Honolulu), March 22, 1901.

11. Moreno, *AIA*, 26–27. For information on Abbona, see Negri 1877 and http://www.provinciaitaliana.omv.org.

12. Faldella 1962, 118.

13. Ibid., 115. Some sources mention more wives. The previously cited article from *Le Siècle* mentions at least three of the Rajah's daughters. Attilio Brunialti (1897, 321) writes that Moreno married "I don't know how many indigenous princesses." More circumspectly, Roberto Battaglia (1954, 69) speaks about an indeterminate number of indigenous princesses. On this point, however, Moreno never spoke or felt the need to contradict what was written about him.

14. Reid 2008.

15. A report in a New Zealand weekly referred to an offer of the island that Moreno had just made to the United States: "America," in *Otago Witness* (Dunedin), August 17, 1868.

16. Reid 2008.

17. *Straits Times and Overland Journal*, Singapore, August 9, 1873. Taken from the *New York Herald*, the interview was also published in the Netherlands ("Wat ik aangaande Atchin weet, Een examen," *Algemeen Handelsblad*, Amsterdam, May 31, 1873).

18. "Hawaiian Commercial Advertiser," April 7, 1900. Regarding Moreno's adventures in Sumatra, Anthony Reid, in a letter of January 31, 2005, told Durante about "small boundary skirmishes with the Dutch on the west and east coasts of Sumatra." Presumably, Moreno took part in this action. Reid, however, maintained that "none of the travelers of this era said that [Moreno] had had any influence on Aceh in the period 1859–1862, although the sultan maintained a rather tough attitude towards a British mission which visited him in September 1859, perhaps because he had heard Moreno's version of events in India."

19. Faldella 1962, 134. One of Moreno's many obituaries spoke of the brief war and his escape on the French ship: "His Dream Not Realized," *The Times*, Washington, March 13, 1901. These events were also mentioned in an obituary published in Italy, "La morte di un avventuriero italiano in America," *La Stampa* (Turin), March 14, 1901.

20. Chesneaux, Bastid, and Bergére 1976, 68–70. As the authors note, the heterogeneous population developed a pidgin English, a combination of

English, Malay, and Chinese. It is also probable that this, and not pure Mandarin, was the "Chinese" Moreno learned.

21. On this important chapter in Chinese history, see Selby 1968; You-wen 1973; Reilly 2004; Spence 1998; Reclus 1972.

22. See Smith 1978 and Teng 1971.

23. Abend 1947. See also Cahill 1930 and Smith 1978, 27.

24. Moreno, *AIA*, 32.

25. Lindley 1866, 2:639–647. See also Newsinger 2001.

26. Lindley 1866, 2:652–653. See also Reclus 1972, 207.

27. Moreno, *AIA*, 33.

28. "Sugar and Sandwich," *Brooklyn Daily Eagle*, February 24, 1884.

29. Moreno, *AIA*, 22. On Spelta and his activities, see Marcellino da Civezza 1860, 99–104.

30. Iannettone 1984, 16–18, 84. See also Hess 1973, 96.

31. On these themes, see Segrè 1991 and De Leone 1955. (Despite its title, the latter also addresses the establishment of colonies in the Far East.)

32. De Leone 1955, 31; Surdich 2005, 117 (which offers a complete portrait of the Italian debate over nineteenth-century colonial projects).

33. On this subject, see Karabell 2003.

34. See Surdich 2005, 68–121.

35. Moreno, *AIA*, 20. Moreno followed the canal with great attention. He approved of it and of all Lesseps's projects, including the excavations of the Isthmus of Panama and the Isthmus of Tenasserim, between the Gulf of Siam and the Andaman Sea, which would have eliminated approximately 600,000 miles of traveling on dangerous routes.

36. The document is found in "Informazioni sull'isola di Sumatra (Oceano), Progetti di colonizzazione," Ministero della Marina, Uffici Diversi (1861–1864), Gabinetto b. 5, f. 39. Archivio Centrale dello Stato, Rome (hereafter ACSR).

37. Surdich 2005.

38. Hess 1973, 94–109; Segrè 1991, 125–128. On the other colonial projects during this time, see De Leone, 1955, 38–46. Most of these projects were short-lived except Giovanni Emilio Cerruti's plan for the creation of a penal colony in Borneo. It enjoyed some government support and considered, among other things, the possibility of assimilating or eliminating the natives.

39. Faldella 1962, 121. Although Faldella praised Moreno's "prodigious and detailed memory," his account of the conversation between the traveler and Victor Emanuel seems more creative than literal.

40. *L'Eco d'Italia* (New York), March 2, 1883.

41. Ministro MAIC, "Colonizzazione di Sumatra," 28 April 1867, "Informazione sull'isola di Sumatra," b. 5 f. 39, MM, ACSR. They reference Bixio's shipwreck along the coast of Sumatra.

42. Ministero di AIC to the Ministero della Marina, 24 April 1867, MM, ACSR.

43. G. Quetta, Capitan of the Port of Genoa, "Nota dei Capitani che navigarono nei mari dell'Isola di Sumatra," 1 May 1867; Ministro della Marina to the Ministro di ACI, 10 May 1867; Ministero della Marina to the Gabinetto, 27 May 1867 per il capitano Montechiaro; MM, ACSR. The discussions about Sumatra began with captains from the ports of Genoa, Naples, and Palermo.

44. Capitano di Porto di Palermo to the Ministro della Marina, 29 June 1867, MM, ACSR, with Captain Scorsone's report.

45. Ministro di AIC to the Ministro della Marina, 26 June 1867. The commission's report is signed by all its members and dated 19 June 1867, "Miscellanea di Uffici Diversi," Gabinetto, 1862–1883, b. 4, f. 38, "Progetto di colonizzazione nell'isola di Sumatra," MN, ACSR.

46. Carpi 1888, 35.

47. Moreno would later claim that Bixio had never been a sailor. When asked if Bixio had supported his project, Moreno said that he had but he did not have what it took to implement it. *L'Eco d'Italia* (New York), March 2, 1883; see also Faldella 1962, 124.

48. Dossi 2010, 839–840 n. 5287.

49. Moreno, *AIA*, 17–25, 125. His article against Negri and the SGI is "L'Italia in Africa: La parodia di Scipione l'Africano," *Cristoforo Colombo* (New York), October 5, 1895 (reproduced in *HGW*, 49–50).

50. Moreno, *AIA*, 16.

51. Marquis de Villemer (Charles Yriarte), "Cesare Moreno," in *Le Figaro* (Paris), October 24, 1867.

52. Yriarte 1868.

53. On the strong interest that Napoleon III referred to, see the column "Paris au jour le jour" in *Le Figaro*, March 11, 1868, which reported on the audience granted to Moreno. Another Parisian daily, *Le Petit Journal*, wrote on February 29, 1868, that the emperor received Moreno in a private audience in the Tuileries Palace.

54. A search for evidence of the bestowal of Legion of Honor uncovered no material about Moreno in the archives of the Musée de la Legion d'Honneur, except for the news that Moreno was the captain of a corvette. No other documentation was found about Moreno's mission in Cochinchina. Various sources mention his travels in Korea and the fact that he was the one to open the country to foreign trade, acquiring great influence in the local court. See Letter of Antonio Trinchese, 10 February 2005, and Dondero n.d. Apart from a brief reference to Moreno, there is little on his time in Japan, Siam, Burma, and Cochinchina (see *AIA*, 17, 22, 125).

55. Brunialti 1883, 71–95. For Moreno's citation, see *AIA*, 9.

56. "The Franco-Annamese Conflict," *Catholic World* 38, no. 224 (November 1883): 213.

57. Cotte 1883, 213. The reference to the Mekong reflects what Moreno wrote in *AIA*, 8.

58. "His Dream Not Realized," *The Times* (Washington, DC), March 13, 1901.

3. THE CHALLENGE OF THE PACIFIC

1. Moreno, *HGW*, 28. See also *L'Eco d'Italia* (New York), May 21, 1869.

2. Cesar Moreno, "Moreno's Island," *New York Times*, August 26, 1868.

3. *La Voce del Popolo* (San Francisco), September 17, 1868.

4. *L'Eco d'Italia*, July 2, 1869.

5. *L'Eco d'Italia*, March 2, 1881.

6. *New York Times*, August 4, 1868.

7. Moreno, *AIA*, 6. What follows is a summary of the forty-page booklet.

8. Ibid., 21.

9. Ibid., 28. Moreno's characterization of the Chinese has much in common with the sketch in Mason 1939. Although he never cites Moreno's book, there are very similar phrases. Mason, for example, refers to the Chinese "innate spirit of association" (14), while Moreno alludes to the "the spirit of association that is innate in them." But phrases like these may only be repetitions of widespread platitudes of the time.

10. Ibid., 26.

11. Ibid., 34.

12. Ibid., 5–6.

13. Ibid., 6.

14. Ibid., 10.

15. Ibid., 6–7.

16. Ibid., 10.

17. Ibid., 7.

18. Ibid., 10.

19. Ibid., 31.

20. Ibid., 29.

21. Moreno's advice for Americans to turn their gaze to the Far East as soon as possible was not unprecedented, but he was one of its earliest advocates. Mason (1939, 123–125) reports that "the idea of using China as a place for the investment of foreign capital seems to have emerged in the sixties," and that "by 1870 the business man's method of civilizing China through the

introduction of Western machinery and other material improvements was taking precedence over the missionary way."

22. Moreno, *AIA*, 13.
23. Ibid., 18.
24. Mason 1939, 100–114.
25. Moreno to Charles Sumner, August 20, 1869.
26. Moreno, *AIA*, 19.
27. Mason 1939, 75.
28. "What We Might Do in Asia," *National Republican*, April 23, 1869.
29. "Asian Speculations," *New York Tribune*, July 8, 1869.
30. Moreno to Charles Sumner, September 20, 1868, Charles Sumner Correspondence, 1829–1873, Series L, Houghton Library, Harvard University.
31. Moreno to Charles Sumner, May 11, 1869.
32. Moreno to Charles Sumner, April 18, 1869.
33. Moreno spoke about his friendship with Burlingame in various letters to Sumner.
34. This and the following paragraphs are from Celso Caesar Moreno, *The Trans-Pacific Cable as Projected by Caesar Celso Moreno in Washington, D.C. 1869* (hereafter *TPC*). It is a collection of documents that includes Moreno's testimony before the Committee on Foreign Relations of the U.S. Senate and House of Representatives, February 16 and 17, 1875, the text of the bill, and press coverage from 1873 to 1877. Moreno's testimony runs five and a half pages.
35. Moreno could have been referring to the pioneering work on the telegraph carried out by Antonio Meucci, the Italian political exile who hosted Garibaldi in his house on Staten Island.
36. Speech of Hon. J. Packard in House of Representatives, *Congressional Globe*, February 18, 1873 in Moreno, *TPC*, 8–9. Echoes of the speech are also found in *La Rivista Europea* (May 1873), 631.
37. This and other newspapers cited in *TPC*, 8–16.
38. Celso Cesare Moreno, "L'arbitrato per le foche," *Gazzetta di Dogliani*, August 6, 1892.
39. Moreno to Ricasoli, respectively San Francisco, December 9, 1874, and Virginia (Nevada), February 15, 1876, in Camerani-Rotondi 1978, 336 and 527. The reference is to Marco Minghetti, then prime minister.
40. "The Trans-Pacific Cable," *San Francisco Examiner*, November 15, 1877 (also in *TPC*, 16).
41. Walsh 1897, 596–597.
42. www.Atlantic-Cable.com (Cable Companies, Am-Pac Cable).
43. Scott 1994.
44. Moreno to Ricasoli, San Francisco, 9 December 1874, in Camerani-Rotondi 1978, 336.

45. See Dondero, n.d., in Dossi, 2010. On Dondero, see also Loverci 1985 and Durante 2001, 490–504.

46. *Società italiana di mutua beneficenza: The Early Years* (Colma, CA: Società Italiana di mutua beneficenza, n.d.).

47. Moreno to Sumner, September 28, 1870, and October 23, 1870.

4. THE LITTLE ITALIAN SLAVES

1. Moreno, *HGW*, 10–11.

2. Zucchi 1992. A large part of this chapter draws upon this excellent book.

3. Anonymous (De Luca) 1868. Although the text was attributed to "a long-time Italian resident of the United States," A. E. Cerqua revealed that De Luca was its author (*New York Times*, June 13, 1873); after which De Luca claimed authorship (ibid., June 23, 1873).

4. More copies can also be found in the Carte Pisani-Dossi, busta 5, fasc. 28, 1873–1894, Archivio Centrale dello Stato, Rome. The entire folder contains documents about the problems of exploited emigrant children.

5. Guerzoni 1868, "To the reader." The initial pages are not numbered.

6. "Ministero degli Affari esteri, Legge del 21 Dicembre 1873 sul divieto dell'impiego di fanciulli in professioni girovaghe," Rome, MAE, 1885, in Carte Pisani-Dossi, 1873–1894, busta 5. fasc. 28, ACSR.

7. Moreno to Giuseppe Guerzoni, 13 May 1872. Collezione d'Autografi, Cassetta v.11A, n.40, Biblioteca Nazionale Centrale di Firenze.

8. It is difficult to say when Dora of Istria entered Moreno's life. Married into the Romanian royal family, she was considered beautiful and brilliant. She frequented Europe's courts and literary salons, writing for some of the continent's most prestigious magazines, including the *Nuova Antologia*. Moreno recalled that the princess had sent him a copy of that magazine containing "this clever Signora's *bello studio*," *L'epopea dell'India* (Moreno to Francesco Protonotari, 19 February 1871, Archivio della Letteratura Italiana, Cassetta 140 n. 26, BNCF). No direct correspondence between Moreno and the Princess has been discovered. On Dora of Istria, see Rossi 2005, 257–278.

9. *New York Times*, February 1, 1869. The letter included a report from Cerqua on the terrible condition of the "little Italian harpists." Cerqua, like Guerzoni, was of the opinion that the trafficking in children was the work of an international organization based in Paris.

10. Brace 1872, 195.

11. "Il piccolo genovese," *L'Eco d'Italia*, May 14, 1869, reprinted in Durante 2001, 442–446. Secchi was also the adoptive father of two Italian orphans, Carlo and Teresa Cuneo. See Franchi 2011.

12. Alger 1872. Note that Alger used the expression "white slavery" before Moreno popularized it.

13. See Hoppin 1994. Although Moreno was primarily responsible for the surge in interest that caught Brown's attention, Hoppin does not mention him, but he does cites *History of a Great Wrong*. Changing his subjects in the 1880s, Brown became known as "the boot-black Raphael" and became "the richest and most celebrated genre painter in turn-of-the-century America." (See Roughton Galleries, http://www.fafa.com/browse-by-artist.html.) Before Brown, drawings of Italian children already occasionally appeared in various publications in the 1870s, particularly *Harper's Weekly*.

14. Moreno, *HGW*, 2. In Chicago, for example, the "little Italian slaves" began to attract the attention of the press and charitable organizations in the summer of 1873. See Vecoli 1963.

15. *New York Times*, June 21, 1873.

16. Ibid.

17. See Hoppin 1994, 20; *New York Times*, June 17, 23, and 28 and July 22, 1873); Faldella 1962, 135.

18. *New York Times*, June 12, 1873. The letter accompanied an article about the "child slaves" that had already appeared in *La Voce del Popolo* (San Francisco).

19. *New York Times*, June 13, 1873.

20. Ibid., June 15, 1873.

21. Ibid., June 20, 1873.

22. Ibid., June 21, 1873.

23. Ibid., June 23, 1873.

24. Ibid., June 21, 1873.

25. Caccia was horrified by the sight in New York of "men and women, children and youths dragged into the abominable trade by certain infamous countrymen" who were "for the most part from the coast of Genoa." Caccia 1850, 333–334.

26. *New York Times*, June 18, 1873.

27. Ibid., June 23, 1873.

28. Zucchi tells the story of this fight. Zucchi 1992, 134–137.

29. *New York Times*, June 25, 26, and 27 and 1 July 1873. On the meeting of the Republican Society, see *L'Eco d'Italia*, June 25, 1873. That same day, Secchi's paper also published a speech by the Marchese Roberto Prati di Rovagnasco in support of the Consul, accompanied by a letter that the Director General of the Italian Foreign Ministry, Augusto Peiroleri, had sent him with the same intent.

30. *L'Eco d'Italia*, June 25, 1873.

31. Giuseppe Vallosio, "La Festa dell'Associazione Donnarumma," ibid., July 2, 1873.

32. The Italian consul in that city, Cella, was interviewed by the German-language newspaper *Illinois Staats Zeitung* (August 22, 1873) and

pointed out that there were not 400 to 800 little southern slaves but between 125 and 150, who were not exploited by *padroni* but by their own parents.

33. *New York Times*, December 4, 1873.

34. Capri 1874, 1:72.

35. Ibid., 1:73. Instead, Angelo De Gubernatis, writing in *La Rivista Europea* (January 1874, 415), praised Moreno for his commitment to the Italian children.

36. Moreno to Maestra, 24 June 1873, Gabinetto Particolare di Maestra, Busta 115, fascicolo 764, ACSR, and accompanying documents. Moreno wrote his letter on Astor House letterhead, which advertised "Rooms One Dollar and Upwards."

37. Moreno to Sumner, 14 November 1873, Charles Sumner Papers, Houghton Library, Harvard University. A longer version, with a section about adult emigrants victimized by the padrone system, was published in the *New York Times* on December 4, 1873.

38. Sumner to Moreno, 15 November 1873.

39. Congressional Record, "43rd Congress, 1st Session, 1873–1874," 469.

40. *New National Era*, January 2, 1873. Reprinted from the *New York Tribune*.

41. *New National Era*, June 25 and July 2, 1873. Evidently, they developed a friendship. Moreno wrote letters of introduction to Italian public figures for Douglass's trip to Italy. Returning the compliment, Moreno called him his "old friend, the Moses and liberator of his companions of misfortune . . . the black slaves of which he himself was one." Douglass, Moreno noted, particularly merited Italians' friendship, since he had used his personal influence and his newspaper to support the "Moreno Bill." Since they are not mentioned in his travel journal, Douglass apparently did not take advantage of the introductions. The Frederick Douglass Papers at the Library of Congress, Correspondence and Diary, http://memory.loc.gov/cgi-bin /ampagr

42. *New York Times*, June 24, 1874.

43. Congressional Record, Forty-Third Congress, Session. I Chap. 464, 1874, 251, 443. Though the Thirteenth Amendment to the Constitution prohibited slavery and involuntary servitude, this law provided for its application to "persons of foreign birth."

44. For a detailed account of the case, see Zucchi 1992, 141–142.

45. "Give the Honors to the Right Man," *The Sun* (New York), March 26, 1875.

46. "Padroni," *Brooklyn Daily Eagle*, February 23, 1874. In 1874 the *Times* published just eleven articles about the "Italian slaves."

47. Zucchi 1992, 142.

48. Ibid., 132.

5. THE ENCHANTER OF HAWAII

1. Andrade 1996, 17.

2. Kuykendall 1967, 3:202–226. Kuykendall also looked at a collection of Hawaiian diplomatic correspondence (Kuykendall 1926) that includes "The Hawaiian Episode of 1880," the report by James M. Comly, the United States representative to Hawaii (appendix A, 42–52).

3. "Sugar and Sandwich," *Brooklyn Daily Eagle*, February 24, 1884.

4. Li Hongzhang [Hung-Chang], Encyclopedia of World Biography, http://www.bookrags.com/Li_Hongzhang; Dye 1997 (Chapter 16, "The Moreno Affair," offers an excellent synthesis of how Moreno was involved in Li's plans to expand Chinese commerce); Kuykendall 1967, 208.

5. Moreno lost no time and presented a memorandum to "His Majesty Kalākaua" in which, among other things, he requested a subsidy for the CMSNC. The government, while pledging "customary support" for the initiative, made no commitment to a subsidy. See Samuel G. Wilder to Celso Caeser [*sic*] Moreno, 8 January 1880, Interior Department Letters, No. 17, July 7, 1880–August 1889, Hawaii State Archives.

6. Dye 1997, 147–149.

7. Fuchs 1961, 4. The discussion on the state of the islands is based on the chapter "A Kingdom Passes," 1–34.

8. Ibid., 4–14, 53. For the king's letter: Kalākaua to William N. Armstrong, February 1879, William Nevins Armstrong Papers, Box 1, Folder 2, Manuscripts and Archives, Yale University Library.

9. Adler and Kamins 1986, 118; Allen 1994, 73; Fuchs 1961, 4–14.

10. Kuykendall 1967, 189–190; Fuchs 1961, 25–26 and 189–190.

11. Stevens 1945; Tate 1945.

12. Fuchs 1961, 21–22.

13. See the chapter on immigration in Kuykendall 1967, 46–185.

14. Kalākaua to Armstrong, 27 October 1879, box 1, folder 3, Armstrong Papers.

15. Dye 1997, 196–197.

16. William Little Lee, a Harvard graduate and future chief justice of the Supreme Court of Hawaii, observed in 1849 that prejudice against "copper-colored skin" persisted against what he considered the hope of Hawaii, that is, "the mixing of the Saxon and Hawaiian races." On the other hand, Doctor George Lathrop considered Hawaiians "niggers" and rejected the idea of a society "in which the whites were not politically superior" (Dye 1997, 20, 48). Based on his skin color and appearance, gossip spread that the father of King Kalākaua was an African American blacksmith named Blossom, impossible because the man had arrived in Hawaii years after the king's birth. See Allen 1994, 26.

17. Kuykendall interpreted this movement as an "attempt to separate natives and foreigners and foment racial hatred." Kuykendall 1967, 87.

18. Alexander 1896, 2–3.

19. Dye 1997, 146 (citation from the *Pacific Commercial Advertiser*, January 4, 1880).

20. Kuykendall 1967, 209. The author says other sources describe Moreno as a person of average height, while one describes him as "a man of Herculean size and strength," capable of speaking almost all modern languages, and equipped with the easy self-confidence of a true yankee. (Delso [*sic*] Caesar Moreno, *Chicago Tribune*, September 10, 1880).

21. *Journal*, Armstrong Papers, 52.

22. U.S. Congress, House, Sub-Committee on Ways and Means, 49th Cong., 1st sess., *Hawaiian Treaty*, February 27, 1886, 40.

23. Allen 1994, 16.

24. Ibid., 8, 39.

25. Kuykendall 1967, 117; Dye 1997, 119.

26. Dye also uses the Hawaiian term for masturbation: *pikoikoi*. Dye 1997, 131.

27. In a letter from Paris to his sister Lili'uokalani, he described the "gaiety" of Sundays in Vienna—bands, dances, beer, the lyric opera—and posed a question: "How is it possible that these serene and happy people must finish in the inferno? Certainly not. What a contrast with our poor and sanctimonious community . . . What rubbish they have convinced us to believe." (Letter to Lili'uokalani, 10 August 1881, Foreign Office and Executive Office, Chronological File, 1881, King Kalākaua Letters from trip around the world, July-September 1881, Folder 2, Hawaii State Archive.)

28. Adler 1966; Tate 1945; "Sugar and Sandwich."

29. Adler-Kamins 1986, 44.

30. Ibid., 81–107. On the meeting between Moreno and Gibson, see also Dye 1997, 200, and Allen 1982, 152.

31. Allen 1982, 152.

32. Adler-Kamins 1986, 9; Dye 1997, 200; Fuchs 1961, 23–24.

33. See Anonymous 1887, 3; Allen 1994, xvi; Adler-Kamins 1986, 115.

34. U.S., Congress, House, Sub-Committee on Ways and Means, *Hawaiian Treaty*, 49th Cong, 1st sess., February 27, 1886, 43.

35. William F. Green to E. H. Allen, 22 October 1880, cited in Kuykendall 1967, 310–311.

36. Adler-Kamins 1986, 172.

37. Moreno, *The Position of Men and Affairs in Hawaii* (hereafter *PMAH*), 11–12.

38. "C. C. Moreno Dead," *The Friend* (Honolulu, April 1901), 77. Even by Moreno's standards, this project seems unlikely.

39. Alexander 1896, 5.

40. Dye 1997, 172, 180.

41. Moreno, *THQ*, 25–26. According to Moreno, the king agreed that "the missionaries were at the heart of the Kingdom's troubles." Kalākaua clearly expressed himself on this issue in a letter to Armstrong: "As the history of religion in every country and climate shows, in every matter in which religion has a strong hold on the masses one finds an oppressive majority that originates with the priests' arts" (Kalākaua to Armstrong, 27 October 1879. Armstrong Papers, Box 1, folder 3).

42. Kuykendall 1967, 208.

43. Kuykendall 1926, 47–48; Adler-Kamins 1986, 115–116.

44. Kuykendall 1926, 48.

45. Kuykendall 1967, 211–212.

46. Ibid., 211.

47. Ibid., 211–212.

48. Allen 1994, 75 (citation from the *San Francisco Chronicle*, November 16, 1874). Ten years later, Moreno confirmed that the conversation concerned both the transpacific cable and the navigation line. "We agreed," he recalled, "on many points regarding the innovations to be introduced in the kingdom." See Testimony of Moreno, February 27, 1886, *The Hawaiian Treaty* (of Reciprocity), U.S. Committee on Ways and Means, 49th Cong., 1st Sess., p. 40.

49. *Ka Uwea Telegarapa Pacifika* (1880). The only copy in a library is in the Italian Geographic Society (Società Geografica Italiana) in Rome.

50. Kuykendall 1967, 209–210; Adler-Kamins 1986, 119. These developments are well summarized by Darlene E. Kelly, Historical Collections of the Hawaiian Islands, "The King," parts 13–14. http://ftp.rootsweb.com/pub/usgenweb/hi/keepers/koc74.txt.

51. Kuykendall 1967, 212–213; Registry of Naturalized Subjects in the Hawaiian Kingdom, Moreno. Celso C., 14 August 1880. www.HawaiianKingdom.org/info/registry/pag/fr–msainm.htm; Dye 1997, 150.

52. Lewis L. Rice to "Bro. Clark," 3 August 1880; undated letter; and 12 February 1881, Rice Letters, Hawaiian Historical Society. Rice was a former journalist from Oberlin, Ohio.

53. *Journal*, Armstrong Papers, 71 ff.

54. Alexander 1896, 5.

55. *Journal*, Armstrong Papers, Box 2, folder 16, p. 72.

56. "How Moreno Fell out with Wilcox," *Hawaiian Gazette*, March 19, 1901.

57. Kuykendall 1967, 214 and 223.

58. He also referred to Moreno by the nickname "Willy Don." See Anonymous 1887, 4.

59. Kuykendall 1926, 49.

60. Ibid., 50–51.

61. Moreno's rise and fall echoed in the American and European press, including several Italian newspapers. But none watched this spectacle with a greater sense of schadenfreude than his old adversary Secchi de Casali. With biting sarcasm, he dedicated a satire to the humiliation of the "famous Baboon of the Seven Lakes," portrayed as a "Carnival king" only capable of bragging about improbable endeavors and of posing as an intellectual while "telling you about the Roman general Hamilcar." *L'Eco d'Italia*, September 11, 1880. The European newspapers talked about the strange drama (or farce) that had taken place in Honolulu. The *Globe* of Paris reproduced an article from an Italian publication that denounced Moreno's dismissal as the work of "reverend missionaries, who, like Jesuits, aspired to be the kingdom's landowners." The French consul was condemned for interfering in Hawaii's internal affairs. In Miscellaneous Scrap Book 1879–1883, M-48, Walter Murray Gibson Scrapbook, Hawaii State Archives.

62. Fuchs 1961, 24.

63. Damon 1957, 156.

64. Alexander 1896, 6; Andrade 1996, 22.

65. Kuykendall 1967, 219.

66. Andrade 1996, 23.

67. Kuykendall 1967, 220. Plesur 1971, 132, believes that American opposition to Moreno was motivated by fear that he wanted to negotiate a treaty with Germany.

68. Ibid., 220–221. A search of the official documents of the Ministry of Foreign Affairs did not produce evidence that Moreno had held another office besides that of Minster of Foreign Affairs. The missing decrees, signed by the king and whose restitution had been requested, were not returned. Memorandum in re C. C. Moreno claims (ca. 1887), Foreign Office and Executive Document #80, Hawaii State Archives.

69. Andrade 1996, 23–25. In a letter, Sanford Dole observed that "Moreno left yesterday on the steamboat with three halfblooded youth . . . officially to educate them abroad, in reality to make up for the expenses of the voyage." Damon 1957, 157.

6. Celso's Vendetta

1. Moreno's statement in front of the Subcommittee on Ways and Means, *The Hawaiian Treaty*, 42.

2. On October 7, 1880, the Italian consul in San Francisco wrote to the Ministry of Foreign Affairs to inform it that Moreno's position as ambassador had been revoked by King Kalākaua, and explained that "Moreno arrived in San Francisco last month . . . but not enjoying the best reputation

in this city, he did not see some of his old acquaintances, and he left for Washington, where he took steps to get the American minister in Honolulu revoked," ASMAE, Consolato di San Francisco, Affari in genere, 7 October 1880.

3. *Washington Post*, October 8, 1880. Moreno's testimony in front of the House of Representatives' Subcommittee on Ways and Means, *THT*, 47. This part of the chapter is based on letters, newspaper articles, and documents that Moreno inserted in the record. An example is a long article in the *Washington Herald* on October 3, 1880. It claims that Moreno had been in Washington for years, "and no one has ever questioned his ability or integrity." *THT*, 46.

4. Quigg 1988, 174–175.

5. Faldella 1962, 128.

6. Quigg 1988, 175.

7. "How Moreno Fell Out With Wilcox," *Hawaiian Gazette*, March 19, 1901.

8. Quigg 1998, 175. In the article cited in note 7, Moreno explained that stopping in Germany with the youths would have necessitated an entire year of German instruction first, and for this reason he preferred to take them to Italy.

9. Booth to his father, Berlin, 23 December 1880. Copies of this letter and of other documents related to Booth are in Naples in the Archivio di Giuseppe Catenacci, "memoria storica vivente" in the Collegio della Nunziatella.

10. The Genoese newspaper *Corriere Mercantile* was the first to publicize the group's arrival. The news was then repeated in other newspapers. See "Un italiano ministro delle isole Sandwich," *Gazzetta Piemontese*, January 30, 1881. On their meetings with Verdi and Garibaldi, "Il re delle isole di Sandwich a Garibaldi," *Gazzetta Piemontese*, February 5, 1881, and *Corriere Mercantile*, February 2, 1881.

11. Quigg 1988, 176.

12. This letter, dated July 10, 1882, is reproduced in Tyrrell 1907.

13. Faldella 1962, 129.

14. "How Moreno Fell out with Wilcox."

15. "Il re delle Isole Sandwich al re d'Italia," *Gazzetta Piemontese*, March 25, 1881. The article talks about the message sent from the "Palazzo Kapiolani" to "His Royal Majesty Umberto I King of Italy, Cyprus, and Jerusalem," who is addressed as "My great and good Brother." Also in the *Gazzetta Piemontese*, March 26, 1881, we find correspondence from Rome that reports Quintino Sella's satisfaction upon learning that "the name of the new Italy is boasted about in the farthest countries and in the most olive-colored parlia-

ments for the primacy of our great shipbuilding." In his diary, Wilcox noted Umberto's words: "Seek wisdom until you find it, then return directly to your homeland for the work that is right for you, for King, country, and people" (Quigg 1988, 176).

16. Letter from Booth et al. to "the People of Hawaii," 22 February 1881. Copies of this letter and of other documents related to Booth are in Naples in the Archivio di Giuseppe Catenacci, "Memoria storica vivente," in the Collegio della Nunziatella.

17. "Kakalakua on His Travels," *Washington Post*, February 7, 1881. Among the William Nevins Armstrong Papers, MS 39, Manuscripts and Archives, Yale University Library, there is a letter issued by the Hawaiian Department of Foreign Affairs on January 17, 1881. It announces the king's voyage with the aim of assessing potential emigrants' suitability for Hawaii.

18. Ibid.; Faldella 1962, 142: "The correspondence from Vienna tells how King Kalākaua received numerous calling cards from the odalisques there."

19. Armstrong to William L. Green, Hawaiian Minister of Foreign Affairs, Shanghai, 4 April 1881, and Vienna, 10 August 1881, Foreign Office and Executive Office, Hawaii State Archives. In his open letter to the king, Moreno could have been referring his conversation in Shanghai with "the scoundrel Ferdinando De Luca," whose contents had been reported to the Minister of Foreign Affairs in Rome, and who had harshly rebuked him for his gullibility. See *PMAH*, 13–14.

20. *Washington Post*, February 7, 1881. Mistaking Moreno's origins, the newspaper wrote, "it is clear that Kalākaua still believes in that charming Spaniard."

21. See "Celso Moreno e il re," *Gazzetta Piemontese*, June 27, 1881.

22. "Il Re Kalākaua a Napoli," *Il Movimento* (Genoa), July 3, 1881.

23. Nicola Lazzaro, "Napoli," *Gazzetta Piemontese*, July 3, 1881. According to Faldella, he "descends on Naples in the arms of Moreno who some newspapers mistake for a comandante Doglioni of Dogliani, his homeland" (Faldella 1962, 142).

24. That is according to Armstrong's journal (Armstrong Papers), which dates it June 10, 1881. The *Journal* is the principle source for Armstrong's subsequent book about his trip around the world with the king: Armstrong 1903, 201..

25. Ibid., 202–203.

26. Quigg 1988, 177.

27. Greer 1971, 92.

28. Armstrong Papers.

29. Greer 1971, 92.

30. Genoa's *Il Caffaro* reported (July 4, 1881) that the king, "accompanied by charge d'affairs Cav. Giustini, and by Messrs. Armstrong and Judd," very much admired Pompeii, especially its archeological remains. Then, returning to Naples, he received the American consul, E. W. Schmidt, with Secretary Robert Wickersham, as well as the consul of Sweden and Norway, Clausen. The next morning, he visited the "Annunziatella" [*sic*], where "Colonel Cav. Briganti, the professors, and school officials received him." The king visited "the entire premises," and deigned to participate in "some gymnastic exercises and fencing," finally expressing "his great satisfaction" to Colonel Briganti.

31. *Il Caffaro* (Genoa), July 5, 1881: "The civil marriage of Mr. Pasquale and the young Arata Naski Misak, who last February escaped the harem of the Egyptian viceroy, was celebrated."

32. See *Il Caffaro*, July 4 and 5, 1881.

33. Moreno presented the Hawaiian government with a fait accompli, and, to use his words from a letter of March 7, 1884 to Kalākaua reprinted in *THQ*, he had "personally and voluntarily" relinquished custody of the three youths on July 2, 1881. Faldella (1962, 141) writes that Moreno "enrolled the Hawaiian princes envied by other nations in Italian military institutes." When later talking about returning his credentials to Kalākaua, he added a prudent "maybe" (142). Though Moreno broke off his official relationship with the "boys," he also forgot to send the letter renouncing his guardianship to Honolulu, retaining their loyalty and encouraging their reluctance to follow the instructions they received. Boyd, writing to the king on May 16, 1881 (Armstrong Papers), observed that the youths had all been settled "thanks to the influence of Moreno, your loyal friend" and warned the king about his true enemies, the "evil doers" who were all around him.

34. For both letters, see Greer 1971, 106–109.

35. *Pacific Commercial Advertiser* (Honolulu), December 10, 1881.

36. Quigg 1988, 177.

37. Booth to Kalākaua, Naples, 18 August 1882.

38. "The Future of Our Hawaiian Youth," *Pacific Commercial Advertiser*, September 2, 1882.

39. Quigg 1988, 178.

40. Ibid., 180–182.

41. In his open letter, reprinted in *THQ*, 42–43, Moreno accused the missionaries, with his usual vehemence, of taking advantage of the natives' virgin souls, exploiting them by means of a false religion, planting the seeds of venality in them, tricking them into ruin with loans and mortgages, and contaminating them with venereal diseases.

42. Quigg 1988, 174–184.

43. Booth to Cerulli, Turin, 14 October 1883.

44. Booth to Cerulli, Turin, 6 January, 14 January, 3 February 1884.

45. G. P. Giustini to Cerulli, Naples, 23 July 1884.

46. *Pacific Commercial Advertiser*, November 11, 1884.

47. News of Booth's death can also been found in a September 13, 1884, *New York Times* article, "The Cholera's Ravage," which perpetuated the usual misunderstanding: "Among those dangerously ill with cholera is the son-in-law of King Kalākaua."

48. Mancini to Cerulli, Rome, 22 September 1884. The condolence message was published in the *Pacific Commercial Advertiser* on October 28, 1884.

49. Perli to Cerulli, Naples, 15 October 1884.

50. "For the Album of the Young Hawaiian Prince James K. Booth—Improvised," in Cordano 1884. Cordano was an instructor in the Nunziatella Military Academy in Naples. Giuseppe Catenacci pointed this poem out to me.

7. ELECTORAL INTERMEZZO

1. Faldella 1962, 114–115.

2. Ibid., 116–117.

3. Moreno to Faldella, Rome, 13 April 1881. In the letter, which he sent along with newspapers with passages underlined "in red pencil," he reports that he knew a mysterious "beautiful teacher" (*bella maestra*) who resided in Saluggia, Faldella's hometown. Moreno also sent Faldella a pamphlet titled "i Comprachicos" which we have not been able to find. It was likely an excerpt from a magazine and referred to the Victor Hugo novel *The Man Who Laughs* in which a band of "*comprachicos*," that is, children buyers, appears. The link to the child slavery Moreno denounced in New York is clear. The term reappears in Faldella's letter to Moreno. All of Moreno's letters to Faldella cited in this chapter are held in the Fondo Giovanni Faldella in the Biblioteche Civiche Torinesi, in the Manoscritti e Rari-Fondi personali section. The correspondence is divided into twenty-two packets and is available on microfilm. Here we will cite the letters by date for brevity.

4. Faldella 1962, 128 and 130.

5. Ibid., 126 and 138.

6. Ibid., 137.

7. Ibid., 144–145.

8. *Gazzetta Piemontese*, August 9, 1881.

9. "C. C. Moreno nel suo paese natio," ibid., 1 September 1881.

10. See Faldella 1962, 125.

11. "L'avvenire di Napoli," *Il Popolo Romano*, July 5, 1881; reprinted in *HGW*, 51. In *HGW* we also find numerous articles about Italian "slavery" in America published in various Italian newspapers during those months.

12. "Ferrovia Dogliani-Monchiero," *Gazzetta Piemontese*, March 25, 1882.

13. Faldella 1962, 129.

14. "Lo scrutinio di lista alla prova," *Corriere Mercantile* (Genoa), October 6, 1882.

15. "Per le elezioni—I deputati del Collegio di Bra Alba," *Gazzetta Piemontese*, September 22, 1882.

16. Baldo, "Elezioni," ibid., October 12, 1882.

17. The list was published in *Gazzetta Piemontese* on October 25, 1882. The province of Cuneo, divided into four electoral districts, elected a total of twelve deputies.

18. "Dinnanzi alle urne," *Il Popolo Italiano* (Genoa), October 29, 1882. Faldella 1962 also mentions De Amezaga, calling him "more fortunate in glorious maritime defense than in electoral struggles."

19. *Il Caffaro* (Genoa), October 29, 1882.

20. "I nostri candidati," *Corriere Mercantile* (Genoa), October 24, 1882; *Il Commercio-Gazzetta di Genova*, October 23–24, 1882.

21. "Elezioni Politiche," *Il Gottardo* (Genoa), October 27, 1882.

22. The numbers are the official numbers reported in *Le elezioni politiche al parlamento subalpino e al parlamento italiano*, part 2, *1848–97—Indice generale degli atti parlamentari. Storia dei collegi elettorali* (Rome: Tipografia della Camera dei Deputati, 1898). The pertinent charts are on pages 17 and 292.

23. "Genova e la lotta elettorale," *Gazzetta Piemontese*, January 2, 1883.

24. L. Levi to Faldella, Fondo Giovanni Faldella in the Biblioteche Civiche Torinesi, Sezione manoscritti e Rari—Fondi personali.

25. "I elezioni da Liguria," *O Ficcanaso*, November 4, 1882.

26. "Celso Cesare Moreno," ibid., November 17, 1882.

27. "Elezioni politiche—Programma di Celso Cesare Moreno," ibid., November 23, 1882.

28. "Un programma unico," *Il Popolo Italiano* (Genoa), November 12, 1882.

29. "Cesare Celso Moreno," *O Stafi* (Genoa), November 18, 1882.

30. "Taglio dell'istmo di Malacca," *O Ficcanaso*, December 2, 1882. The article was reprinted in the Roman newspaper *La Lega della Democrazia*.

31. "Elezioni politiche e Maneuvra elettorale," *O Ficcanaso*, December 23 and 30, 1882.

32. "Elezioni politiche e La linea di demarcazione," *Il Movimento* (Genoa), January 3 and 5, 1883.

33. "Cronaca e notizie varie," *Corriere Mercantile*, January 5, 1883.

34. "Lettera di C. C. Moreno al ministro Baccarini," *O Ficcanaso*, January 7, 1883. The letter is dated "Rome 28 November 1882."

35. Information obtained respectively from *Il Caffaro* and *Il Gottardo*, January 9, 1883. Guglielmo Oberdank, better known as Oberdan, was an Italian irredentist hanged in Trieste for high treason on December 20, 1882. In recent weeks the Italian newspapers had dedicated ample space to his cause.

36. "I elezioni."

37. "Il ballottaggio e La proclamazione," *Il Mare*, January 15 and 16, 1883.

38. See Beccaria 1994, 223.

39. Moreno to Faldella, Washington, DC, 8 February 1886.

8. THE NEW ITALIAN AMERICA

1. Moreno to Faldella, Washington, 19 October 1885.

2. Faldella 1962, 143.

3. News of the meeting, held on September 29, was in the *New York Star* and in the *New York Sun*, and also reprinted by the *Chicago Tribune* ("Italians and Poles," October 2, 1884). On Moreno's support of the Democratic Party, see "Per un nostro concittadino," *Gazzetta di Dogliani*, January 16, 1893, which reproduces an article that appeared in the *Courier Journal* of Louisville, Kentucky.

4. Moreno to Faldella, Washington, 19 October 1885.

5. Moreno to Faldella, 24 September 1885.

6. "Giudizi americani sulla condanna di Sbarbaro," *Gazzetta Piemontese*, December 16, 1885.

7. See *HGW*, 43.

8. Moreno to Faldella, 22 October 1885.

9. Moreno to Faldella, 28 January 1888.

10. Moreno to Faldella, 28 March 1886.

11. Moreno to Faldella, 8 February 1886.

12. "Imported Contract Labor," *New York Herald*, June 22, 1884, reprinted in *HGW*, 14–15.

13. Ibid.

14. "The Italian Padroni," *Washington Post*, January 29, 1885.

15. "The Italian Padroni and Slaves," *The Craftsman*, May 9, 1885, reprinted in *HGW*, 4.

16. *HGW*, 18–19.

17. "80,000 Italian Slaves," *Chicago Daily Tribune*, and "Slaves to Padrones," *New York Times*, February 27, 1886.

18. "Italian Slavery in America," *Washington Post*, February 28, 1886.

19. "The Padrone System," *Chicago Daily Tribune*, February 28, 1886.

20. See Andreas 1884–86, 2, 118.

21. On Moreno's accusations and the *padrone* system in Chicago, see also Lombardo 2010.

22. Franzina 1995, 187; Rossi 1892, 68–69.

23. "Italian Slavery in America."

24. Many books that address the Italian experience in America dedicate ample space to Palma di Cesnola. For a more recent and specific contribution, see Palombi 2006. It discusses the bitter conflict over the illegal exportation of art from Italy to America that pitted Cesnola against Rodolfo Lanciani. On Suzzara Verdi, see Durante 2001, 505–516. On the Suzzara-Weston marriage, see "Alfred Jerome Weston of This City Married to Miss Verdi," *New York Times*, June 7, 1891.

25. For the first, see "The Italian Padroni and Their Accomplices," *Alexandria Gazette*, July 18, 1894. For the second, see *HGW*, 9.

26. Celso Caesar Moreno, "The Organ of the Italian Padroni," *Chicago Daily Tribune*, October 30, 1886.

27. Iorizzo 1980, 75.

28. Ibid.

29. Moreno's article, accompanied by Speroni's testimony, is in *HGW*, 39–40. The resulting narrative is in Ciambelli 1893, I, 22–24. The South Carolina case raised an uproar; other horrific testimony was reported in *L'Eco d'Italia* ("L'atroce martirio di 150 braccianti italiani nel South Carolina," December 15, 1891).

30. *Washington Post*, August 2, 1888, and "Italian Slavery in California," ibid., October 17, 1888.

31. Celso Caesar Moreno, "A Letter to King Humbert," ibid., August 3, 1888. The previous letter to the king may be found in *HGW*, 17–18.

32. See Cacioli 1988.

33. Moreno to Faldella, 5 May 1888.

34. Moreno to Faldella, 2 February 1888.

35. Moreno to Faldella, 24 November 1891.

36. Fitzgerald 1996, 122.

37. *HGW*, 21–24.

38. Celso Caesar Moreno, "The Italian Press in America," *Washington Post*, April 30, 1889.

39. On Fava, see Loverci 1977 and Thomas 2010.

40. "Minister Fava Not Recalled," *Washington Post*, June 9, 1890.

41. "Il *Non possumus* del Papa e la conciliazione," in *La Civiltà Cattolica* VII, no. 966 (1890): 641–658. *L'Osservatore Romano*, the Holy See's daily newspaper, had already published Moreno's 1886 arguments in front of the Chamber of Deputies. See *HGW*, 37.

42. Faldella 1962, 137.

43. *HGW*, 47.

44. Moreno to Bonghi, 4 April 1890, Archivio di Stato di Napoli, Archivio privato Ruggiero Bonghi, busta 11, 667.

45. Crispi 1892, 82.

46. The discussion of Bonghi's inquiry is in Crispi 1892, 377–379.

47. Moreno to Bonghi, 31 January 1891, ASN, Archivio privato Ruggiero Bonghi, busta 11, 668.

48. Moreno to Bonghi, 20 December 1891, ASN, Archivio privato Ruggiero Bonghi, busta 11, 669.

49. See *HGW*, 38–39.

50. Celso Caesar Moreno, "Italy's New Premier," *Washington Post*, February 3, 1891.

51. Loverci 1977, 254–256.

52. There is an ample bibliography on anti-Italian violence in the United States. Among the most recent contributions, see Salvetti 2003 and the impressive "Timeline of Tears" in Borsella 2005, 52. Moreno (*HGW*, 32) also lists many episodes of violence.

53. Bosi 1921, 124–125.

54. "Baron Fava's Recall," *Los Angeles Times*, April 3, 1891.

55. "Charges Against an Italian Consul," *Chicago Daily Tribune*, October 10, 1891. Moreno had already told the story of Fava's undignified lodgings, described as a "furnished room," to *Cristoforo Colombo* on April 10 and then to the *Washington Herald* on May 3, 1891. He talked about "a simple boardinghouse" with San Francisco's *La Voce del Popolo* on May 25 under the title "Le meschinità di Fava."

56. Loverci 1977, 256–257.

57. Bosi 1921, 126.

58. Thomas 2010, 61–62.

59. See Fava 1904.

60. "Baron Fava's Trip Home," *New York Times*, September 19, 1892.

61. "An Unwelcome Visitor to Mr. Moreno," *Washington Post*, September 30, 1893.

62. "Caesar Celso Moreno Warned," ibid., September 13, 1894.

63. Published on November 17, 894, the article was reprinted in *HGW*, 9–10.

64. Abruzzo made his views on the issue known. See his letter "Le Infamie dei Bosses," *L'Eco d'Italia* (New York), March 1, 1891.

65. On Fava's activities in Bucharest and the Jewish question in Romania and the Balkans, see the last two chapters of Ardizzone 2008.

66. Thomas 2010, 63. See "For Libeling Baron Fava," *New York Times*, July 12, 1895.

67. "Celso Caesar Moreno Gives Bail," *Washington Post*, July 13, 1895.

68. Thomas 2010, 60.

69. "Not in Government Employ" and "Moreno and the Immigration Bureau," *Washington Post*, September 19 and October 13, 1894.

70. Thomas 2010, 66. The Moreno-Stump exchange is in *HGW*, 27.

71. "At the National Capital," *New York Times*, July 20, 1895.

72. "Libelled Baron Fava," *The Sun*, New York; "Fava's Libeler Guilty," *Chicago Daily Tribune*; "Moreno Guilty," *Los Angeles Times*; and especially "Moreno Guilty of Libel," *The Morning Times* and "Don Celso Moreno Still in Jail," *The Evening Times* (Washington, DC), all October 30, 1895.

73. "Moreno May Be Sentenced Monday," *Washington Post*, November 10, 1895.

74. "Moreno Goes to Jail for Ninety Days," *New York Times*; "Moreno Sent to Jail," *Washington Post*; "Moreno Sent to Jail," *Morning Times*, all November 12, 1895.

75. "Smith D. Fry, His Career Closed," *Barton County Democrat*, June 21, 1901.

76. "Kalākaua's Ex-Minister," *Los Angeles Times*, November 16, 1895.

77. "Sunday Behind Walls," *Washington Post*, November 18, 1895.

78. "Has an Island for Sale," ibid., December 16, 1895.

79. The repeated references in *HGW* to the wife of the then-Minister of Foreign Affairs Alberto Blanc, the Cuban Dolores Natalia (Natividad) Terry y Dorticos, are dark. See page 50 in particular.

80. Luigi Einaudi, "Italiani in America," *La Stampa* (Turin), June 4, 1897.

81. *HGW*, 8.

82. Ibid., 25.

9. THE DESTINY OF HAWAII

1. Moreno, *PMAH*, 3.

2. Ibid., 4.

3. Ibid., 7.

4. Ibid., 10.

5. Ibid., 11.

6. Andrade 1996, 42–43.

7. The information summarized in these pages is based on Kuykendall 1967, 322–338.

8. Moreno, *PMAH*, 11–12. Ocean Island, today Banaba Island, is a coral island belonging to Republic of Kiribati.

9. Ibid., 14.

10. Kuykendall 1967l, 405–406; Zambucka 2003, 82–85; "A Period of Intrigue," *Washington Post*, November 16, 1893.

11. Moreno, *PMAH*, 15.

12. Ibid., 16.

13. Ibid., 17.

14. Celso Caesar Moreno, "Hawaii Past and Present," *Washington Post*, December 16, 1889.

15. Celso Caesar Moreno, "King Malietoa and Germany," ibid., February 25, 1890.

16. Quigg 198, 184.

17. Andrade 1996, 58.

18. "Excitement in Hawaii," *New York Times*, August 11, 1889. See also Wong-Rayson 1987, 194–198, and, obviously, Andrade 1996.

19. Chapin 1996, 84–92.

20. On the "racial" turn in Wilcox's political thought, see Andrade 1996, 71 ff.

21. "England and Hawaii," *Los Angeles Times*, September 18, 1891; "The Hawaiian Story," *Wichita Daily Eagle*, September 21, 1891.

22. C.C. Moreno, "La questione delle isole Sandwich," *Gazzetta di Dogliani*, December 5 and 19, 1891.

23. "Wilcox Makes Denial," *Washington Post*, January 13, 1892.

24. Celso Caesar Moreno, "The Hawaiian Dominions," ibid., August 26, 1892.

25. "Hawaiians May Visit Washington," ibid., August 31, 1892.

26. "Affairs in Hawaii," ibid., November 18, 1892.

27. Andrade 1996, 126.

28. Celso Caesar Moreno, "Blount's Mission to Hawaii," *Washington Post*, March 25, 1893.

29. "The Situation in Hawaii," ibid., September 10, 1893; "From the Queen's Cabinet Officer," ibid., September 26, 1893.

30. Andrade 1996, 139.

31. "Trusting the United States," *Washington Post*, October 26, 1893. Alexander, born in Hawaii, was the son of a Presbyterian minister and studied at Yale. In 1891 he published *A Brief History of the Hawaiian People*. In 1896, he published *History of the Later Years of the Hawaiian Monarchy and the Revolution of 1893*.

32. "Ridiculed by Wilcox," *Washington Post*, December 21, 1893; Celso Caesar Moreno, "The Army of Hawaii," ibid., December 30, 1893.

33. Moreno, *THQ*. The *Washington Post* highlighted the pamphlet's publication in a short article, "The Hawaiian Question," February 3, 1894.

34. "An Open Letter to His Majesty the Emperor of Japan," *Alexandria Gazette*, April 27, 1895.

35. "Lili'uokalani's Character," *Washington Post*, February 19, 1894; "Will Protect the Queen," ibid., April 15, 1894.

36. "Fred Douglass on Hawaii," ibid., March 17, 1894.

37. "Mr. Cleveland's Convert," *The Morning Call* (San Francisco), March 24, 1894.

38. Daws 1968, 281.

39. "Will Protect the Queen," *Washington Post*, April 15, 1894; "Bob's Backslide," *Los Angeles Times*, May 8, 1894.

40. "The Uprising in Hawaii," *New York Times*, January 20, 1895.

10. THE SUNSET ROAD

1. "Haunt the Halls of Congress," *Chicago Daily Tribune*, April 28, 1896.

2. "Nicolleti's Push Queered Him," *Los Angeles Times*, August 18, 1896, and "A Literary Los Angeleno," *The Herald* (Los Angeles), August 19, 1896.

3. "Celso Caesar Moreno" and "Next Italian Ambassador," *Washington Bee*, August 8 and November 28, 1896. The newspaper viewed Moreno's appointment very favorably, saying that since 1871 he "with devotion, energy and self-sacrificing spirit, has all over the United States protected his countrymen in need of protection and aid."

4. "Human Liberty," *The Washington Bee*, May 30, 1896.

5. Celso Cesare Moreno, "Le foche e il Mare di Behring [*sic*]," *Gazzetta di Dogliani*, March 7 and March 28, 1891; "L'Arbitrato per le Foche," ibid., August 6, 1892; "Socialismo ed utopia," ibid., June 23, 1894.

6. "All the Fruit Vendors to be Tagged," *Washington Post*, May 8, 1889; Celso Caesar Moreno, "L'Influenza Morbus" and "The Antipirina and the Influenza," *Washington Post*, December 30, 1889, and February 2, 1890; "The Columbus Monument at Genoa," ibid., June 8, 1890. On the same subject, see the *Gazzetta di Dogliani*, June 28, 1890.

7. "The Strange Career of Caesar Moreno," *Seattle Star*, March 22, 1901.

8. "Hearings in the 'Hung Up' Cases," *Washington Post*, December 23, 1893.

9. "Plea for Tony Tomasola," *Washington Post*, December 29, 1897. The case had some resonance and also appears in the New York *Sun* ("A Question To Be Decided," December 12, 1897).

10. "Diana Romi Remains Free," *Evening Times* (Washington, DC), February 5, 1897.

11. "Former Friar Heavily Sentenced," *Washington Post*, March 5, 1899.

12. "Fruit Peddlers Must Move," ibid., November 26, 1899, and "He Wants Protection," *The Times* (Washington, DC), February 15, 1898.

13. "Italians Take a Hand," *Washington Post*, April 6, 1900. That same day, the *Times* of Washington also reported that Moreno, asked to speak, excused himself, claiming that he was unwell.

14. Celso Cesare Moreno, "La China secondo il Cap. Celso Cesare Moreno," *Il Giornale* (Genoa), February 9, 1900.

15. Celso Cesare Moreno, "Divagazioni cinesi," ibid., June 26, 1900.

16. Celso Cesare Moreno, "La Cina, l'Inghilterra e l'Italia," ibid., June 29, 1900.

17. The Peruna ad appeared in many American newspapers from 1900 until 1902, even after Moreno's death. See, for example, the *San Francisco Call*, October 3, 1901, and *The Colored American*, March 22, 1902. Regarding the ads in Hawaiian newspapers, see the *Gazzetta di Dogliani*, March 21, 1891. The negative comment appeared in *The Hawaiian Star*, March 28, 1900.

18. "A Prophet on Crown Lands," *The Independent* (Honolulu), May 1, 1899. See also *Speech on the question of the Crown-lands in the Hawaiian islands and territorial expansion before the Committee on territories of the United States House of Representatives on Friday the sixth day of January, 1899.*

19. "The Foes of Hawaii," *Hawaiian Gazette*, February 9, 1900.

20. "LaBob Wilcox," ibid., March 2, 1900.

21. "Natives in Convention Lay Plans For Severance From the Haoles," ibid., June 8, 1900.

22. "Tell of Hawaiian Hopes," *Evening Bulletin* (Honolulu), July 29, 1900.

23. "The First Gun," *Hawaiian Star*, October 1, 1900.

24. "Wilcox Denounced a Hypocrite and Deceiver," *Honolulu Republican*, October 19, 1900.

25. "How Moreno Fell Out With Wilcox," *Hawaiian Gazette*, March 19, 1901. Curiously, this article was published a few days after Moreno's death.

26. "Look out for This Man," *Scranton Tribune*, October 19, 1900.

27. "A Preposterous Protest and Petition" and "Endorse the Delegate," *The Independent* (Honolulu), December 1 and November 22, 1900.

28. "His Life One Adventure," *Dubuque Herald*, December 21, 1900. With minor variations, this article, which originally appeared in a New York newspaper, was published in other provincial newspapers with the title "Wilcox in the World." See *Hawaiian Gazette*, January 15, 1901.

29. *Hawaiian Star*, January 8, 1901.

30. See the introduction to Mantea 2007, 43; the articles "Hawaii's Delegate to Congress May Be Refused a Seat," *San Francisco Call*, November 17, 1900; "New Delegate in Congress from Hawaii," *Omaha Daily Bee*, December 2, 1900.

31. See "After Wilikoki's Scalp," *Hawaiian Star*, December 22, 1900.

32. See "Triumphant Republicanism Tells Its Story," *Hawaiian Gazette*, October 19, 1900.

33. See Andrade, chapter XIII. On the accusations of treason, see "Calls Wilcox Traitor," *Washington Post*, and "Faces Charges of Treason," *Chicago Daily Tribune*, February 2, 1901.

34. "Let Wilcox Alone," *Hawaiian Gazette*, December 26, 1900.

35. See "Wilcox in Washington"; *The Independent* (Honolulu), January 8, 1901; "Give Us A Rest," ibid., February 9, 1901.

36. "Hawaii's Delegate to Congress May Be Refused a Seat," *San Francisco Call*, November 17, 1900.

37. "His Dream Not Realized"; "'Bob' Wilcox Friend"; "Five Days a Premier—Once Headed Revolt in Sumatra"; "A Soldier of Fortune Dead"; "Death of Moreno Extremely Pitiful," respectively *The Times* (Washington, DC), *Los Angeles Times*, *Washington Post*, and *New York Times*, March 13, 1901, and *Evening Bulletin* (Honolulu), April 2, 1901. That day, news of Moreno's death appeared in various minor newspapers (for example, the *Mansfield News* of Mansfield, Ohio).

38. "His Dream Not Realized," "Funeral of Celso Moreno," *The Times* and *The Evening Times* (Washington, DC), March 13, 1901; "Celso Caesar Moreno's Funeral," *Washington Post*, March 15, 1901.

39. Faldella 1962, 115.

40. "A Premier . . . of Polynesia," *Manitoba Morning Free Press* (Winnipeg), July 13, 1901.

41. "His Dream Not Realized."

42. "Death of Celso Caesar Moreno" and "The Carpet Bagger," *Hawaiian Gazette*, March 22 and May 10, 1901; untitled piece in *The Hawaiian Star*, March 22, 1901; "Celso Moreno Closes His Career," *Honolulu Republican* (reprinted in the *San Francisco Chronicle*), March 22, 1901; "Topics of the Day," *The Independent* (Honolulu), March 22, 1901.

43. Unsigned editorial, *Daily Yellowstone Journal*, March 21, 1886.

BIBLIOGRAPHY

WORKS BY CELSO CESARE MORENO

AIA *American Interests in Asia*. New York: C. S. Westcott & Co., 1869.

HGW History of a Great Wrong: *Italian Slavery in America*. Washington, DC: U.S. Department of Labor, 1896.

PMAH The Position of Men and Affairs in Hawaii: Open Letter to His Majesty King Kakalaua, August 7, 1886, *Post Scriptum*, April 7, 1887. Washington, D.C. [1887].

THQ *The Hawaiian Question, or The Position of Men and Affairs in Hawaii.* Washington, DC: Hartmann & Cadick, 1894.

TPC *The Trans-Pacific Cable as Projected by Caesar Celso Moreno in Washington, D.C. 1869*. n.p.

ARCHIVAL SOURCES

ACSR Archivio Centrale dello Stato, Rome, "Ministero della Marina, Uffici Diversi (1861–1864)."

APQP Archivio della Parrocchia di San Quirico e Paolo, Dogliani (Books of Baptisms, Marriages, and Deaths).

Archivio di Stato Genova, "Camera di Commercio di Genova," "Inventario della Scuola di Nautica. Regolamento," and Fondo Università di Genova, Registri dei Matricolati.

Archivio di Stato di Torino, "Intendenza Generale d'Armata, Campagna 1855–1856."

ASCD Archivio Storico del Comune di Dogliani ("Stato della Popolazione", "Anagrafe," "Registro della Popolazione," "Liste di Leva"; and other records on "Catasti" (i.e. real estate transactions) and "Imposta dui fabbricati").

ASMAE Archivio Storico del Ministero degli Affari esteri Roma.

Correspondence between Moreno and various individuals (sources identified in footnotes).

PRINTED SOURCES

Abba, Giuseppe Cesare. *Dal Bonaparte a Carlo Alberto—Cronache a memoria.* In *Meditazioni sul Risorgimento*. Turin: S.T.E.N., 1913.

———. *Le alpi nostre: Uomini e soldati*. Brescia: Morcelliana, 1996.

———. *Vita di Nino Bixio. Opere di Giuseppe Cesare Abba*, vol. 2. Brescia: Morcelliana, 1983.

Abend, Hallett. *The God from the West: A Biography of Frederick Townsend Ward*, Garden City, NY: Doubleday & Company, 1947.

Adler, Jacob. *Claus Spreckels: The Sugar King in Hawaii*. Honolulu: University of Hawaii Press, 1966.

Adler, Jacob, and Robert M. Kamins. *The Fantastic Life of Walter Murray Gibson: Hawaii's Minister of Everything*. Honolulu: University of Hawaii Press, 1986.

Alexander, W. D. *History of Later Years of the Hawaiian Monarchy and the Revolution of 1893*. Honolulu: Hawaiian Gazette Company, 1896.

Alger, Horatio. *Phil the Fiddler, or the Story of a Young Street Musician*. Philadelphia: Porter & Boston, 1872.

Allen, Helena G. *The Betrayal of Queen Liliuokalani: Last Queen of Hawaii 1838–1917*. Honolulu: Mutual Publishing, 1982.

———. *Renaissance King*. Honolulu: Mutual Publishing, 1994.

Andrade Jr., Ernest. *Unconquerable Rebel: Robert W. Wilcox and Hawaiian Politics, 1880–1903*. Niwot: University Press of Colorado, 1996.

Andreas, Alfred T. *History of Chicago from the Earliest Period to the Present Time*. 2 vols. Chicago: Andreas, 1884–86.

Anonimo (Ferdinando De Luca). *Sulla emigrazione dei fanciulli*. Florence: Ministero degli Affari Esteri, 1868.

Anonymous. *A Sketch of Recent Events, being a short account of the events which culminated on June 30, 1887, together with a full report of the Great Reform Meeting, and the two Constitutions in parallel columns*. Honolulu: Hawaiian Gazette Print, 1887.

Ardizzone, Pietro. *Formazione del Regno di Romania: La posizione italiana*. Digital Library Intratext, 2008. http://www.intratext.com/IXT/ITA3149.

Armstrong, William Nevins. *Around the World with a King*. Rutland, VT: Tuttle, 1903.

Battaglia, Roberto. *La prima guerra d'Africa*. Turin: Einaudi, 1954.

Bayley, C. C. *Mercenaries for the Crimea, 1854–1856*. Montreal: McGill-Queen's University Press, 1977.

Beccaria, Roberto. *I periodici genovesi dal 1473 al 1899*. Genoa: Associazione Italiana Biblioteche–Sezione Ligure, 1994.

Bettazzi, Luigi. *Obbediente in Ivrea: Monsignor Luigi Moreno vescovo dal 1838 al 1878*. Turin: Società Editrice Internazionale, 1989.

Borsella, Cristogianni. *On Persecution, Identity & Activism: Aspects of the Italian American Experience from the Late 19th Century to Today*. Wellesley, MA: Dante University Press, 2005.

Bosi, Alfredo. *Cinquant'anni di vita italiana in America*. New York: Bagnasco Press, 1921.

Brace, Charles Loring. *The Dangerous Classes of New York and Twenty Years' Work Among Them*. New York: Wynkoop & Hattenbeck, 1872.

Brunialti, Attilio. "La questione dei possedimenti coloniali: La Francia e le altre potenze." *Nuova Antologia* 1883, 71–95.

———, *Le colonie degli italiani*. Turin: UTET, 1897.

Caccia, Antonio. *Europa ed America: Scene della vita dal 1848 al 1850*. Monaco: Giorgio Franz Tipografo-Editore, 1850.

Cacioli, Manuela, ed. *La rete consolare nel periodo crispino (1886–1891)*. Rome: Istituto Poligrafico dello Stato, 1988.

Cahill, Holger. *A Yankee Adventurer: The Story of Ward and the Taiping Rebellion*. New York: Macaulay Company, 1930.

Camerani-Clementina Rotondi, Giulia, ed. *Carteggi di Bettino Ricasoli*. Rome: Istituto Storico Italiano per l'età moderna e contemporanea, 1978.

Carpi, Leonardo. *Cesare Correnti: Note storico-biografiche*. Milan: Vallardi, 1888.

Carpi, Leone. *Delle colonie e dell'emigrazione d'Italiani all'estero*. Milan: Editrice Lombarda, 1874.

Carter, Samuel. *Cyrus Field: Man of Two Worlds*. New York: Putnam, 1968.

Casalis, Goffredo. *Dizionario Geografico Storico-Statistico-Commerciale degli Stati di S.M. il Re di Sardegna*, vol. 6. Turin: Cassone e Marzorati, 1840.

Cerri, Domenico. *Biografia di Monsignor Luigi Moreno*. Ivrea: Tipografia del Seminario, 1878.

Chapin, Helen Geracimos. *Shaping History: The Role of Newspapers in Hawai'i*. Honolulu: University of Hawaii Press, 1996.

Chesneaux, Jean, Marianne Bastid, and Marie-Claire Bergére. *China from the Opium Wars to the 1911 Revolution*. New York: Pantheon Books, 1976.

Ciambelli, Bernardino. *I misteri di Mulberry Street*. New York: Frugone & Balletto, 1893.

Conterno, Giovanni. *Dogliani una terra e la sua storia*. Dogliani: Amici del Museo, 1986.

Cordano, Luigi. *Ricordo agli amici: Versi e prose*. Naples: Morano, 1884.

Cotte, Alfred M. "The Franco-Annamese Conflict." *Catholic World* 38, no. 224 (November 1883): 202–217.

Crispi, Francesco. *Discorsi di politica estera pronunciati da Francesco Crispi presidente del Consiglio, ministro dell'interno e ministro* ad interim *degli affari esteri. Aprile 1887–gennaio 1891*. Rome: Tipografia delle Mantellate, 1892.

Damon, Ethel M. *Stanford Ballard Dole and His Hawaii*. Palo Alto, CA: Pacific Books, 1957.

Daws, Gavan. *Shoal of Time: A History of the Hawaiian Islands*. New York: Macmillan, 1968.

de Leone, Enrico. *L'Italia in Africa. Le prime ricerche di una colonia e la esplorazione geografica politica ed economica*, vol. 2. Rome: Istituto Poligrafico dello Stato, 1955.

Degli Alberti, Mario. *Per la storia dell'alleanza e della campagna di Crimea, 1853–1856*. Turin: Fratelli Bocca Librari, 1910.

Del Boca, Angelo. *Gli italiani in Africa Orientale, 1: Dall'unità alla marcia su Roma*. Rome: Laterza, 1985.

Dizionario Biografico degli Italiani (DBI). Rome: Istituto della Enciclopedia Italiana, 1960.

Dondero, Carlo. *Cap. Cesare Moreno*. In Carlo Dossi, *Note azzurre*. Milan: Adelphi, 2010.

Durante, Francesco. *Italoamericana: Storia e letteratura degli italiani negli Stati Uniti*, vol. 1. Milan: Mondadori, 2001.

Dye, Bob. *Merchant Prince of the Sandalwood Mountains: Afong and the Chinese in Hawaii*. Honolulu: University of Hawaii Press, 1997.

Einaudi, Luigi. *Monografia economico-agraria del Comune di Dogliani*. Mondovì: Tipografia e Libreria G. Issoglio, 1894.

Embree, Ainslie. *British East India Company Raj*. In *Encyclopedia of India* 1:176–183. Detroit: Gale, 2006.

Faldella, Giovanni. *Roma borghese*. Bologna: Cappelli, 1962.

Fava, Saverio. "Le colonie agricole italiane nell'America del Nord." *Nuova Antologia* 113 (October 1904).

Fenton, Edwin. *Immigrants and Unions*. Cambridge, MA: Harvard University Press, 1957.

Ferrari, Mario Enrico. "L'interesse genovese per l'Australia (1850–1860): I progetti e l'opera di Nino Bixio e Giuseppe Carcassi." *Miscellanea di Storia delle esplorazioni* 12 (1987): 143–180.

Fitzgerald, Keith. *The Face of the Nation: Immigration, the State, and the National Identity*. Stanford, CA: Stanford University Press, 1996.

Franchi, Jacopo. "Gian Francesco Secchi de Casali il pioniere della stampa italiana in America (Piacenza, 1819–Elizabeth, New Jersey, 1885)." *Bollettino storico piacentino* 2 (2011): 1–29.

Franzina, Emilio. *Gli italiani al nuovo mondo: L'emigrazione italiana in America 1492–1942*. Milan: Mondadori, 1995.

Fuchs, Lawrence H. *Hawaii Pono: A Social History*. New York: Harcourt, Brace & World, 1961.

Greer, Richard A. *Royal Tourists: Letters Home from Tokio to London*. Honolulu: Hawaiian Historical Society, 1971.

Guerzoni, Giuseppe. *La tratta dei fanciulli: Pagine del problema sociale*. Florence: Tipografia di Giovanni Polizzi, 1868.

Gupta, Pratul Chandra. *Nana Sahib and the Rising at Cawnpore*. Oxford: Clarendon Press, 1963.

Hearn, Chester G. *Circuits in the Sea: The Men, the Ships, and the Atlantic Cable*. Westport, CT: Praeger, 2004.

Hess, Robert L. "Italian Imperialism in Its Ethiopian Context." *International Journal of African Studies* 6, no. 1 (1973): 94–109.

Hoppin, Martha J. "The 'Little White Slaves' of New York: Paintings of Child Street Musicians by J. G. Brown." *American Art Journal* 26, nos. 1–2 (1994): 5–43.

Iannettone, Giovanni. *Presenze italiane lungo le vie dell'Oriente nei secoli XVIII e XIX*. Naples: Edizioni Scientifiche, 1984.

Iorizzo, Luciano. *Italian Immigration and the Impact of the Padrone System*. New York: Arno Press, 1980.

Jian, Youwen. *The Taiping Revolutionary Movement*. New Haven: Yale University Press, 1973.

Karabell, Zachary. *The Parting of the Desert: The Creation of the Suez Canal*. New York: Knopf, 2003.

Khan, Syed Ahmed. *The Causes of the Indian Revolt*. New York: Oxford University Press, 2001.

Kuykendall, Ralph S. *Hawaiian Diplomatic Correspondence*. Honolulu, Honolulu Star-Bulletin, 1926.

———. *The Hawaiian Kingdom*. Vol. 3, *The Dynasty 1874–1893*. Honolulu: University of Hawaii Press, 1967.

Labanca, Nicola. *Oltremare: Storia dell'espansione coloniale italiana*. Bologna: Il Mulino, 2007.

Lebrun, Joseph. *Souvenirs des guerres de Crimée et d'Italie*. Paris: Edentu, 1889.

Lindley, Augustus F. *Ti-ping Tien-Kwoh: A History of the Tai-Ping Revolution*. 2 vols. London: Day & Son, 1866.

Lombardo, Robert M. *The Black Hand: Terror by Letter in Chicago*. Champaign: University of Illinois Press, 2010.

Loverci, Francesca. "Il primo ambasciatore italiano a Washington: Saverio Fava." *Clio* 13, no. 3 (July–September 1977): 239–276.

———. "Un pioniere del giornalismo italiano in California, Carlo Andrea Dondero (1842–1939)." In *Miscellanea in onore di Ruggero Moscati*, 453–459. Naples: Edizioni Scientifiche Italiane, 1985.

Mantea (Gina Sobrero). *Espatriata: Da Torino a Honolulu*. Edited by Ombretta Frau. Rome: Salerno, 2007.

Marcellino da Civezza, P. *Storia universale delle missioni francescane*, vol. 4. Rome: Tipografia Tiberina, 1860.

Martin Koszta—Correspondence, etc. Message from the President of the United States, transmitting Copies of correspondence, etc. growing out of the seizure and rescue of Martin Koszta, House of Representatives, 33rd Congress, 1st Session, Ex. Doc. no. 91, Washington, DC, 1854.

Mason, Mary Gertrude. *Western Concepts and the Chinese, 1840–1876*. New York: Author, 1939.

Misra, Anand Swarup. *Nana Saheb Peshwa and the Fight for Freedom*. Lucknow: Uttar Pradesh, 1961.

Mukharya, P. S. *The Revolt of 1857*. Delhi: Sharada, 2001.

Negri, Cristoforo. "Dei meriti del Rev. P. Abbona missionario della Birmania." *L'Ateneo illustrato* 1877, 117–119.

Newsinger, John. "Taiping Revolutionary: Augustus Lindley in China." *Race & Class* 42, no. 4 (2001): 57–72.

Nye, Gideon. *The Memorable Year*. Macao, 1858.

Palombi, Domenico. *Rodolfo Lanciani: l'archeologia a Roma tra Ottocento e Novecento*. Rome: L'Erma di Bretschneider, 2006.

Plesur, Milton. *America's Outward Thrust: Approaches to Foreign Affairs, 1865–1890*. DeKalb: Northern Illinois University Press, 1971.

Quigg, Agnes. "Kalakua's Hawaiian Studies Abroad Program." *Hawaiian Journal of History* 22 (1988): 170–208.

Reclus, Jacques. *La révolte des Tai-Ping (1851–1864)*. Paris: Le Pavillon, 1972.

Reid, Anthony. *The Contest for North Sumatra, 1858–1898*. Kuala Lumpur: Oxford University Press, 1969.

———. "Merchant Princes and Magic Mediators: Outsiders and Powers in Sumatra and Beyond." *Indonesia and the Malay World* 36, no. 105 (July 2008): 253–267.

Reilly, Thomas H. *The Taiping Heavenly Kingdom*. Seattle: University of Washington Press, 2004.

Rossetti, Carlo. *Corea e coreani: Impressioni e ricerche sull'impero del Gran Han*. 2 vols. Bergamo: Istituto italiano d'arti grafiche, 1904–1905.

Rossi, Adolfo. *Un italiano in America*. Milan: Treves, 1892/1899.

Rossi, Luisa. *L'altra mappa: Esploratrici, viaggiatrici, geografe*. Reggio Emilia: Diabasis, 2005.

Salvetti, Patrizia. *Corda e sapone: Storie di linciaggi degli italiani negli Stati Uniti*. Rome: Donzelli, 2003.

Saul, David. *The Indian Mutiny: 1857*. New York: Penguin, 2003.

Scott, R. Bruce. *Gentlemen on Imperial Service: A story of the Trans-Pacific Telecommunication Cable*. Victoria, BC: Sono Nis Press, 1994.

Segre, Claudio G. "*Il colonialismo e la politica estera*." In *La politica estera italiana, 1860–1895*, edited by Richard J. B. Bosworth and Sergio Romano, 121–146. Bologna: Il Mulino, 1991.

Selby, John. *The Paper Dragon: An Account of the China Wars, 1840–1900*. New York: Praeger, 1968.

Shastitko, Pyotr. *Nana Sahib*. Pune: Shubhada-Saraswat Publications, 1980.

Smith, Richard J. *Mercenaries and Mandarins*. Millwood, NY: KTO Press, 1978.

Smith, Robert Barr. "Avenging Cawpore." *Military History* 20, no. 6 (February 2004): 58–64.

Solero, Don Pietro. *Appunti sulla storia di Tonengo Canavese*. Mazzè: Associazione Mattiaca, n.d.

Spence, Jonathan D. *The Taiping Vision of a Christian China, 1836–1864*. Waco, TX: Baylor University Press, 1998.

Stevens, Sylvester K. *American Expansion in Hawaii 1842–1898*. Harrisburg: Archives Publishing Company of Pennsylvania, 1945.

Surdich, Francesco. "Il dibattito sull'espansione coloniale italiana alla Società di Letture e Conversazioni Scientifiche di Genova (1868–1912)." In *Filosofia e politica a Genova nell'età del postivisimo*, Atti del Convegno dell'Associazione Filosofica Ligure, Genova 14–16 maggio 1987, ed. Dino Cofrancesco, 1:269–295. Genoa: Compagnia dei Librai, 1988.

———. *L'attività missionaria, politico-diplomatico e scientifica di Giuseppe Sapeto*. Cairo Montenotte: Comunità Montana Alta Val Bormida, 2005.

Tate, Merze. *Hawaii: Reciprocity or Annexation*. East Lansing: Michigan State University Press, 1968.

———. "The Opposition to Hawaiian Reciprocity." *Pacific Historical Review* 14 (June 1945): 157–183.

Teng, Ssuyu. *The Taiping Rebellion and the Western Powers*. Oxford: Clarendon Press, 1971.

Thomas, Teresa Fava. "Arresting the *Padroni* Problem and Rescuing the White Slaves in America: Italian Diplomats, Immigration Restrictionists & the Italian Bureau 1881–1901." *Altreitalie* 40 (January–June 2010): 57–79.

Tognoli, Pietro Angelo. *Cairo nella storia della Liguria e della nazione*. Cairo Montenotte: Ed. Lagio, 1971.

Tyrrell, Henry. "Garibaldi in New York." *The Century* 74, no. 2 (June 1907): 174–184.

Vecoli, Rudolph J. "Chicago's Italians Prior to World War One." PhD dissertation, University of Wisconsin, 1963.

Walsh, George Ethelbert. "Girdling the Globe with Submarine Cables." *New England Magazine* 16 (March–August 1897): 584–597.

Wong-Ann Rayson, Helen. *Hawaii's Royal History*. Revised edition. Honolulu: Bess Press, 1987.

Zambucka, Kristin. *Hawaii's Last King*. Honolulu: Mana Publishing, 2003.

Zucchi, John. *The Little Slaves of the Harp, Italian Street Musicians in Nineteenth Century Paris, London, and New York*. Montreal: McGill-Queen's University Press, 1992.

INDEX